IMAGES
of America

MERIDIAN

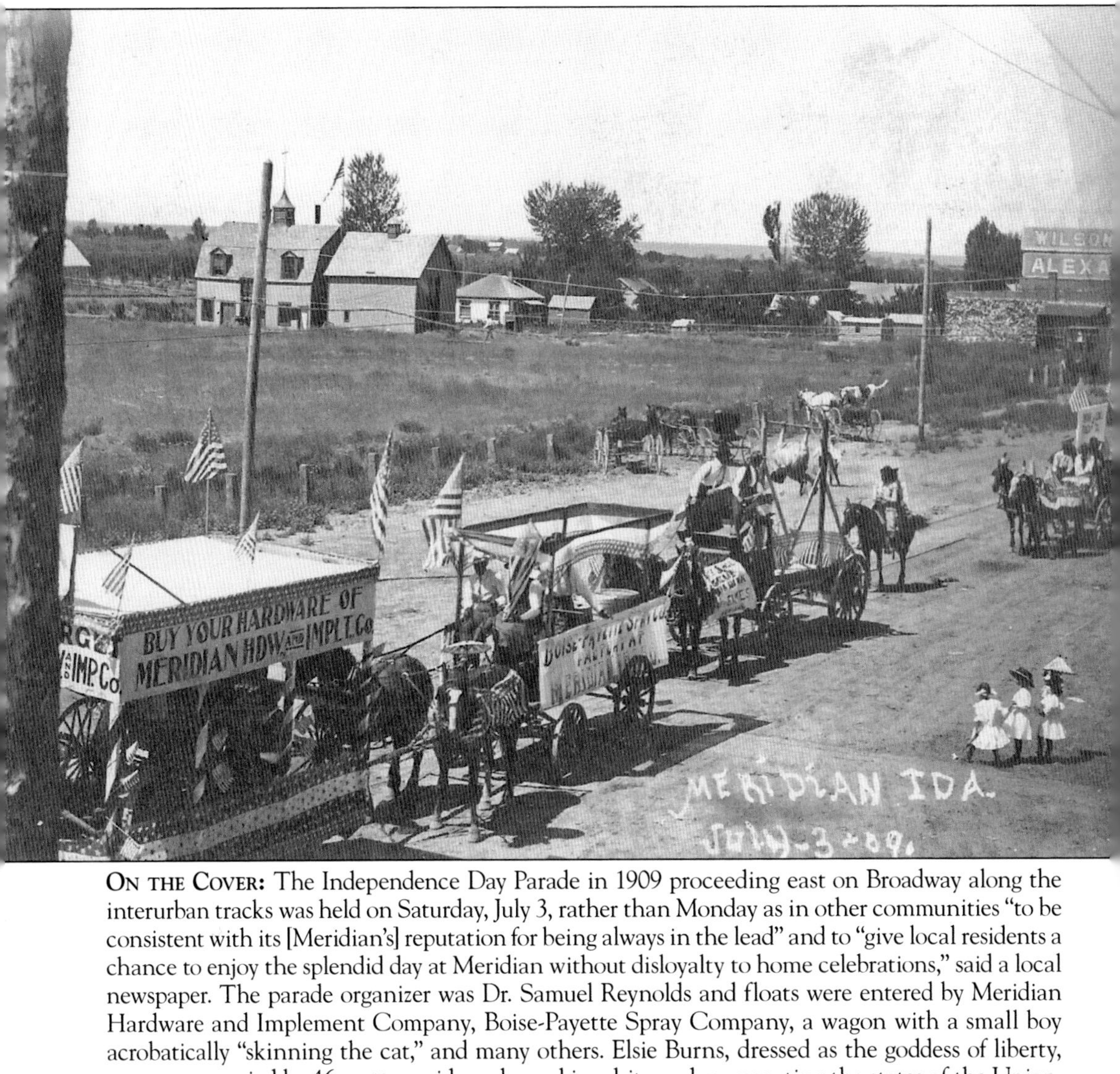

On the Cover: The Independence Day Parade in 1909 proceeding east on Broadway along the interurban tracks was held on Saturday, July 3, rather than Monday as in other communities "to be consistent with its [Meridian's] reputation for being always in the lead" and to "give local residents a chance to enjoy the splendid day at Meridian without disloyalty to home celebrations," said a local newspaper. The parade organizer was Dr. Samuel Reynolds and floats were entered by Meridian Hardware and Implement Company, Boise-Payette Spray Company, a wagon with a small boy acrobatically "skinning the cat," and many others. Elsie Burns, dressed as the goddess of liberty, was accompanied by 46 pretty maidens dressed in white and representing the states of the Union. Other participants that would be considered politically incorrect today were children dressed as "pickaninnies" and "southern darkie characters." The parade marshal, J. J. Jones, was called "the tall sycamore." Note the three "Little Miss Liberties" at the bottom right among the spectators. Coincidentally, 1909 was the year the Lincoln penny was issued. (Meridian History Center.)

IMAGES
of America

MERIDIAN

Frank Thomason and
Polly Ambrose Peterson

ARCADIA
PUBLISHING

ISBN 978-0-7385-8012-8

Published by Arcadia Publishing
Charleston, South Carolina

Printed in the United States of America

Library of Congress Control Number: 2009935203

For all general information contact Arcadia Publishing at:
Telephone 843-853-2070
Fax 843-853-0044
E-mail sales@arcadiapublishing.com
For customer service and orders:
Toll-Free 1-888-313-2665

Visit us on the Internet at www.arcadiapublishing.com

This book is dedicated to Lila Hill for her enduring contributions to area history, including helping to establish the Meridian Historical Society in 1986 and, with the City of Meridian, the Meridian History Center in 2008.

Contents

Acknowledgments		6
Introduction		7
1.	From Sagebrush to Settlement	9
2.	Railways and Early Meridian	27
3.	Education in Early Meridian	41
4.	People and Places in Meridian Village	57
5.	Between the Wars and Beyond	79
6.	From Creamery to City Hall	103
7.	Church and Community	115
Bibliography		127

Acknowledgments

Acknowledgment is extended to the Meridian Historical Society; the Meridian History Center (MHC); the Meridian Historic Preservation Commission (MHPC); the Public Archives and Research Library (PARL); the State Historic Preservation Office (SHPO) of the Idaho State Historical Society (ISHS); Lila Hill for text review, insight and information; Brent and Gwen Alger; Carol Jetton; and Terry P. Smith and Carolyn Bowler of PARL. Ann Swanson and Belinda Davis of SHPO were also helpful, as was Walter Lindgren, chairman of the MHPC, and James Thomason of Integrity Computer Consulting. Thanks also to the Pine Street School curator-docent and former teacher, Betty Kusler, and longtime resident Jean Fisher.

Special thanks also to Richard Nourse for sharing his extensive family history information and photographs, and to Pastor Burton Roberts of Meridian Gospel Tabernacle, Pastor Steve Moore of Ten Mile Christian Church, Pastor Tim Pusey (with help from Dale and Mary Ownby and Larry Woodard) of Valley Shepherd Church of the Nazarene, Randy Cook of the First Baptist Church, and representatives of Holy Apostles Church and the United Methodist Church. Unless otherwise noted, all photographs appear courtesy of the Meridian Historical Society/Meridian History Center. The key to identification of other sources is Hummel Architects (HA), Holy Apostles Catholic Church (HACC), Idaho State Historical Society (ISHS), Church of Jesus Christ of Latter-day Saints (LDSC), Meridian First Baptist Church (FNBC), Meridian Gospel Tabernacle (MGT), the Meridian Presbyterian Church (MPC), Polly A. Peterson (PAP), Richard Nourse (RN), Ten Mile Christian Church (TMCC), and the Valley Shepherd Church of the Nazarene (VSCN) and United Methodist Church photographs are from the Meridian History Center.

INTRODUCTION

In the 1890s, Meridian consisted of a collection of primitive buildings as settlers struggled to replace sagebrush and jackrabbits with businesses and homes. The late Clysta Gray recalled, "In the early days, Meridian was surprisingly like the little Western cow towns you see in the movies. They had an abundance of saloons at one time and a fine big livery stable where the creamery (city hall) is now. Meridian had several rooming houses for travelers and a hotel."

Gray also remembered going to movies starring William S. Hart. "I wanted to be Gloria Swanson, so I glued my eyes with tape. There were silent movies and a bowling alley on Main Street in later years. We rode the trolley to the Nat (Natatorium) and had a bowl of chili." From its inception until suburbia arrived in the 1970s, Meridian was essentially rural and agriculture in character, even within the village, with a primary emphasis on family and children. The first Boy Scout troop in Idaho was organized in Meridian on July 20, 1917, with Harold Salisbury as scoutmaster and Fred Hunt as patrol leader.

"Sometimes on Halloween, kids would pull pranks like disassembling a hay wagon piece by piece and reassembling it on top of Baird's building downtown," Gray said, referring to longtime *Meridian Times* publisher and editor John Baird. "Kids would scatter the plumber's pipes all over town."

Another longtime resident, Anna Koskela, daughter of Serafim Lopez, said, "That was mischievous but it's not like that anymore. Now kids break into homes, rob, and bring guns to school."

The late Pastor Evert Roberts recalled band concerts, plays, and Chautauquas that brought entertainment and culture for the whole community, with speakers, teachers, musicians, entertainers, preachers, and specialists of the day. Clysta Gray said two performers who later became famous were television announcer Johnny Olson and actor Forrest Tucker, decades before Clint Eastwood used part of downtown Meridian as a backdrop for his 1980 movie, *Bronco Billy*. Well-known Meridian High School (MHS) graduates include Bill Agee, made famous by his role in the demise of the Morrison-Knudsen Corporation, and Renn Ross, who retired as chief of the Boise Fire Department in 2007.

Pastor Roberts said, "Meridian was a beautiful place to live as I grew up." Roberts came to Meridian as a boy in 1921 and spent 50 years as a pastor. After attending church conferences in many states west of the Mississippi River, Roberts said, "The beauty of it all was coming home, the feeling of contentment and peace I never felt in any other place. Maybe it's all sentiment, but I don't think it is. This was a wonderful place to raise children."

Clysta Gray, whose mother died two years after the family moved to Meridian, said, "I had so many 'mothers' I didn't suffer much. Frank Johnson's grandmother taught me how to bake bread. If your stove was on fire, you would just yell and the neighbors would carry the flaming stove out. There were a lot of widows in Meridian, and I can't think of one of their children that didn't turn out just fine."

The following chapters focus on seven areas of Meridian's development. The first, From Sagebrush to Settlement, illustrates the monumental achievement by settlers who dug ditches by hand and with horses, an enterprise akin to surface mining with fewer trenches to cave in on top of diggers than in underground mining. Early arrivals also had to contend with myriads of ravenous jackrabbits. As late as 1931, Ada County paid a 1¢ bounty on magpie and crow heads and eggs. "I don't remember a bounty on rabbits, but we had one on magpie heads and eggs," said Pastor Roberts. But rabbits were still plentiful in his youth. "I had two uncles near the New York Canal and Cloverdale and we'd go out there just after dark, cross the bridge and turn the lights on the hayfield," he said. "There were so many rabbits, we couldn't believe it."

Chapter two, Railways and Early Meridian, follows the arrival and importance of railroads from the 1880s and the electric trolley from 1908 to 1928. Railcars shipped orchard produce and other goods to regional and national markets, while the famous interurban streetcar revolutionized society and the economy in Meridian and the entire Boise valley. "It was the best thing we had," said Clysta Gray. She and Roberts recalled the trolley, the creamery whistle, and the ringing of bells at the Methodist and Nazarene churches. "There was something beautiful about them," he said. "After it's all over, it's too late."

Chapter three, Education in Early Meridian, looks at conditions and challenges facing parents and school boards in the early decades, when common schools dotted the countryside and pupils studied in one and two-room buildings, whose heritage is now preserved by the Pine Street School curator and docent, Betty Kusler. Population explosion crowded the school system into consolidation by the mid-20th century and a succession of bond attempts to pay for needed facilities ensued, but issues continued, including financing, local control, and the rural-urban dichotomy.

The fourth chapter, People and Places in Meridian Village, is a compilation of photographs and information about individuals and families as well as buildings and landmarks, which depict the flavor and character of life from the 1890s until the World War I. This period is arguably Meridian's halcyon era, a golden age marked by peace and prosperity, embodied in a growing local economy and the fabled electric trolley system, before global conflict and economic downturn generated more growth, as well as chaos and calamity.

Chapter five, Between the Wars and Beyond, deals with the decades between 1916 and the 1950s, when the advent of the automobile and the termination of trolley systems nationwide ushered in a larger and different form of society and economy. Photographs in this chapter focus on the effects of these processes and World War II on Meridian as it evolved from a village to a city.

The sixth chapter, From Creamery to City Hall, captures the importance of the dairy industry and the creamery in Meridian to the later village and the surrounding area. In 1970, when Meridian's population was still only 2,616 (up from 2,082 in 1960), creamery operations moved to Caldwell, and the old facility began a long period of deterioration that ended only when a farsighted series of mayors and city councils saved enough money to purchase the site and erect a magnificent municipal complex. The result honors the city's heritage and will inspire mixed-use downtown development.

The final chapter, Church and Community, surveys several prominent denominations that were active as the village and city evolved in the 19th century. Religious and civic institutions were forced to cope with a population that had risen by 1980 to 6,686, and by 1990 to 9,596. Meridian's explosion had only begun, reaching 9,596 in 1990 and 34,919 in 2000. Growth continues at a slower pace, with an estimated population in 2008 of 66,916 and a projected population in 2010 of 80,136. That is quite a leap for a village whose population in 1900 was 200 and in 1910, only 619. No longer a bedroom community to Boise, Meridian today is experiencing transportation transformation, from the Ten Mile Interchange on the west side to the split corridor downtown, and corporations as well as small businesses are still flocking to and springing up within its confines.

One

From Sagebrush to Settlement

An estimated 300,000 travelers crossed the Oregon Trail to points west in the 1840s and 1850s. All were seeking a new or better life, and many were virtuous and hardworking, unlike Yale University president Timothy Dwight's 1821 characterization of all pioneers and Westerns as "too idle, too talkative, too passionate, too prodigal, and too shiftless to acquire either property or character."

Persuaded by empty promises of splendor and plenty in a land described as fabulous in promotional brochures, immigrants discovered to their dismay that life and conditions in the dry West were harsh and unyielding. Most travelers continued through the Boise Valley, which was largely settled by returning sojourners who found its climate and soil relatively attractive after seeing what eastern Oregon had to offer.

Meridian today is a mirage. It wears a mask of landscaped and "greened-up" subdivisions and commercial development that covers its physical or geographic nature of a desert.

The harshness of early settlers' lives and their determination to adjust and conquer, to "make the desert bloom," cannot be overstated. Many filed for patents from the U.S. Land Office, which required a source of water, such as irrigation, prior to issuance of a patent. Many failed to prove themselves on homesteads and were no stranger to relinquishment, today known as foreclosure.

In the 1880s, all that was seen in and around what became Meridian was jackrabbit-infested sagebrush. Clearing the land by "grubbing" the desert vegetation and clubbing the rabbits was not enough. Early settlers built shacks and primitive business structures along Five Mile Creek and completed the Settlers' Ditch by 1890. The Ridenbaugh Canal (Nampa-Meridian) began delivering water in the area about the same time and presently serves the immediate Meridian area through the Hunter lateral. In 1900, the New York Canal, which was dug by men, opened larger tracts for agricultural pursuits.

In the 1880s, the railroad passed through the area, and the village became a mail drop called Hunter, after a railroad official along the Oregon Short Line route, before becoming a small growing agricultural center after 1900.

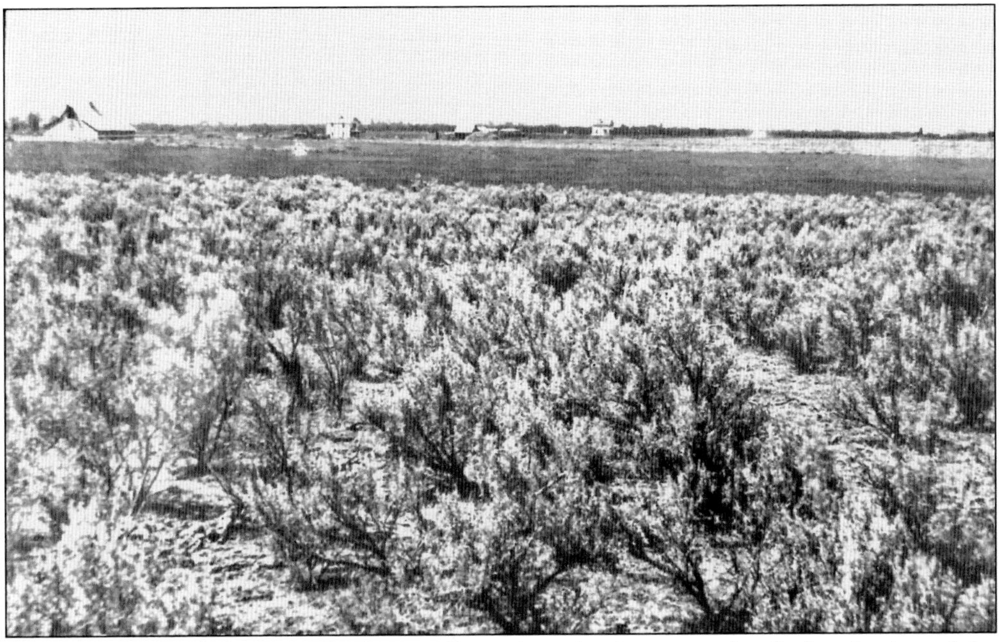

Sagebrush, pictured above, is a shrub or small tree from the Asteraceae family that dominated the area that became Meridian and still abounds south of Kuna, 9 miles from Meridian. Settlers had to clear, or "grub," the coarse, hardy, silvery-gray bush and its yellow flowers, as lumber merchant J. A. Fenton did in the spring of 1894 when he planted a commercial orchard in the later downtown area. Below, farmers employ horses and a grub hoe to conquer the sagebrush. A versatile plant, sagebrush was used for fuel and even construction of primitive shacks and outbuildings. Even the first sidewalks in Meridian were made of sagebrush. One extended from the Independent Order of Odd Fellows (IOOF) hall to the railroad station. The late Clysta Gray remembered, "In the old days, roads were built of poles . . . and were called corduroy roads, so Meridian had a sagebrush corduroy sidewalk."

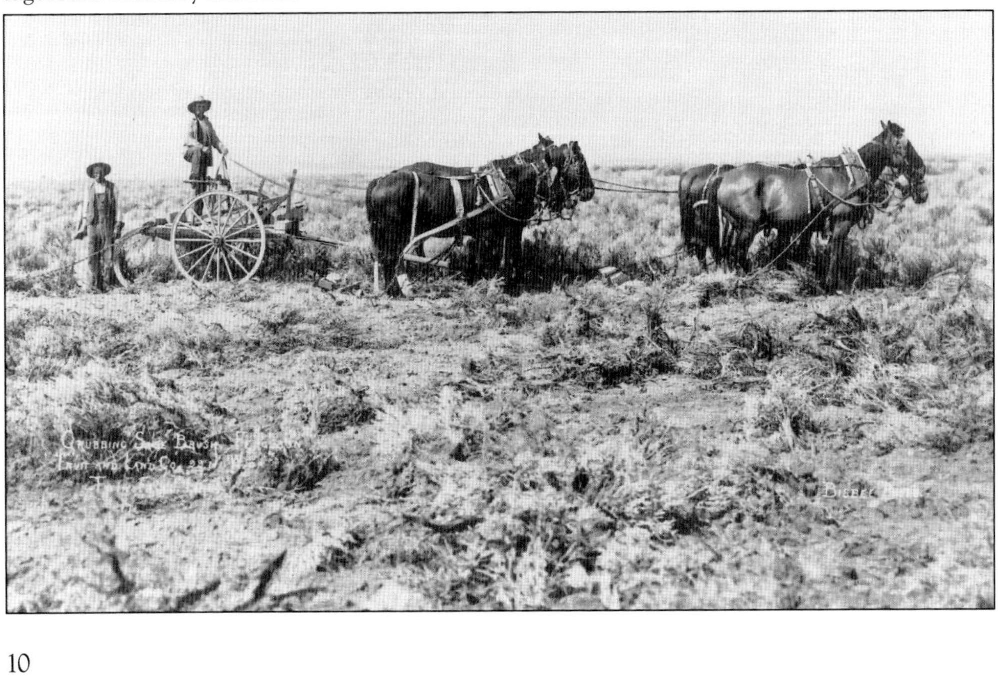

The animals competed with humans and domesticated critters for scarce food stocks, and to early residents and business people, it was a case of "us against them." At right, a portion of an Ada County rabbit bounty list from 1886 shows that Luther Snyder was paid $272.75 and George Robertson, $340.05. At 1.25¢ to 5¢ per pair of rabbit ears, the payments from the fund indicate the seriousness with which rabbit extermination was pursued. However, every 10 years if not more frequently, a resurgent rabbit population brought out the old and young men with their clubs, guns, and horses. Below, a local daily newspaper advertisement in 1895 promises an "awful slaughter" and a "proposed sport" in the Meridian area. It also mentions the farmers' intention "to be avenged for the losses inflicted by the mule ear tribe."

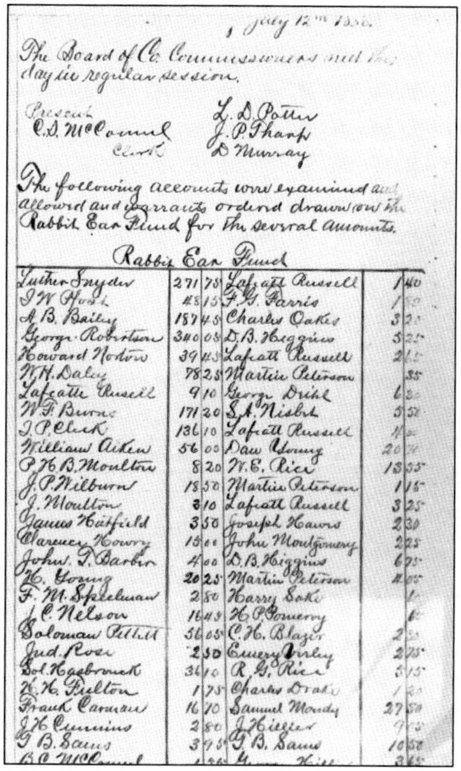

July 12th 1886

The Board of Co. Commissioners met this day in regular session.

Present: L. D. Potter, J. P. Tharp, D. Murray; C. D. McConnell, Clerk

The following accounts were examined and allowed and warrants ordered drawn on the Rabbit Ear Fund for the several amounts.

Rabbit Ear Fund

Luther Snyder	271 75	Lafeatt Russell	1 40
J W Frost	48 15	F. G. Parris	[illegible]
A. B. Bailey	187 45	Charles Oakes	[illegible]
George Robertson	340 05	D. B. Higgins	5 25
Howard Norton	39 45	Lafeatt Russell	[illegible]
W. H. Daley	78 25	Martin Peterson	35
Lafeatte Russell	9 10	George Driht	[illegible]
W. F. Burns	171 20	S. A. Nisbit	[illegible]
J. P. Clark	136 10	Lafeatt Russell	[illegible]
William Aiken	56 05	Dan Young	[illegible]
P. H. B. Moulton	8 20	W. E. Rice	13 35
J. P. Wilburn	18 50	Martin Peterson	1 15
J. Moulton	3 10	Lafeatt Russell	3 25
James Hatfield	3 50	Joseph Hawes	2 30
Clarence Howry	15 00	John Montgomery	2 25
John T. Barber	4 00	D. B. Higgins	6 75
H. Young	20 25	Martin Peterson	[illegible]
F. M. Spileman	2 80	Harry Sake	[illegible]
J. C. Nelson	16 45	H. P. Pomeroy	[illegible]
Soloman Tittell	56 05	C. H. Blazer	[illegible]
Jud. Rose	2 50	Emery Virley	2 75
Sol. Hasbrouck	36 10	R. G. Rice	[illegible]
H. H. Fulton	1 75	Charles Drake	[illegible]
Frank Carman	16 70	Samuel Mondy	27 50
J. H. Cummins	2 80	J. Hiller	[illegible]
J. B. Sams	3 95	J. B. Sams	10 50

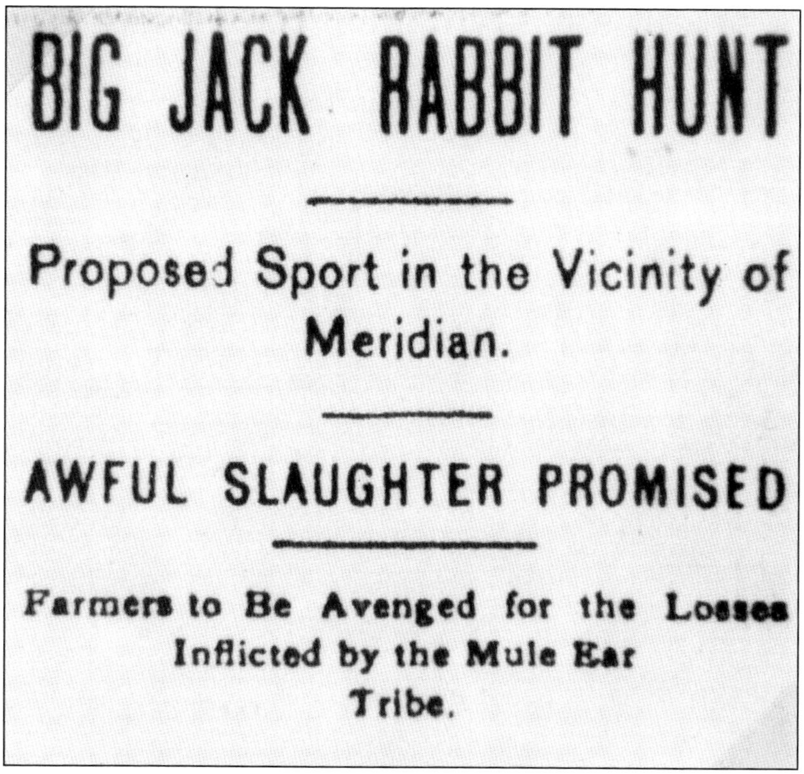

BIG JACK RABBIT HUNT

Proposed Sport in the Vicinity of Meridian.

AWFUL SLAUGHTER PROMISED

Farmers to Be Avenged for the Losses Inflicted by the Mule Ear Tribe.

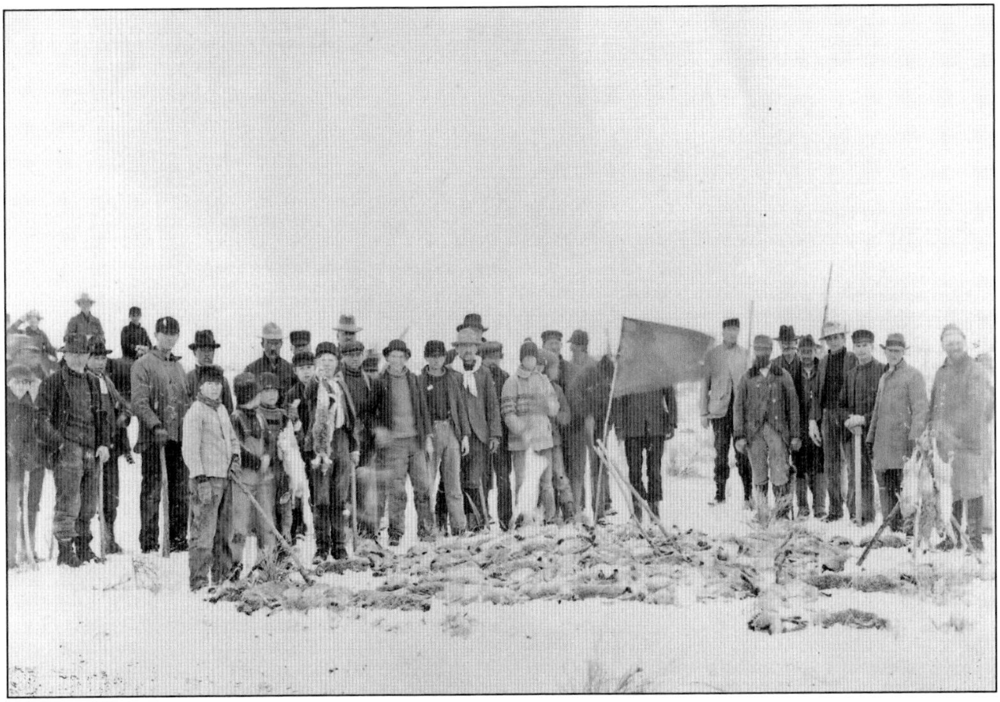

Above and below, settlers contended with ever-growing populations of jackrabbits that took over an area, chewing bark from young fruit trees and decimating entire gardens. Rabbit drives were held as late as the mid-1930s. The *Meridian Times* reported on July 6, 1934, "Several rabbit drives have been staged near Kuna of late. Two were put through last week out toward Ten Mile and Mora. On Monday evening, over 800 animals were killed and on Thursday evening another 1,600. Another drive is planned for Monday and Tuesday evenings." Hunters scattered poisoned alfalfa around Hubbard Lake and elsewhere. "Methods used in Idaho to exterminate thousands of the state's five million jackrabbits to prevent extensive destruction of trees and crops clash with those endorsed by the American Humane Association," which objected to the use of clubs in the presence of children.

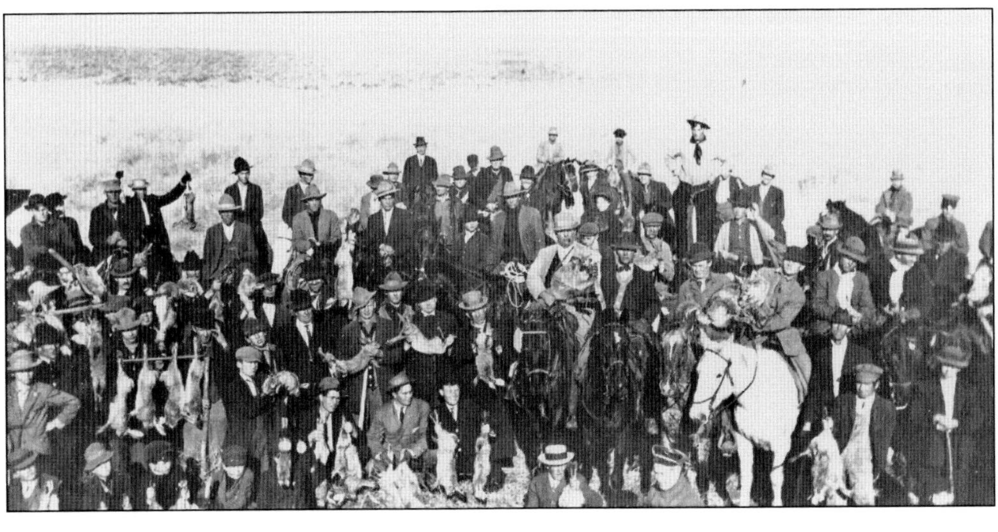

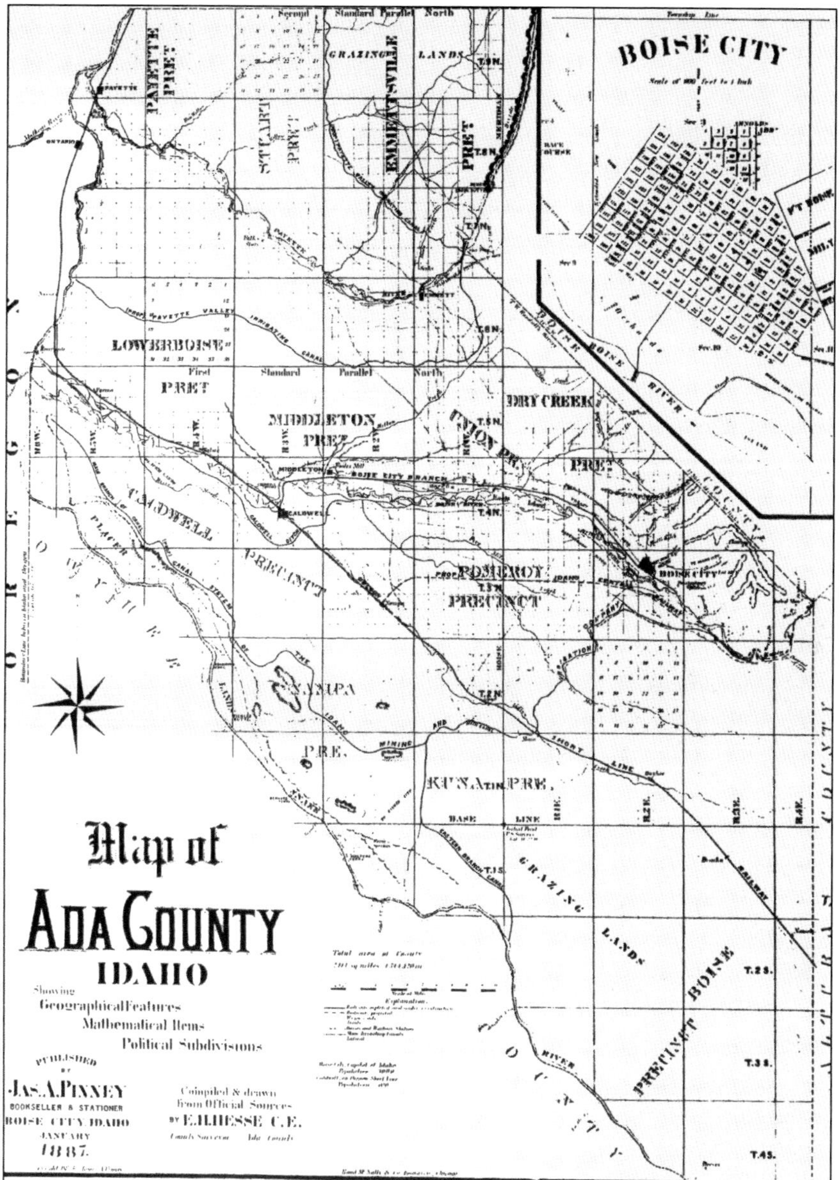

The above map of Ada County, dated January 1887, was compiled and drawn by county surveyor E. H. Hesse and published by Boise bookseller and stationer J. A. Pinney. It depicts "geographical features, mathematical items, and political subdivisions," including precincts west and south of Boise City. Meridian is not yet evident and the area is designated as Pomeroy Precinct, including the intersection of the railroad and Meridian Road where the new creamery was built in 1929 and the new city hall in 2008. The map also shows railway lines running north and south from Payette through Ontario, Oregon, and back into Idaho through Caldwell. The map shows points southeast, as well as the Boise City branch of the Oregon Short Line from Caldwell through Middleton, Star, and Eagle to Boise and the stub line of the Idaho Central Railway extending eastward from Nampa through Meridian to a junction southeast of Boise City.

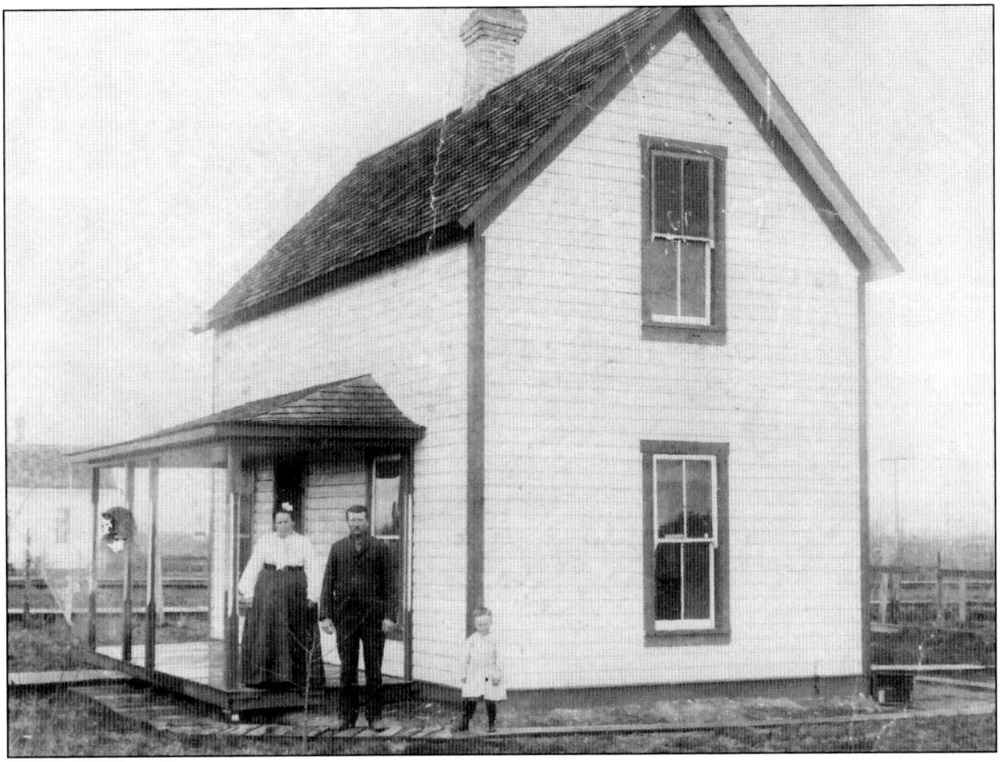

Above is the Whitely home *c.* 1886 with young Amos Whitely to the right of his parents. Arlene Kyle donated this photograph, one of the earliest of a Meridian residence. The architectural style is of "the modified federal two-story house like those in the Ohio and Mississippi river valleys . . . varied with porches or verandas," wrote Lila Hill. Below is an early street scene taken in 1896 looking north on the east side of Main Street from the railroad tracks. Stewart Clelan, grandson of W. H. Mateer, donated this photograph. The Methodist Church is on the left, and the 1894 Grade School is on the right. (Above, ISHS; below, MHC.)

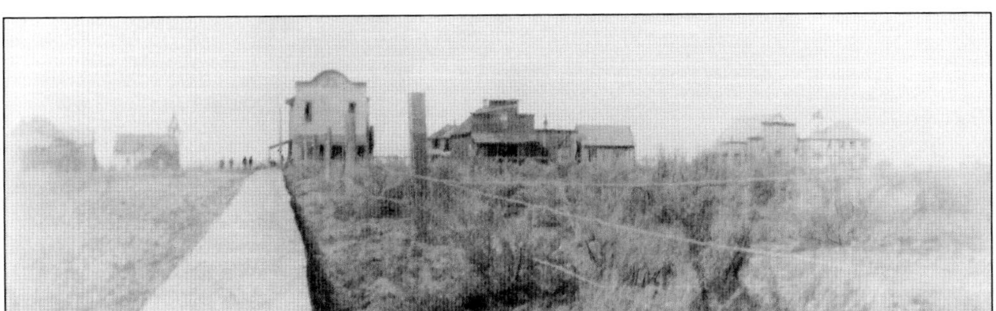

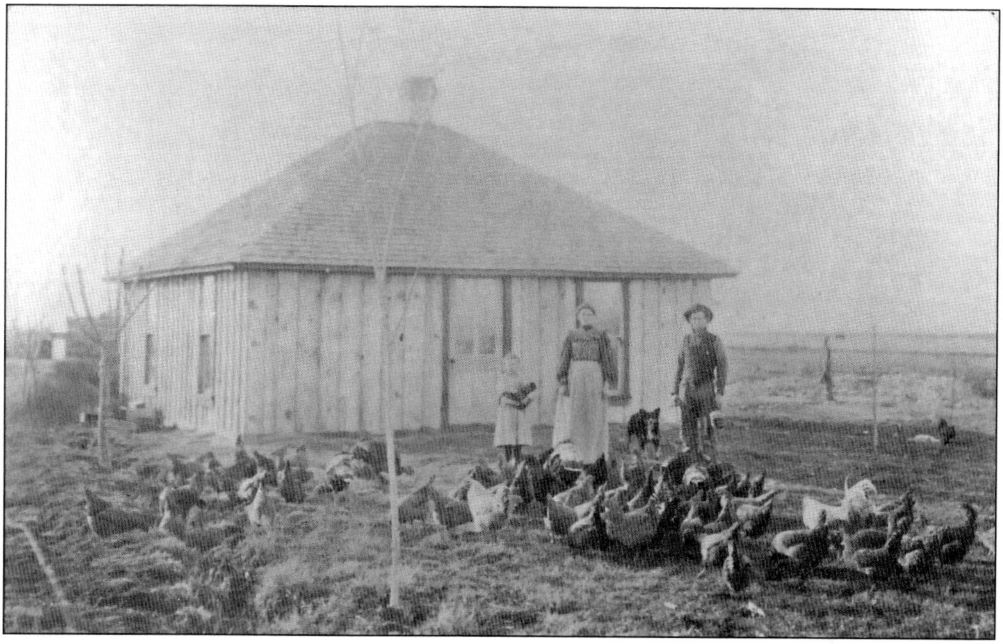

Above, the Anderson homestead is pictured on the west side of Ten Mile Road between Cherry Lane and Pine Avenue. Pictured here are, from left to right, Naomi Anderson Johnson, age seven, and Naomi's mother and father, Martha Davidson Anderson and James Matthew Anderson, a real estate agent and dealer in horses. Below, teams of horses and crews of men labor on the first irrigation ditches in the Meridian area. In the 1880s, it was a thirsty, barren region of sagebrush where settlers used the same basin full of water to wash dishes, then bathe, and finally to water the garden. Lila Hill wrote, "Soiled diapers would be hung out to dry for later use."

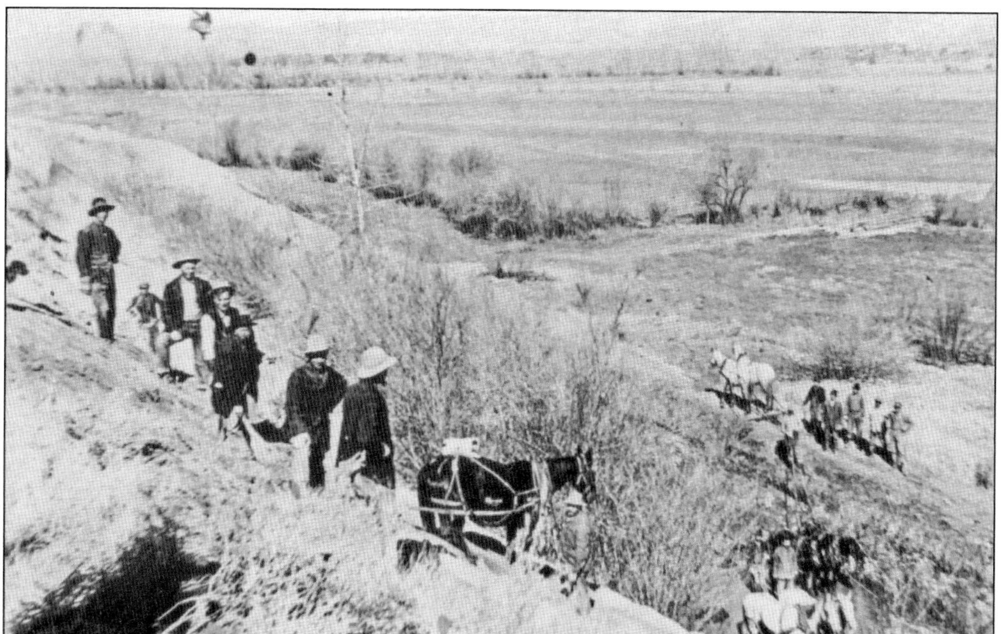

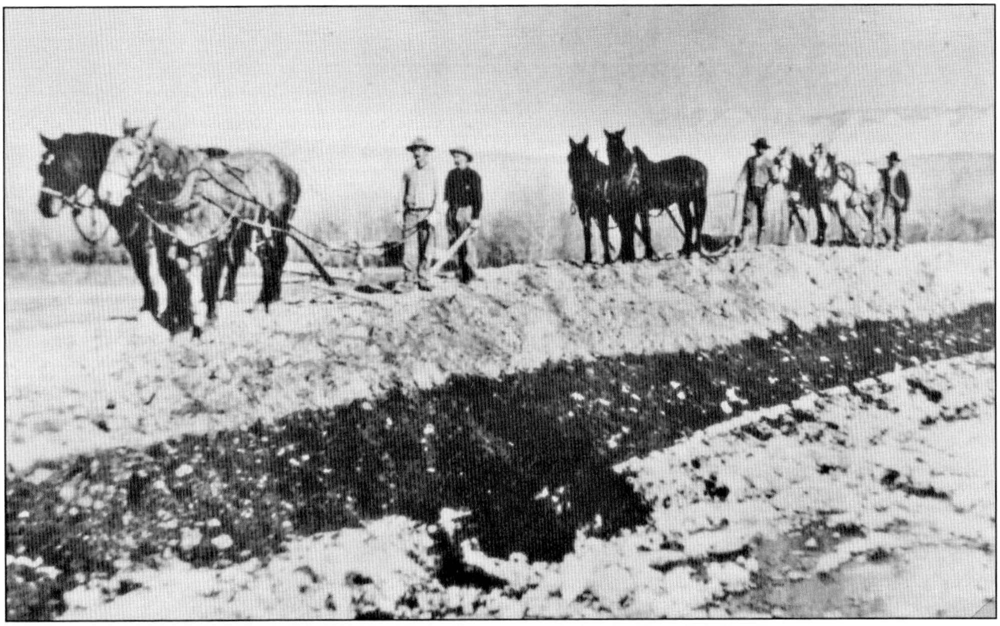

Above, workers use horses and primitive implements to dig ditches for the first irrigation system in the area. Clysta Gray said, "Water came to Meridian for irrigation via the Settlers' Ditch, and by way of the Ridenbaugh," both in the 1890s. The first water for irrigation was via sloughs and consisted mostly of wastewater from the McBirney orchards, first owned by a man named Rossi. The first fences were mostly of sagebrush piled high around the reclaimed land. Below, the headgate for the farmers' lateral ditch is pictured. Diversion of precious water into a nearby and growing network of canals extended the arable land to the south and west of Meridian. (Above, MHC; below, ISHS.)

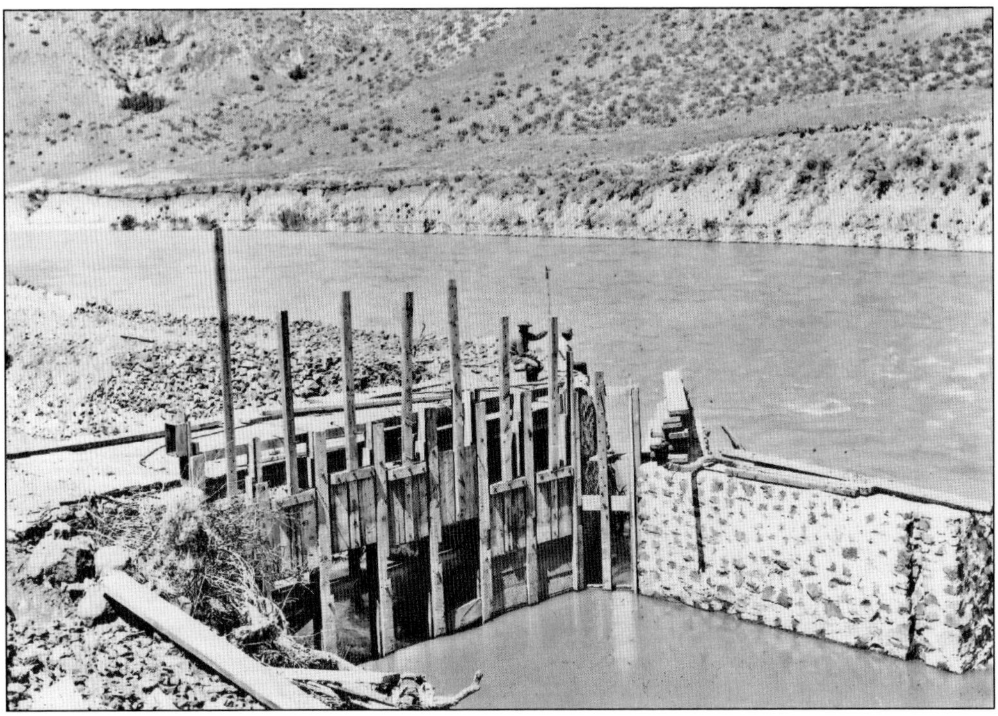

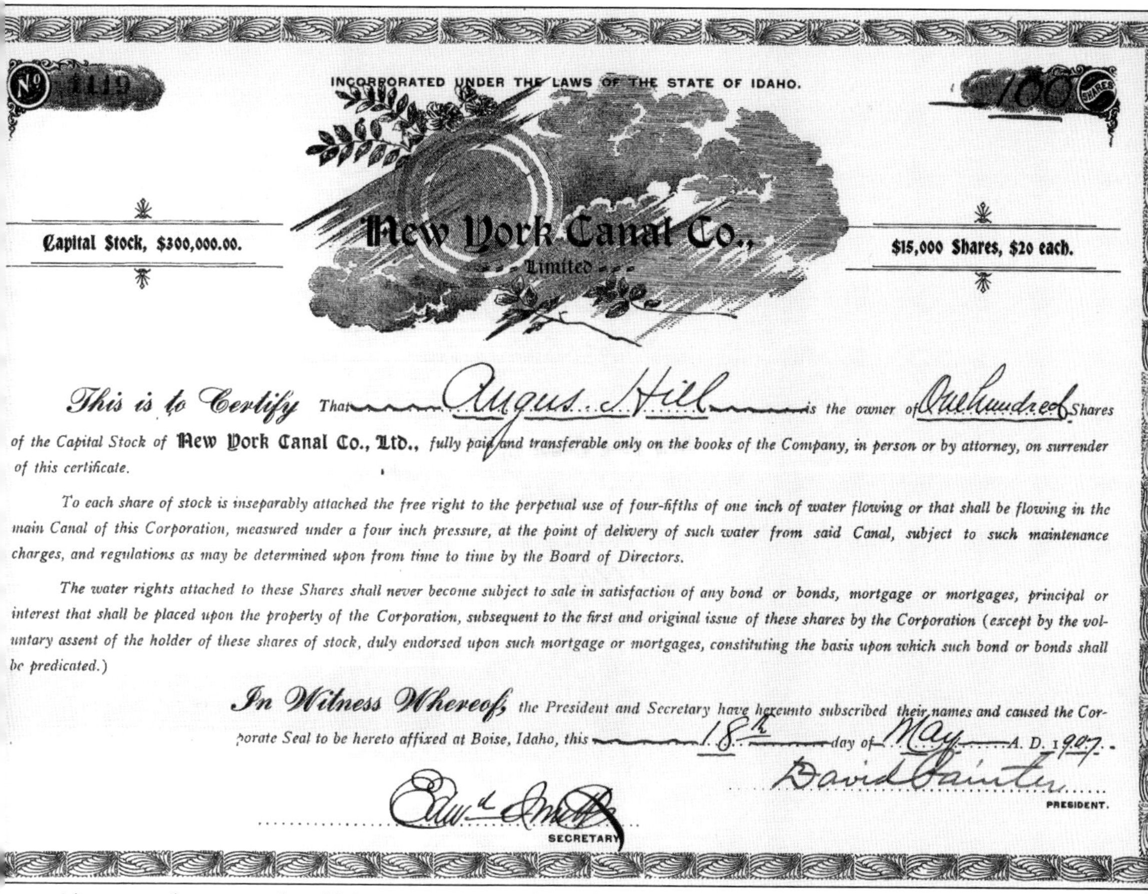
No 1119

INCORPORATED UNDER THE LAWS OF THE STATE OF IDAHO.

100 SHARES

Capital Stock, $300,000.00.

New York Canal Co., Limited

$15,000 Shares, $20 each.

This is to Certify That Angus Hill is the owner of One hundred Shares of the Capital Stock of New York Canal Co., Ltd., fully paid and transferable only on the books of the Company, in person or by attorney, on surrender of this certificate.

To each share of stock is inseparably attached the free right to the perpetual use of four-fifths of one inch of water flowing or that shall be flowing in the main Canal of this Corporation, measured under a four inch pressure, at the point of delivery of such water from said Canal, subject to such maintenance charges, and regulations as may be determined upon from time to time by the Board of Directors.

The water rights attached to these Shares shall never become subject to sale in satisfaction of any bond or bonds, mortgage or mortgages, principal or interest that shall be placed upon the property of the Corporation, subsequent to the first and original issue of these shares by the Corporation (except by the voluntary assent of the holder of these shares of stock, duly endorsed upon such mortgage or mortgages, constituting the basis upon which such bond or bonds shall be predicated.)

In Witness Whereof, the President and Secretary have hereunto subscribed their names and caused the Corporate Seal to be hereto affixed at Boise, Idaho, this 18th day of May A. D. 1907.

David Painter
PRESIDENT.

Edw. Smith
SECRETARY

Above is a document dated May 18, 1907, certifying farmer Angus Hill as the owner of 100 shares of capital stock of the New York Canal Company Limited. Angus arrived in Idaho in 1888 from Powersville, Putnam County, Missouri, and owned sheep in the Mountain Home area before filing a homestead claim on Ten Mile Creek in 1891. He died in 1938 and his eldest son, Angus, took over the family farm, where he raised hay and grain and milked cows. As a single man, he followed the example of earlier landowners and donated the first acre of land for the Hillsdale School. After several years of marriage and seven children later, he donated another acre so there was enough land for a ball field and play area adjacent to the school. Descendants of homesteader Angus still live on the family-owned farm 118 years after he filed for the property. (Lila Hill.)

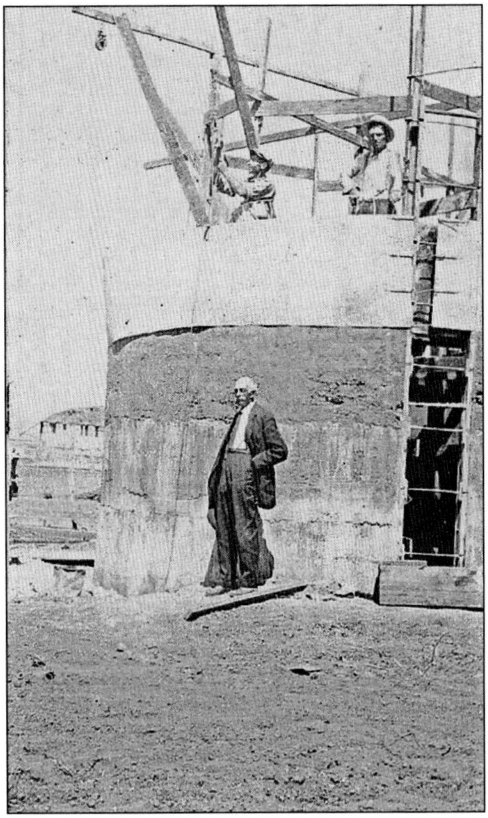

Left is Frank Alonzo Nourse during the initial construction of the silo on his property at the southeast corner of McMillan and Meridian Roads. Born in Illinois, he came to Idaho in 1881 and lived in Boise. He had a large forwarding house there, which furnished supplies to the mines northeast of Boise before the railroad came to Boise. Frank had another forwarding house in Kuna and was associated with the Idaho Building and Loan Association. A 1920 history of Idaho said, "At one time he owned nearly the whole town of Meridian and still has in his possession a large amount of property there." After selling 320 acres to his son, George A. Nourse, he retained possession of 400 acres and was described as "a most resourceful and enterprising merchant" and a successful farmer and stock raiser. Below are workers atop and below the nearly completed silo on the F. A. Nourse ranch. (Both RN.)

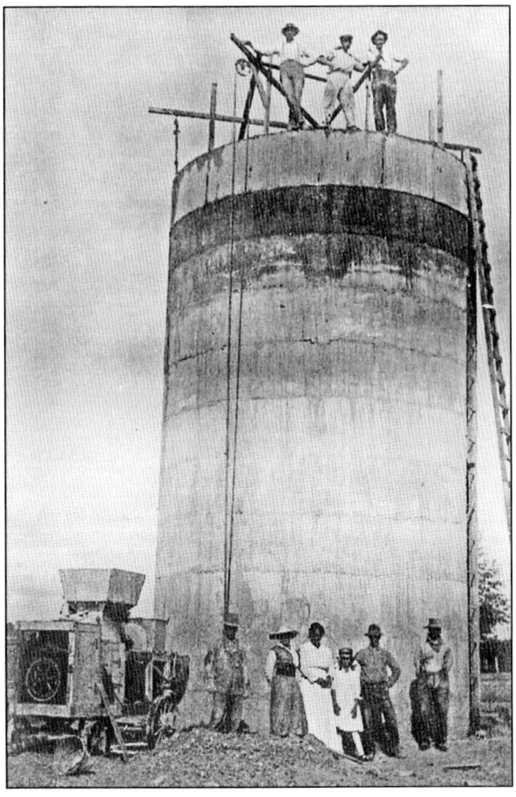

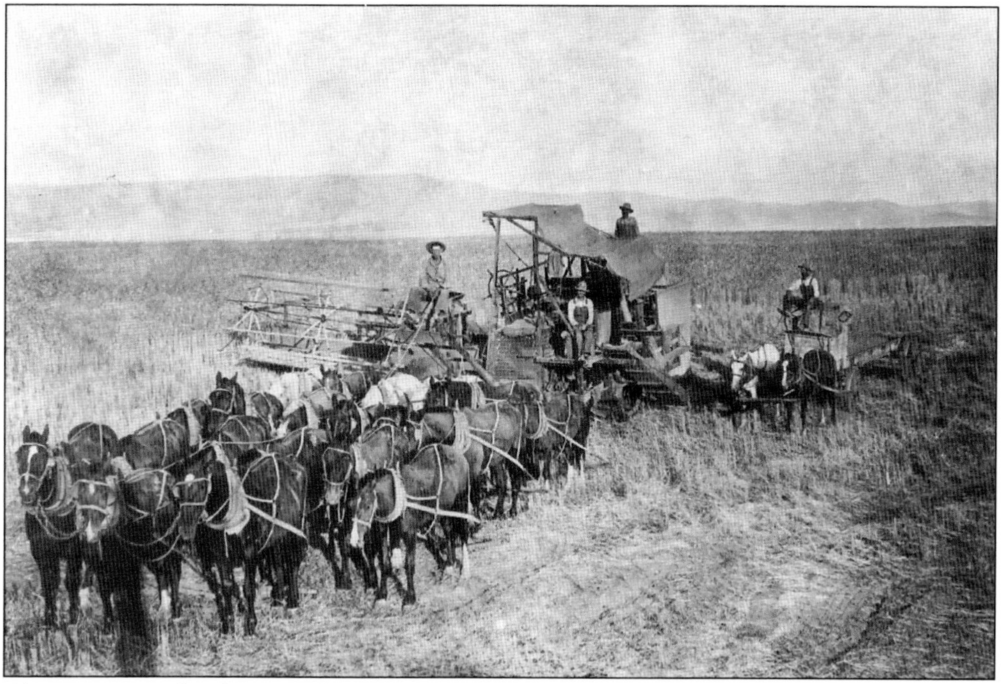

Above, a team of 12 horses pulls a binder during harvest time at the Elliott farm. Farmers grew and fed livestock within the village limits and increasingly in the expanding area to the north, west, and south of Meridian. Below, farmers use horsepower to pull a wagon overflowing with cut hay and a Mormon derrick to stack the alfalfa in a gigantic and growing hay pile. Meridian's reputation as a dairy center in the first half of the 20th century has overshadowed the row-crop industries, including the production of hay for use on farms and where horses were maintained.

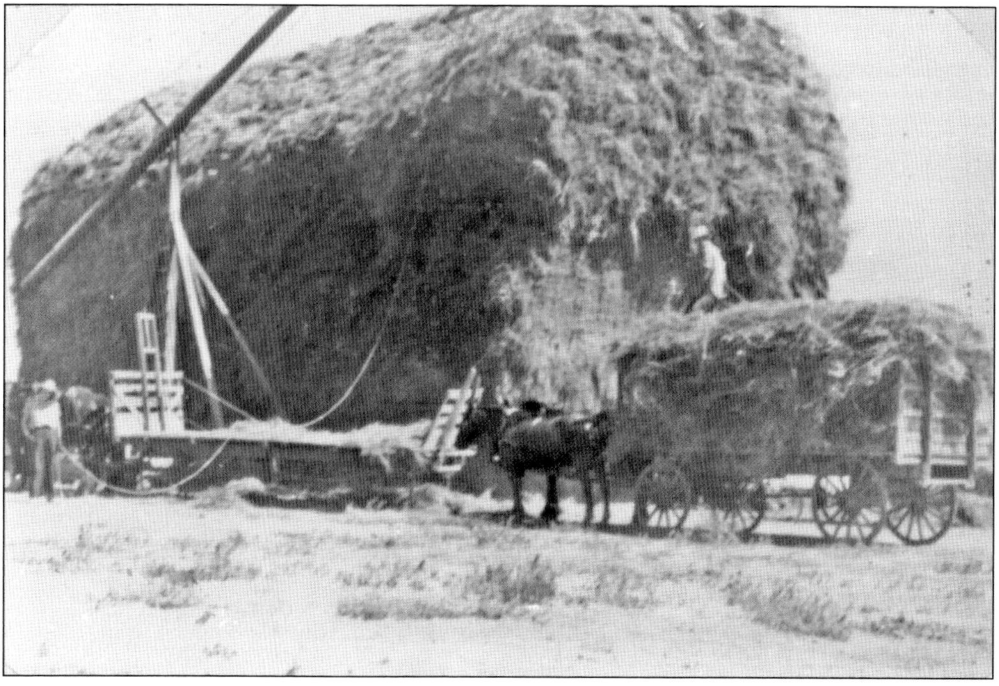

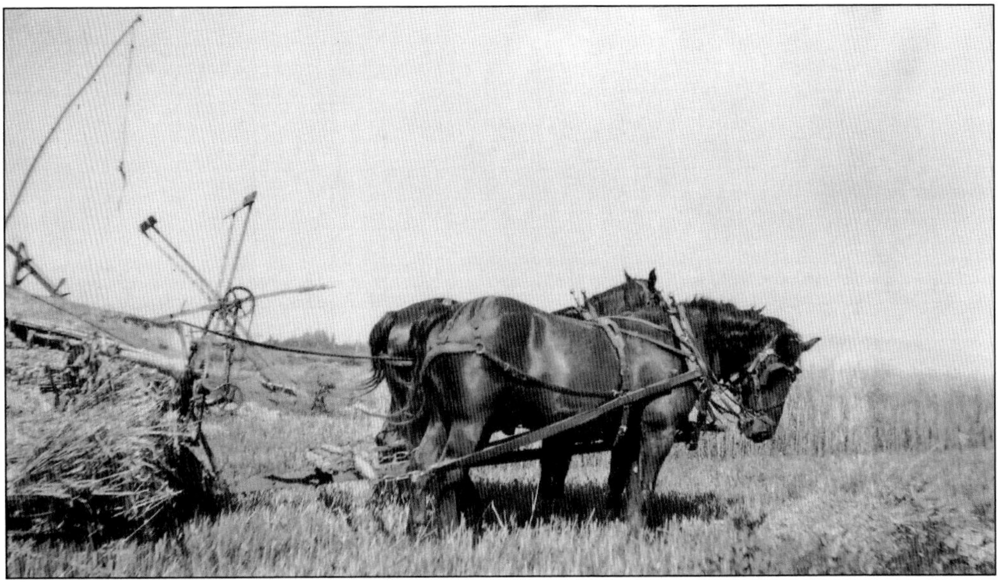

Above, a team of two stout horses pulls a sled during the wheat threshing harvest. Early settlers from Missouri, Kansas, Nebraska, and elsewhere were familiar with horses and adapted well to this aspect of rugged area farming. Farmers were familiar with collars and other leather horse goods, and these requirements generated business for more than one village harness and tack shop. Below, the term "horsepower" is expanded during hay harvest time to include an early steam tractor. However, the word's origin and namesake is still visible to the left and right, along with 19 adults armed with pitchforks, reins, a long pole, and even a coffee can.

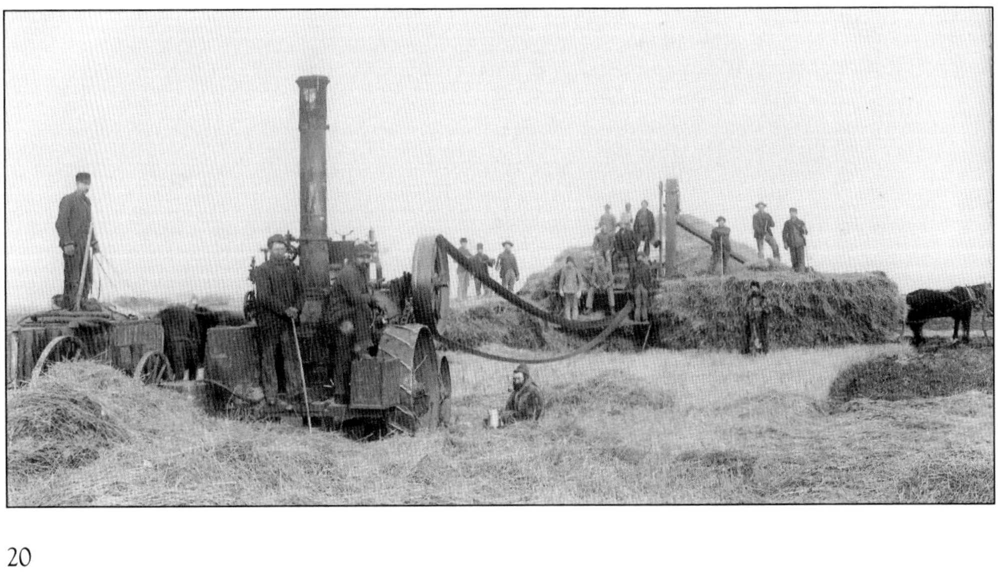

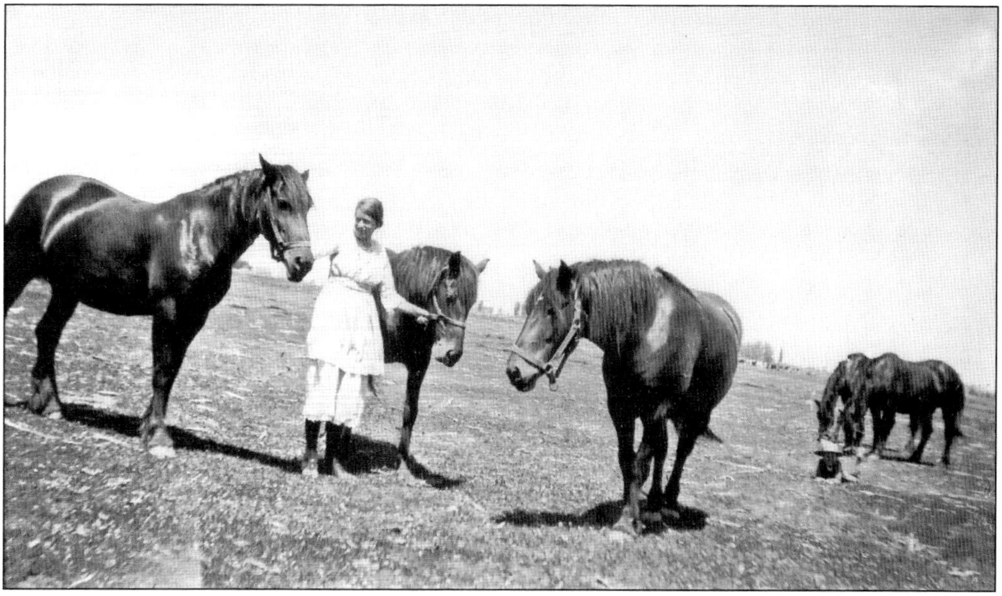

Above, an unidentified woman holds the halters of two horses. Note the young boy lying on his elbows and stomach to the right in front of the two other horses. Horses were everywhere on early area farms, providing literal horsepower for farming operations as well as transportation to and from the village, and also serving as pets that were often considered part of the family. Below, a barn on the west side of Eagle Road, south of Interstate 84, sits with a manure spreader and a wagon behind a dilapidated fence. To the right, two newer split-level homes contrast sharply with the farm-era outbuilding and remnants.

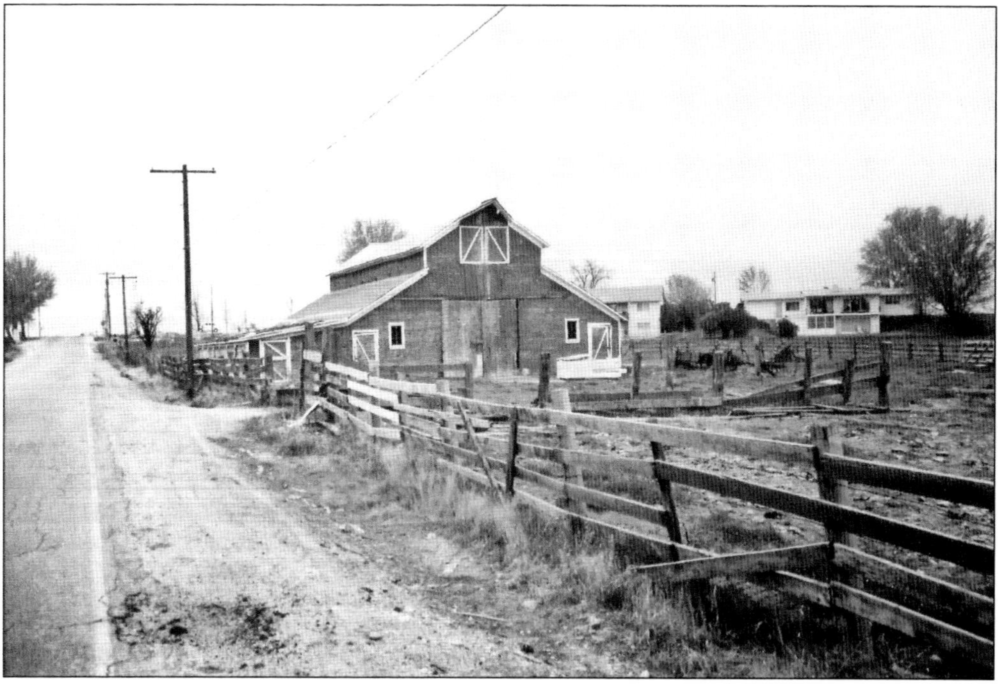

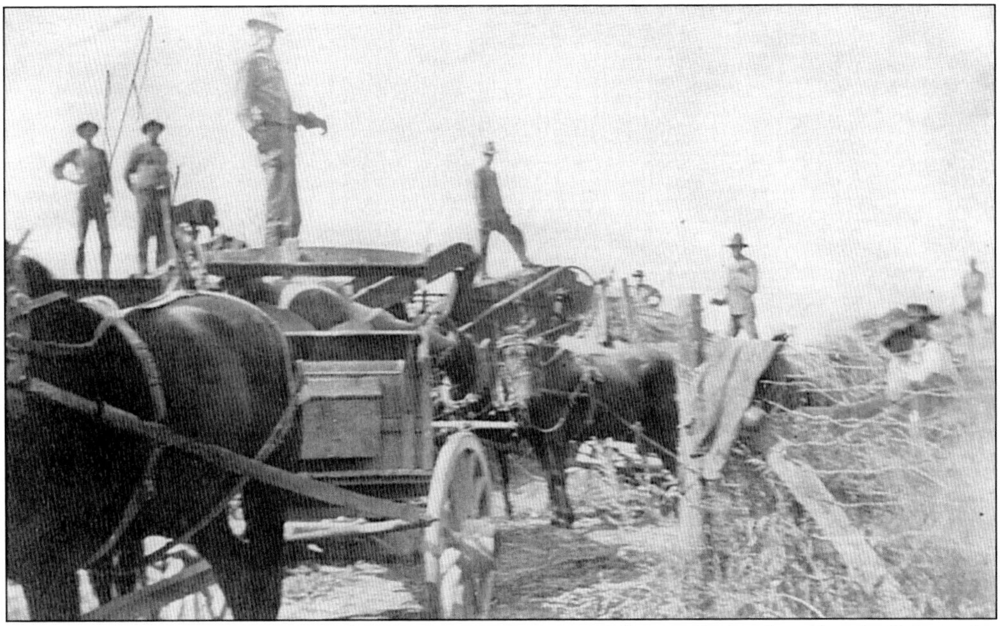

Above is a thresher operating at the Nourse ranch at McMillan and Meridian Roads. Below, the Mittleider Farmstead historic register property is south of Meridian and east of the Meridian-Kuna Highway. Atop a small knoll on the rolling hills of the Snake River Plain that extends southwest of Boise, the farmstead used irrigation water from the Boise-Kuna Irrigation District and included a two-story, balloon-framed banked barn with a gambrel roof and a foundation of poured concrete. Christian Mittleider constructed all of the outbuildings between 1945 and 1950 (the house was built between 1937 and 1940). The barn's construction design is reflective of plans developed by the University of Wisconsin's Agricultural Experiment Station, popular throughout the United States and used in Idaho from 1910 to the 1940s. (Above, RN; below, MHPC.)

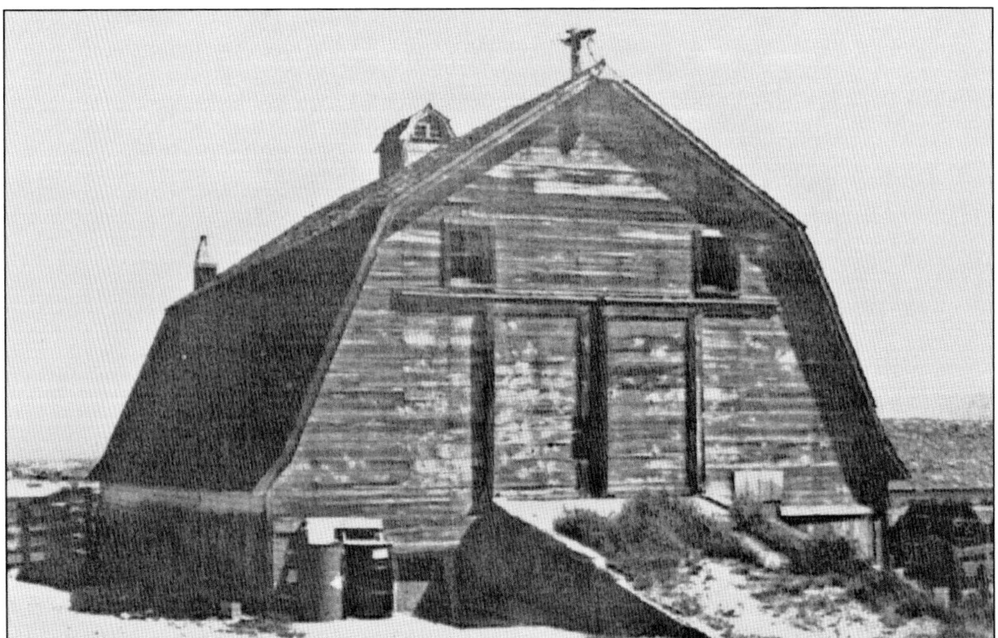

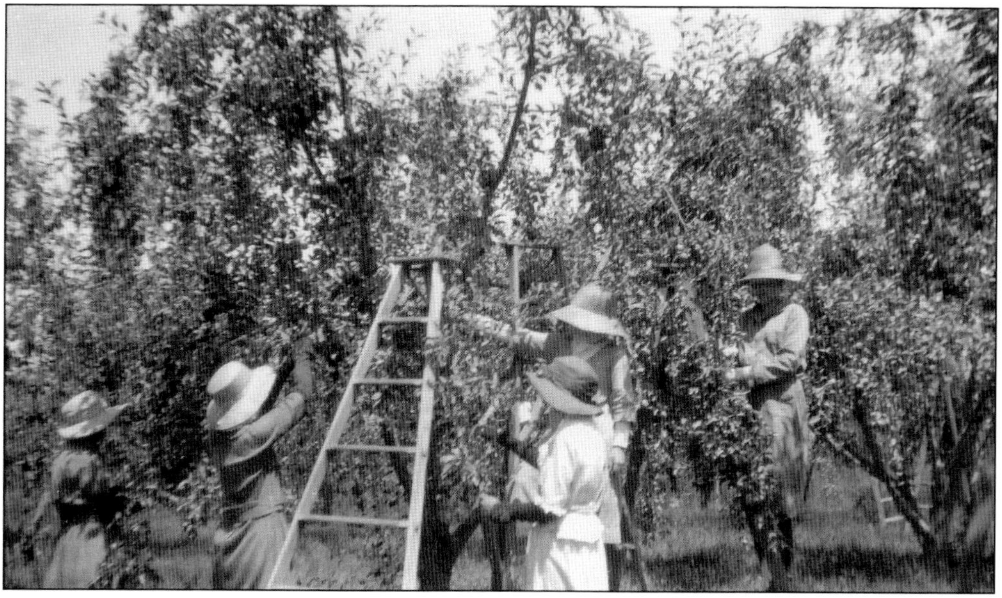

Above, five women wearing sun hats, one wearing elbow-length gloves, and another perched on a ladder's lower rung pick fruit. Below, a group photograph of workers at the packinghouse of Saxton and Riggs shows the overwhelming majority of the workforce was composed of women. Area evaporators, where the picked fruit was dried and processed for shipping, provided other industry-related jobs. Clysta Gray recalled that in early October 1921, "My father worked in the prune dryer. There were five in McDermott at that time for fruit trees, prunes, and apples. I picked cherries for two years at an 80-acre orchard at Cherry Lane."

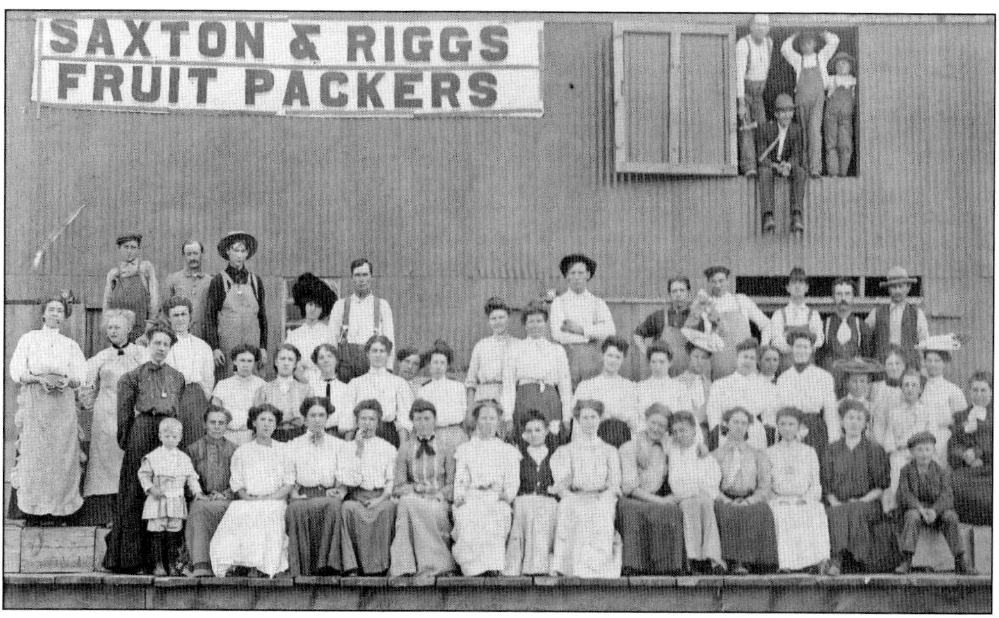

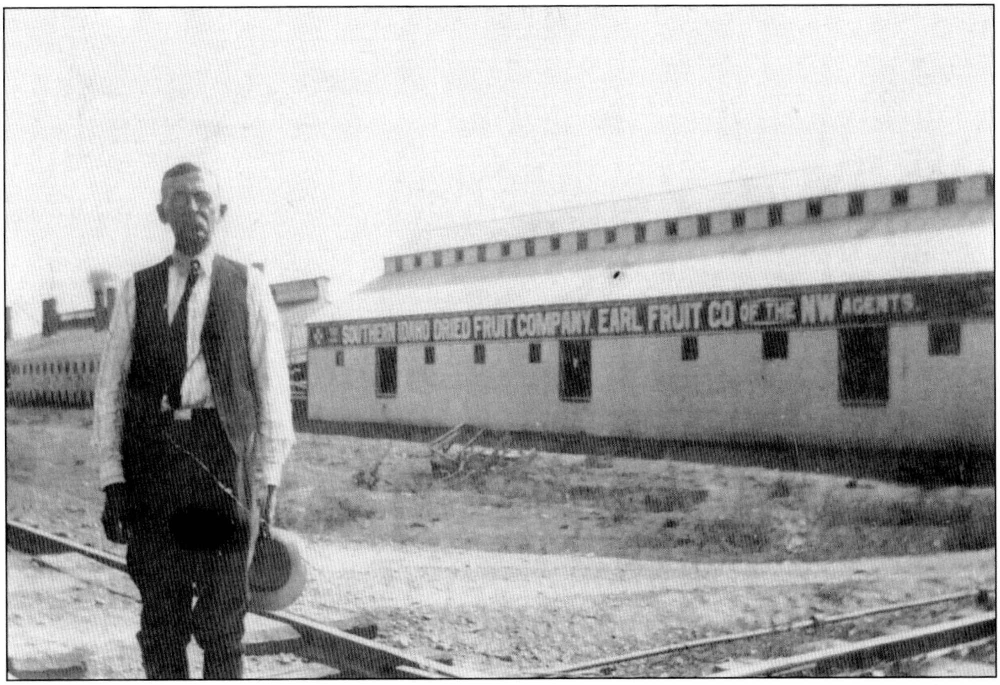

Above is an unidentified man in front of the Southern Idaho Dried Fruit Company, Earl Fruit Company of the NW Agents. The Earl Fruit Company packing shed was south of the railroad tracks between East Third and West Third Streets. Around 1924, a crew of about 20 workers, including several women, is pictured below in front of the shed. Not all fruit picking and packing were done by larger companies. Clysta Gray said, "Kids picked prunes and mothers packed 'em. My uncle gave me a nickel a day to pack prunes." Many decades later, in 1993, she confessed, "I still eat prunes."

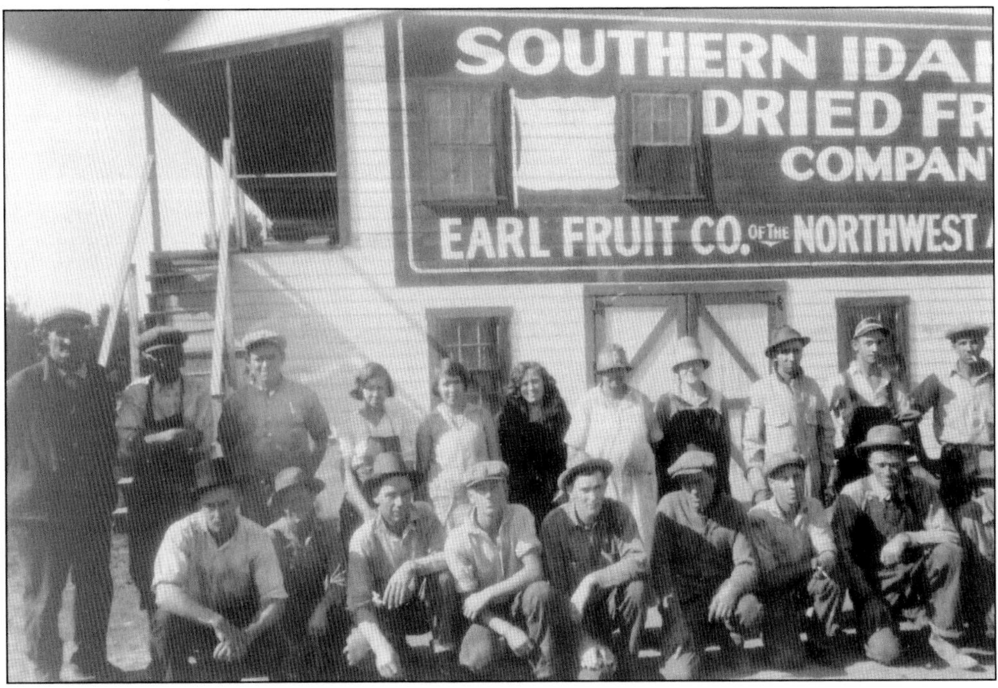

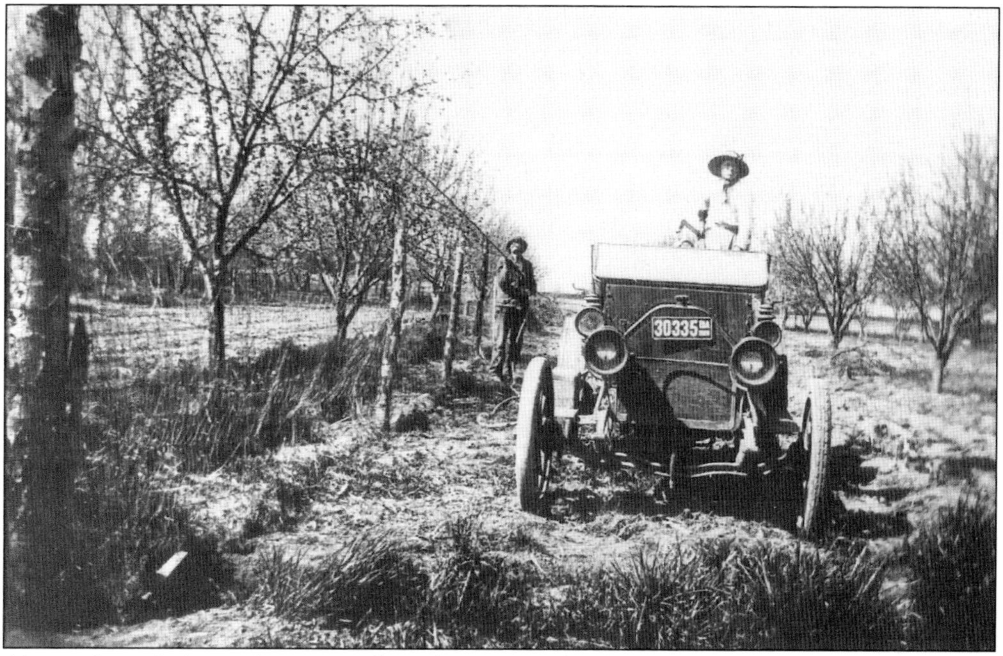

Above, the wife drives the auto, pulling the spray tank, while the husband wields the extended wand sprayer in one of the many orchards in the Meridian area in 1928. Below, a crew of mostly women wearing hair nets sort prunes in a large bin separated by wooden slats on September 21, 1939. The late Reverend Roberts said, "What changed the atmosphere in Meridian was the Dairymen's Creamery Association. The orchards began to disappear as dairy farms grew. There were 840 acres in apples in Kuna owned by the Stark brothers and 1400 where the Nampa airport is. Everyone started getting rid of their trees, especially prune, then apple." By the mid-1940s, refrigeration helped bring an end to the market of dried fruits. (Above, MHC; below, ISHS.)

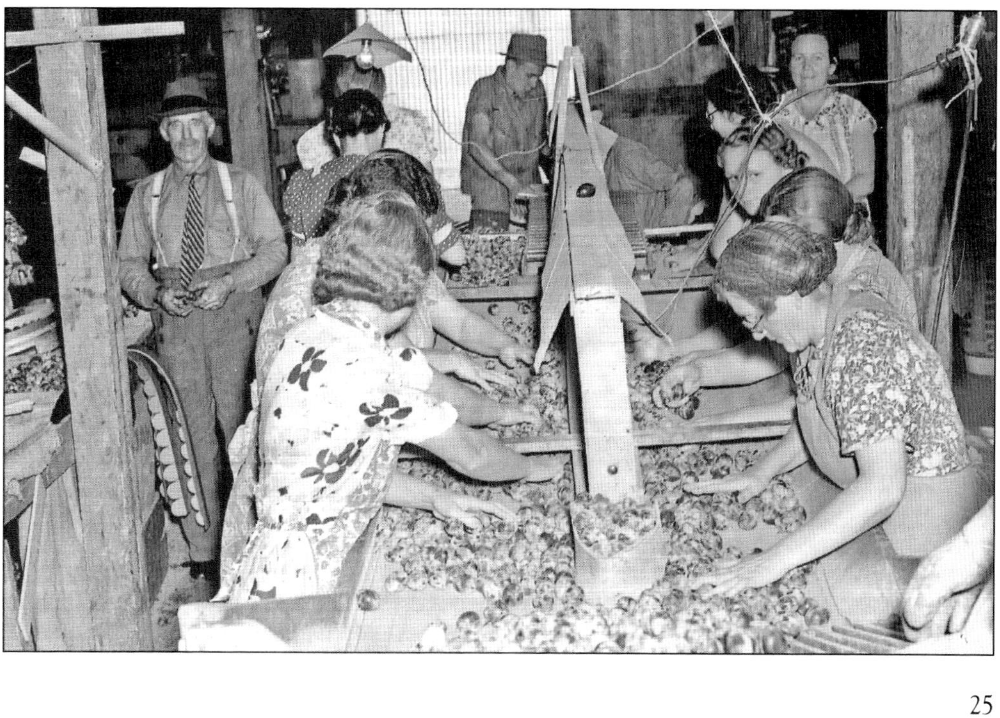

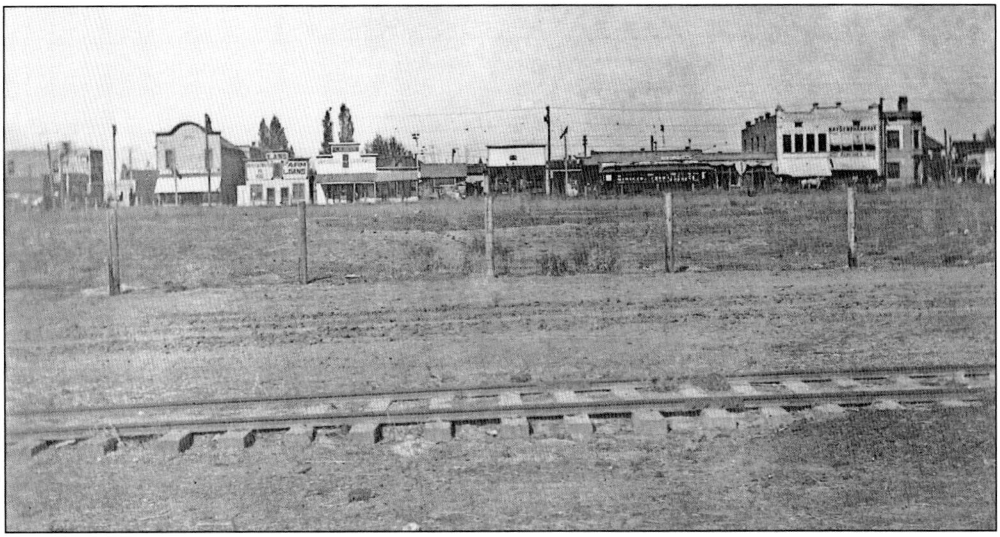

The railroad track, pictured above, is in the foreground and to the north, with an interurban car near the end of its short-lived route at Broadway Avenue and East Second Street. "Streetcars hauled carload after carload of prunes, apples, and lettuce to be loaded on freight cars and shipped to other places," recalled the late Rev. Evert Roberts. "Very few people owned cars." Below is a bird's-eye view of downtown Meridian between 1910 and 1915. On the far left is the IOOF Hall, the first public building in the village. The local IOOF chapter began at Isaac Daly's home at an 1893 Independence Day picnic. The lodge held its first meeting at the Rowan home at the current intersection of Nola Lane and Pine Avenue. A building followed in the spring of 1894, after Lizzie Badley organized the Rebekah Lodge for women in January. The IOOF established the village cemetery in 1893 and provided its members insurance and other family-oriented programs. The IOOF structure burned in 1923.

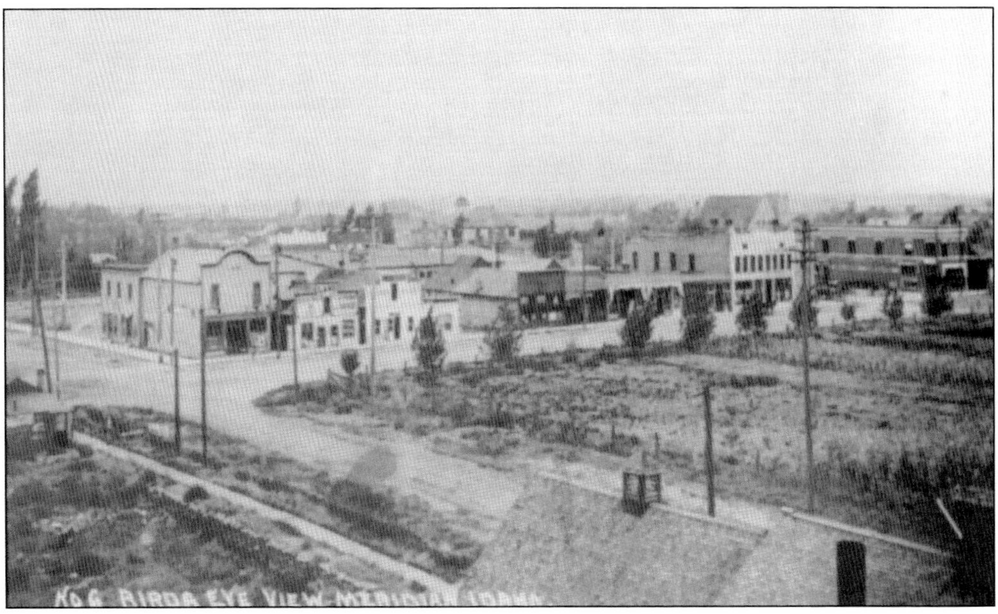

Two

Railways and Early Meridian

Transportation systems are about linkages between population centers and sources of materials and markets, and among grower, shipper, and customer. In Boise and Ada County, pack trains supplied the mining areas in the Boise Valley, while stage and wagon lines connected Boise above its western bench to points west and south. The west and south points included Ten Mile Station, the future site of Kuna, which was 10 miles southwest of Boise and Fifteen Mile Station, which was 5 miles farther to the southwest, toward present-day Melba.

By the 1880s, railroad tracks were replacing stage lines. By 1883, the Oregon Short Line Railroad (OSL) arrived at the Fifteen Mile Stage Station. OSL tracks reached Nampa in September 1883, but Boise was not connected until 1887, when the newly incorporated Idaho Central Railway Company laid tracks from Boise to the OSL line in Nampa. The two companies merged in 1889.

Meridian benefited from its location between two larger cities. In the 1880s, village settlement shifted with the arrival of the railway from Onwiler at Ustick and Meridian Roads south to what became East First Street and the railroad tracks. The railroad gave the area its first name, Hunter, after a local railroad superintendent, and brought in lumber, bricks, and stones for local houses and stores. It also opened a sparsely populated sagebrush site to area, regional, and even national markets for local produce.

Internal valley transportation took a giant leap with the advent of the interurban, which began in the early 1890s in Boise and, by July 1908, included Meridian in its famous loop around the Boise Valley. Local businesses raised $4,000 to help pay for the tracks from Onwiler, the farm of William and Eliza Onwiler, to the downtown area.

The interurban carried people, produce, milk cans, lumber, students, bicycles, and much more in far less time than required by horse and buggy. Large groups of passengers rode the trolley from Meridian to Boise and back for funerals, fairs, and other significant social events. They rode in mud- and dust-free comfort in pollution-free cars powered by overhead lines, with the only noise generated by the clanking of wheels on railway lines.

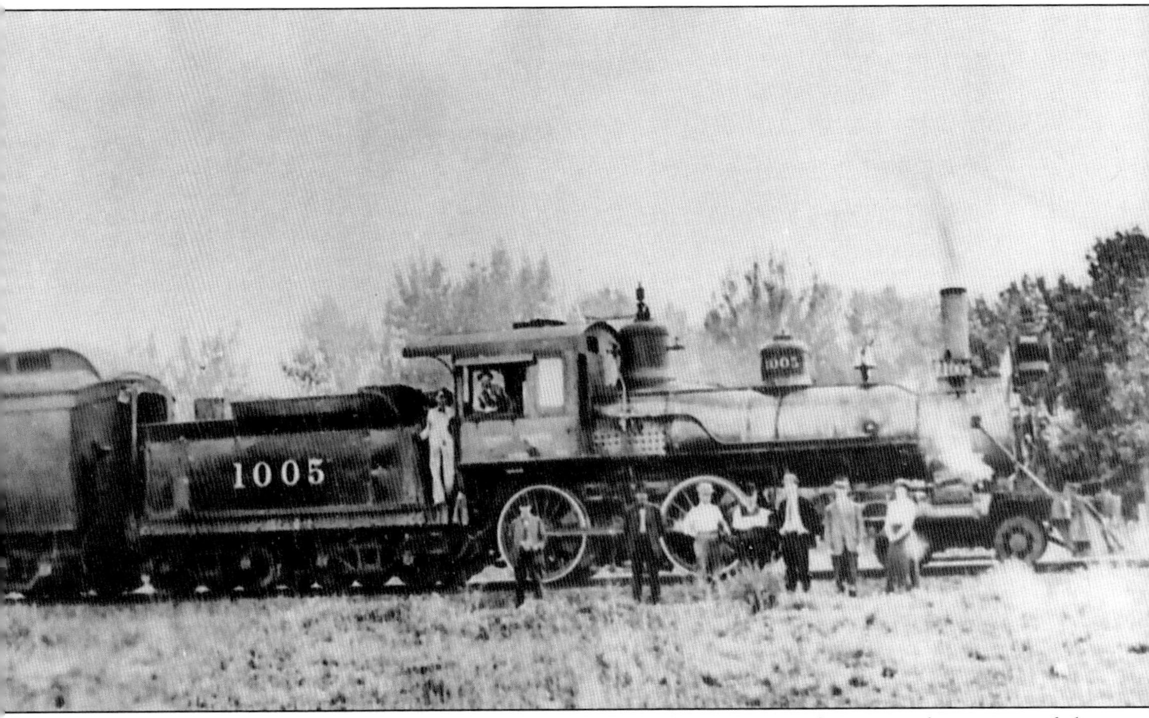

The transcontinental railroad was completed in Utah in 1869 and 11 years later, cars of the Utah and Northern Railway were operating in southeastern Idaho. But it required several more years for railway transportation to reach the Boise Valley. In December 1884, the Oregon Short Line, a branch of Union Pacific, began running cars between Omaha and Portland. But it took private investment and seemingly reckless faith to extend a rail line or spur from the main line to connect Boise and Nampa in 1886–1887. The Idaho Central Railroad dropped off and picked up mail sacks at the little Hunter station. The train cars carried emigrants and manufactured goods into agrarian areas and hauled large loads of fruit and other raw materials to regional and later national markets. In 1889, Union Pacific acquired Idaho Central Railroad.

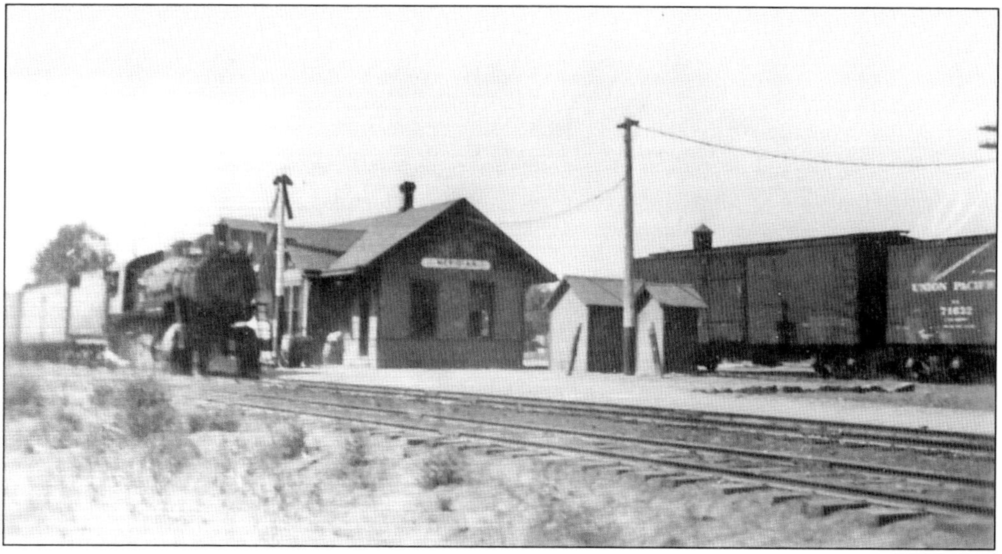

Above, the small wooden depot on the Union Pacific (Oregon Short Line) route from Boise to Nampa passed through Meridian, unloading freight and passengers in the early 1900s. The postmaster was there to receive the mail and sometimes invited weary travelers to his house, "a wooden structure with five-gallon tin cans flattened out to use as siding," according to Mary French in describing her arrival to Meridian on January 1, 1894. Below are transport workers of F. M. Slater City Dray. Mary French wrote that in 1894, when she stepped off the train in Meridian, "The usual gathering of young men were there waiting for the mail to be distributed, and one that I have never forgotten was George Deck. He was the life of the crowd in those days."

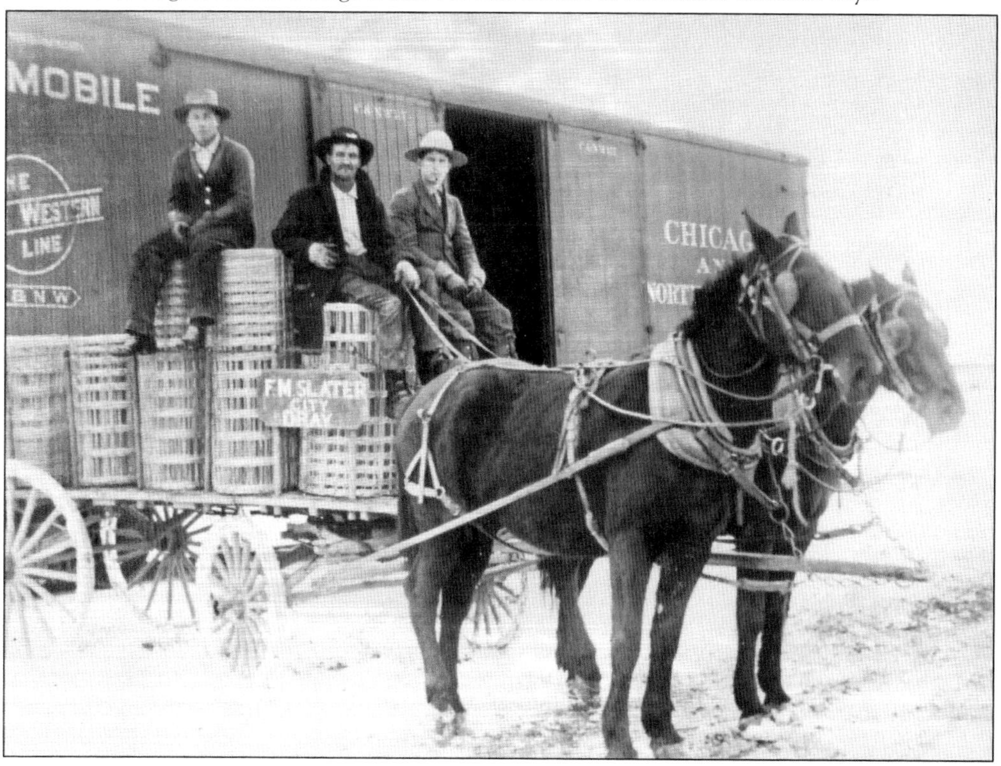

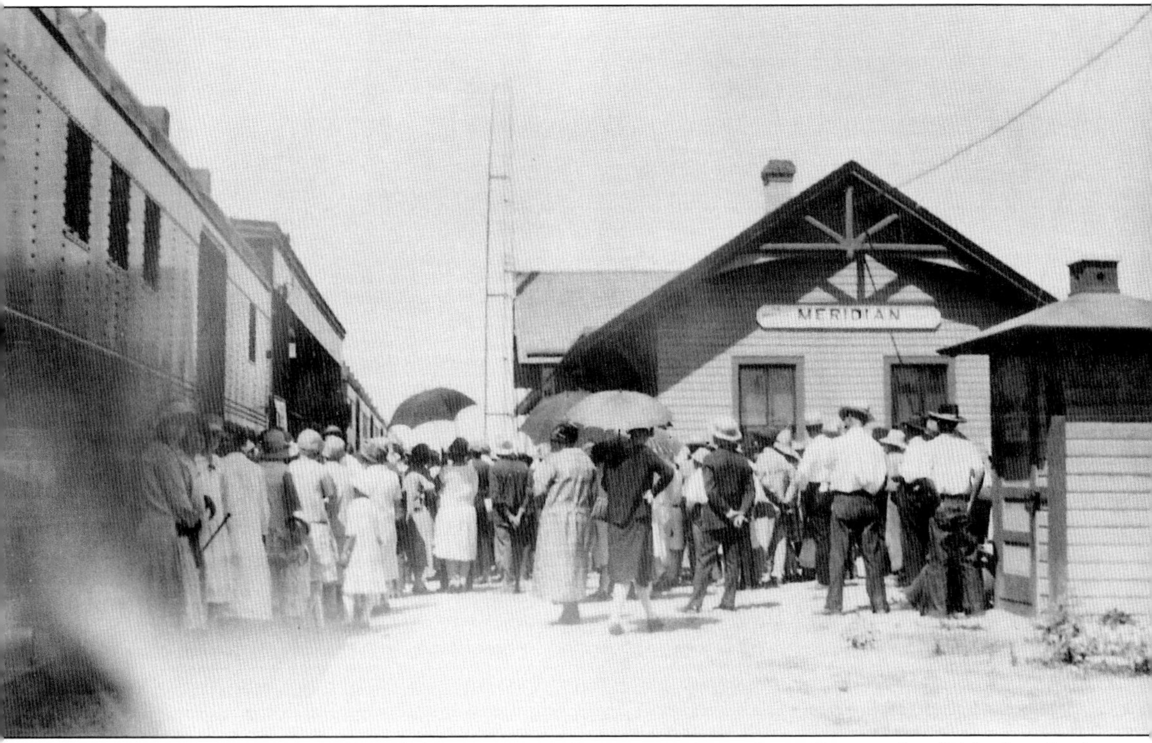

Meridian-area students board the Union Pacific Moscow Special car. During the 1930s, hundreds of local scholars traveled to and from the University of Idaho in Moscow via railway. Such a long journey to northern Idaho and back by rail fostered a strong sense of camaraderie, especially among devoted University of Idaho Vandal fans. The intense rivalry with Boise State University evolved in that era and intensified over the decades. Notice the abundance of hats and parasols among the passengers as well as onlookers to the side. Observe also how virtually everyone appears to be attired in Sunday finery for a very special occasion as the dense throng packs into the waiting railcar. This practice continued until railway service ended in the 1970s. In 2008, university students still traveled in groups along a chartered bus route. (ISHS.)

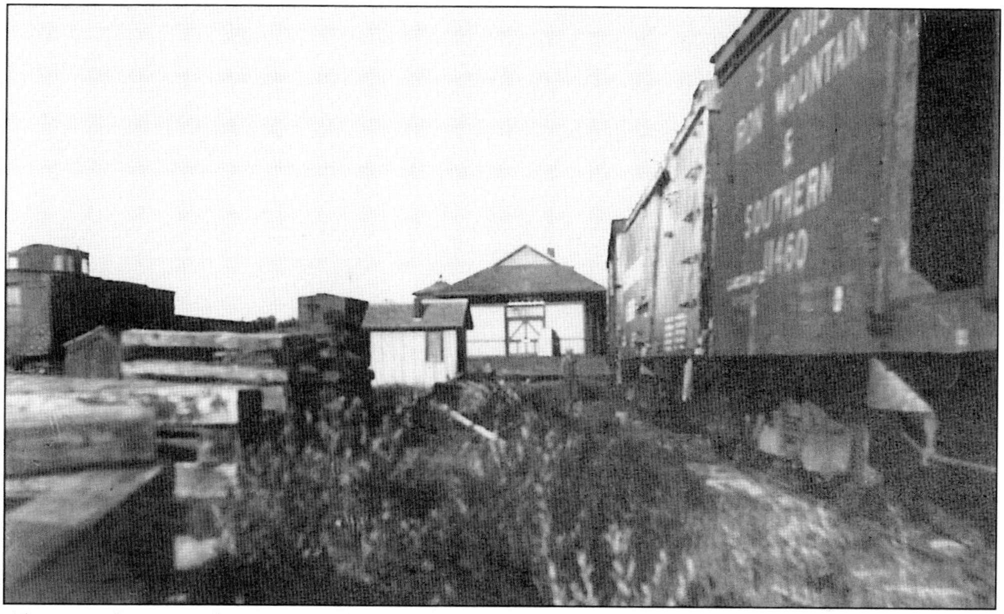

Above is the train depot around 1930. During the previous three decades, freight cars carried many shipments of hay, perishable goods, coal, lumber, and a vast variety of other commodities to and from Meridian and other stations in the Boise Valley. They also brought settlers from the east and connected a steadily but slowly growing community with economic and social centers in Idaho and surrounding states. Below, this later photograph of the Meridian Oregon Short Line Depot shows the depot on the left with a coiled hose hanging on a hook and the 1915 water tower in the distance to the right. The Challenge Butter smokestack's top portion is visible behind and to the left of the depot. These local landmarks plus the coal building and automobile on the right indicate the railroad's economic and social importance.

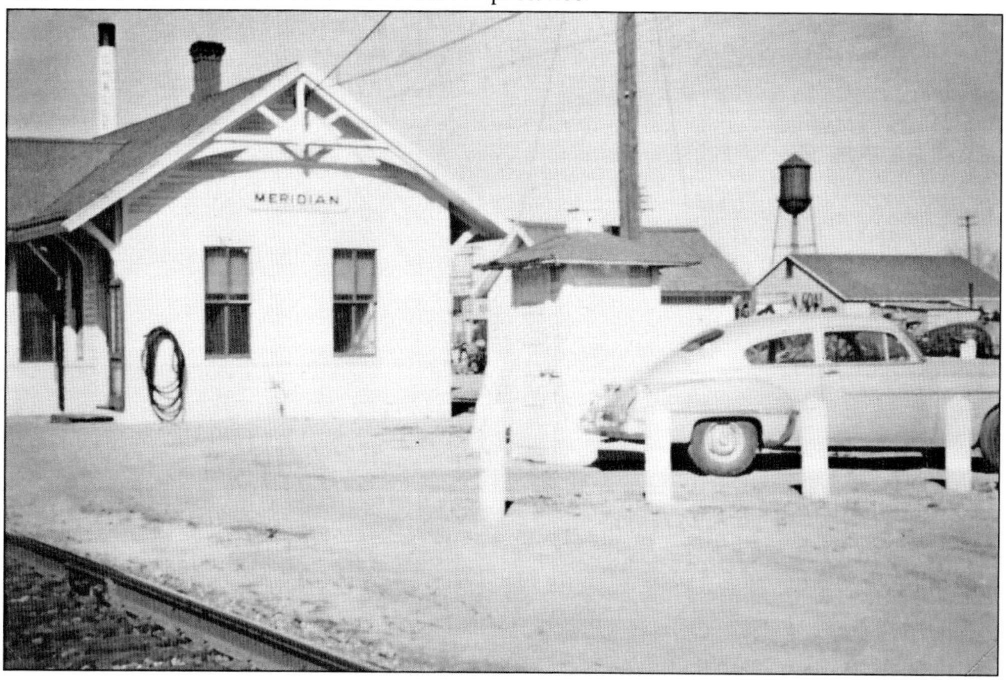

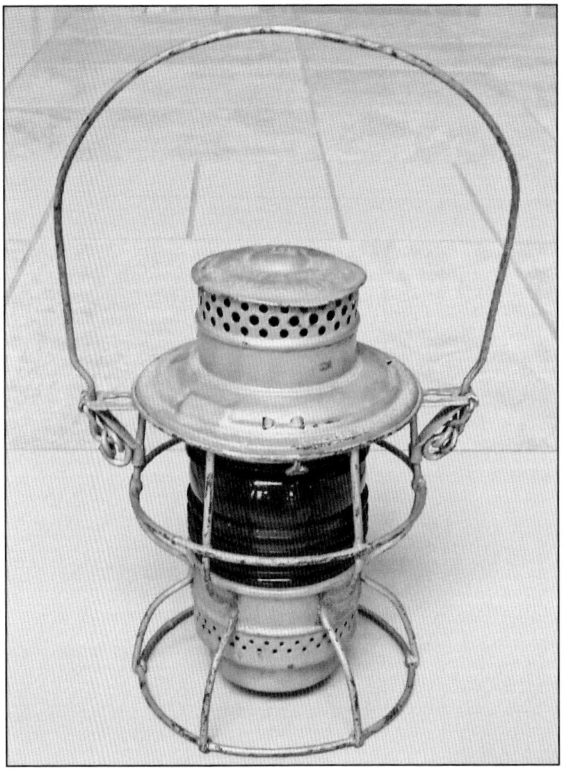

Fran Linn donated the Union Pacific Adlake candle lantern pictured at left to the Meridian History Center in memory of her late husband, John Linn, a former Meridian Union Pacific freight agent. Charles "Red" and Louise Gambill, parents of Sue (Gerry) Mattison, donated the caboose lantern pictured below. Railroad lanterns are basically a metal cage with a translucent globe that protects a source of light. They were used for relaying signals and inspecting trains at night. Collectors look for earlier types of lanterns that burned kerosene, signal oil, or other fuel types. Most are trainmen's lanterns used by railroad crewmembers, but some are conductors' lanterns used in passenger service and inspectors' lanterns used for inspecting cars in terminals and train yards. Today any globe or lantern with a railroad marking is highly prized by collectors of early railway artifacts. (Both PAP.)

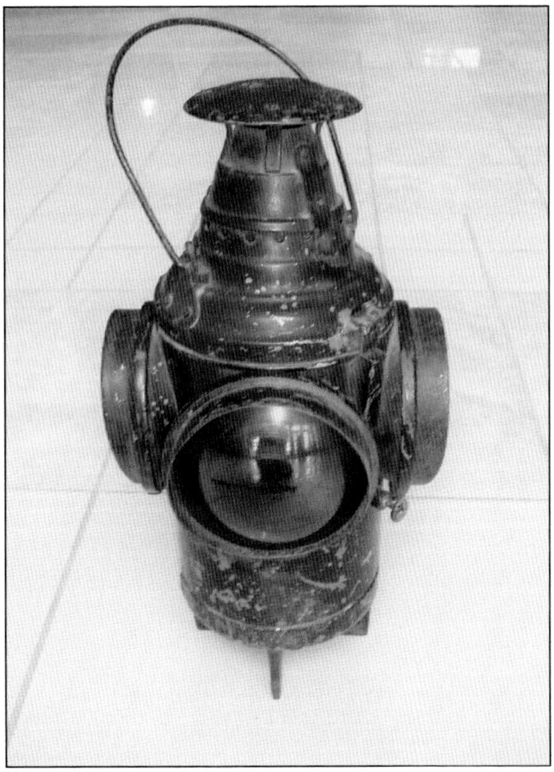

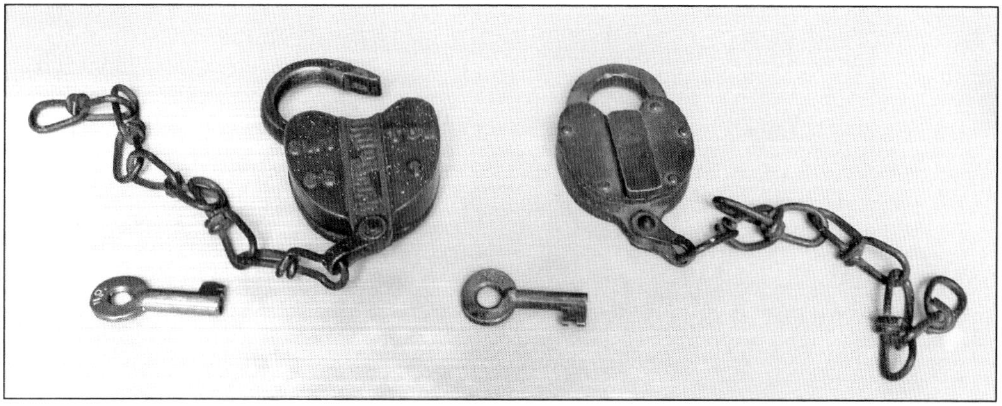

Union Pacific (UP) switch locks with keys, pictured above, were used to prevent unauthorized persons from changing switches on the train. Workers on the caboose were issued keys to these locks, which is why it was so important to have someone in the rear car. Today the switches are controlled electronically. A railroad switch or turnout is a mechanical installation at a point where one rail track divides into two. The correct setting of points on the switches is fundamental to the safe operation of a railway. Below is the UP switch cleanout tool donated by Dean and Opal Merrell of Meridian. It was used to remove dirt and sludge buildup in the switches. (Both PAP.)

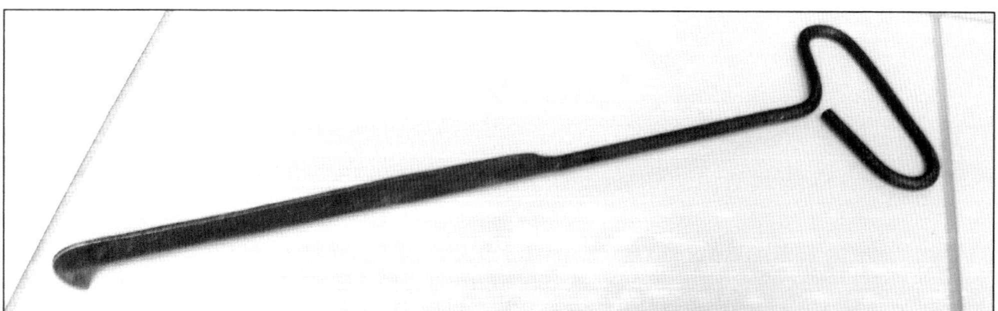

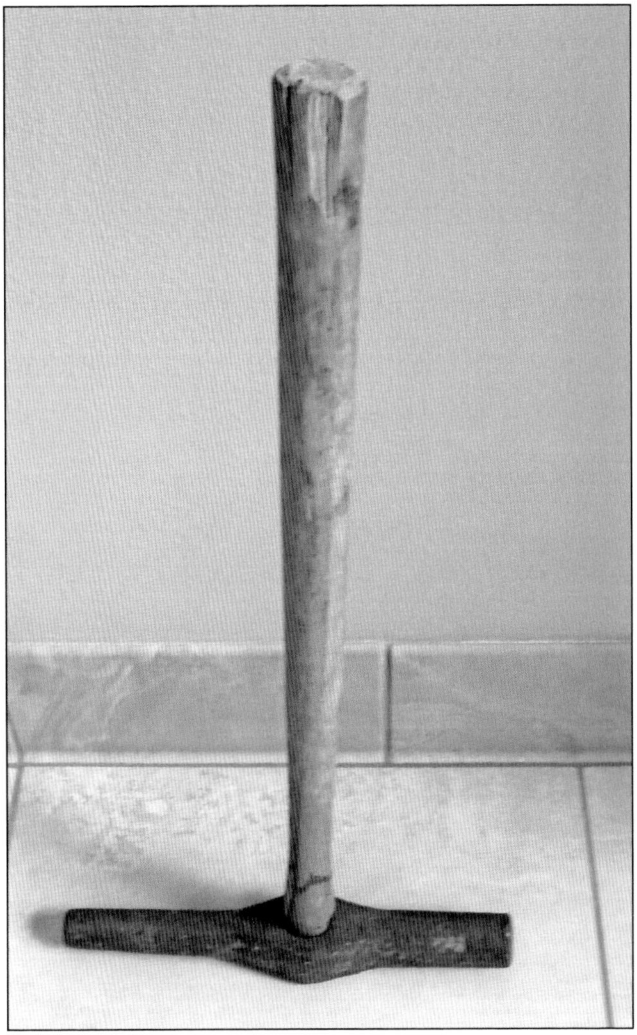

Left, a spike driver, used to drive nails through the track sections into the wooden ties, was donated by Jim and Diane Weseman to the Meridian History Center. Note the split wooden handle end, indicating a lot of use over time. The driver was an essential tool for construction crews and a handy item for the constant repair of broken sections of line. Fran Linn donated the UP freight car door lock bands, each engraved with Union Pacific, which are pictured below. These and other railroad memorabilia and artifacts are on display in the Meridian History Center at city hall. (Both PAP.)

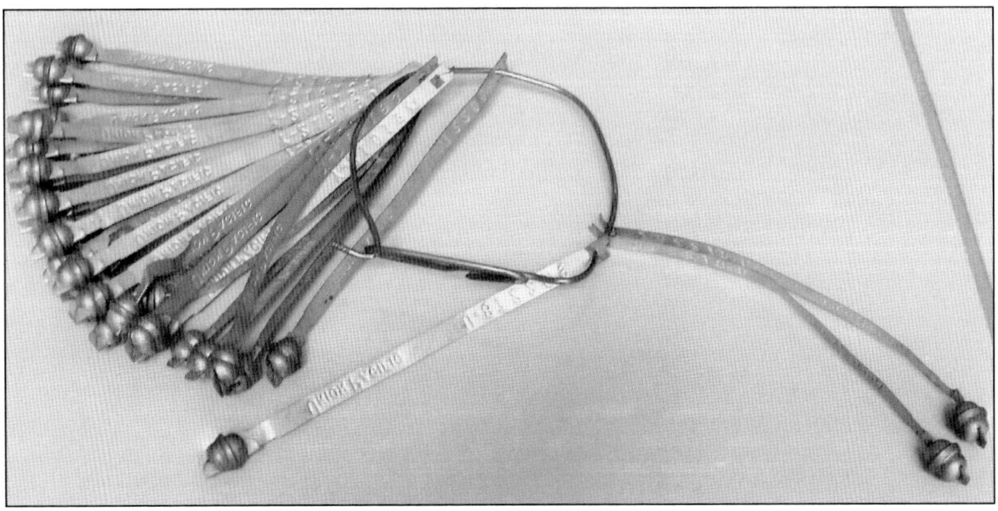

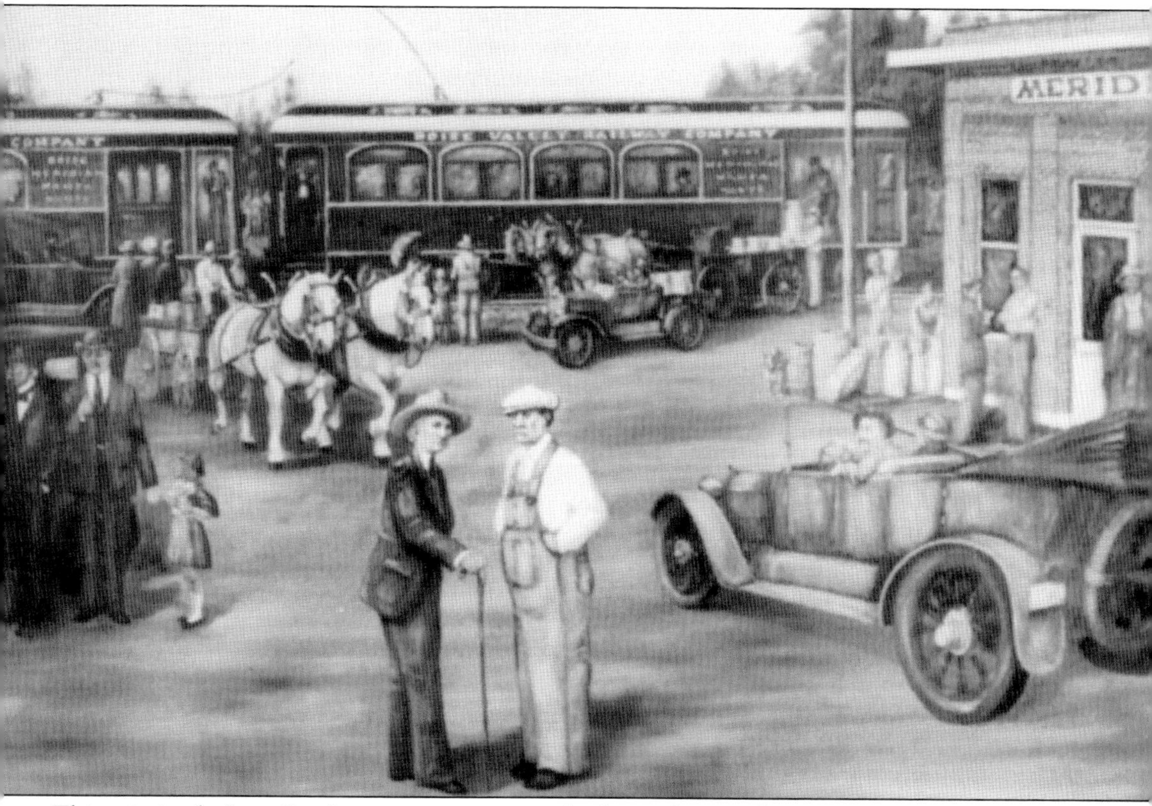

This painting by Jerry Snodgrass is on permanent display in the Meridian City Council chambers. A commissioned original artwork for the community centennial of 1993, it depicts people and conveyances, including automobiles, a horse-drawn cart, and a Boise Valley Railway Company (interurban) car, all converging at the intersection of Meridian Road and Idaho Avenue. The building on the right was the trolley depot that later formed the western half of the community library, which was established by the ladies of the Occident Club in the 1930s, after the demise of the mass transit railroad system. Note the milk cans and other freight items at the building's corner awaiting transport. Snodgrass, a graduate of Meridian High School, is also a well-known sculptor specializing in Western themes. His works include statues of Julia Ann Davis in Boise and Thomas Aiken in downtown Eagle.

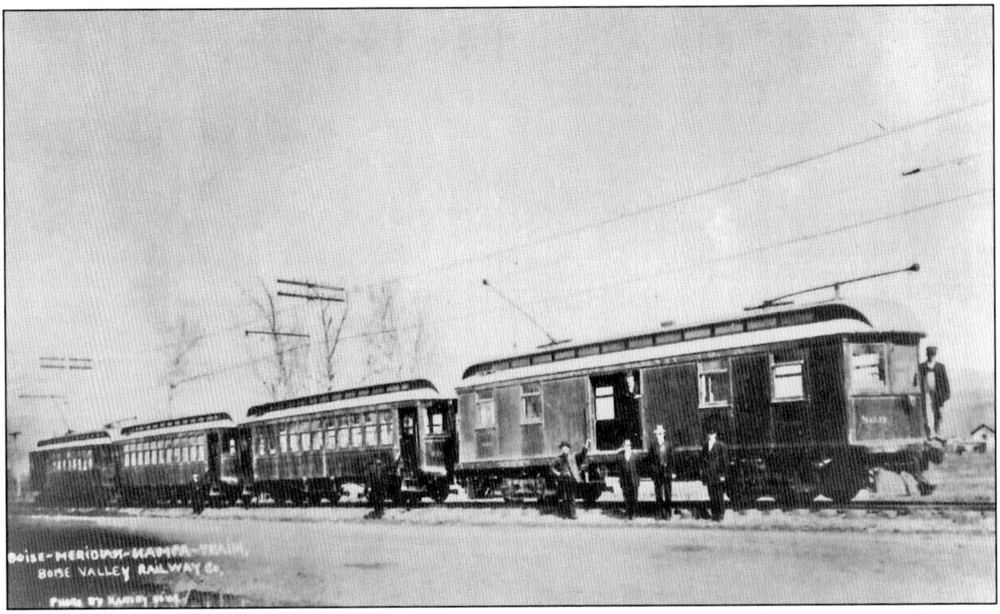

Above, this photograph of a Boise Valley Railway Company electric trolley car shows the crew that operated the Boise-Meridian-Nampa route. Boise developed the interurban in the 1890s, and the railway service developed a loop that ran from Boise west through Eagle, Star, and Caldwell before returning eventually through Nampa and Meridian. Below, a trolley car of the other interurban firm, the Boise Valley Traction Company, is stopped at the Ballantyne Station west of Eagle. Note how the pole connecting the car and rails to the overhead wire is in down or stopped mode. Releasing the pole to reconnect with the line restarted the trolley.

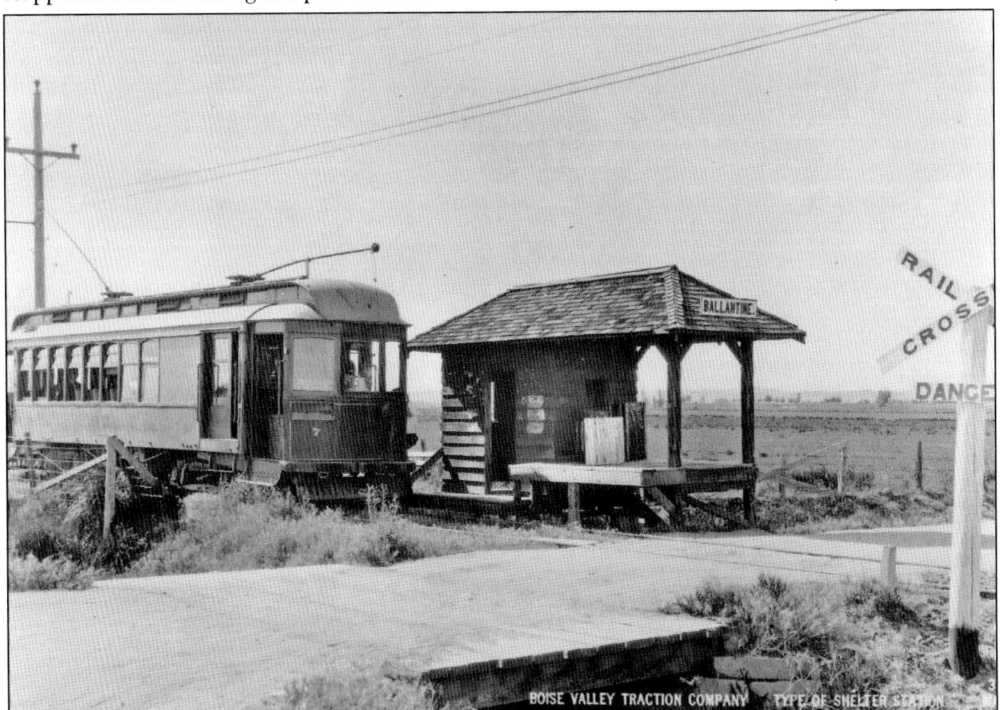

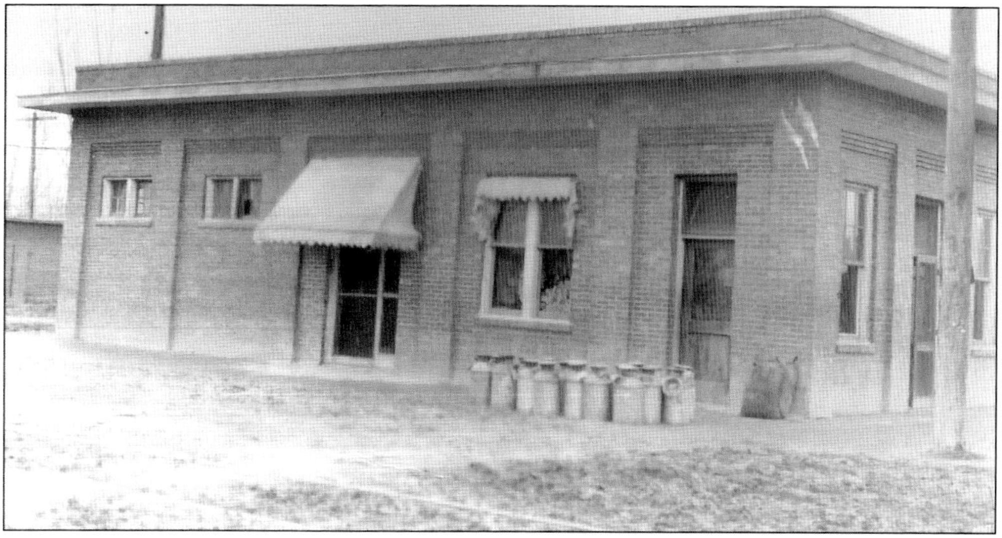

Above is the Boise Valley Traction Company depot on the northeast corner of Meridian Road and Idaho Avenue. Note the milk cans on the corner awaiting pickup by the trolley car. After the railway company was forced into bankruptcy in 1928, the building became the west end of the Meridian Library, thanks to years of hard work and bake sales by ladies of the Occident Club. Below, three interurban cars, including a flatbed for freight in the middle, are parked between Broadway Avenue and East Second Street. At the left is a horse-drawn wagon in front of Hayden's Pharmacy, which advertised its toilet articles.

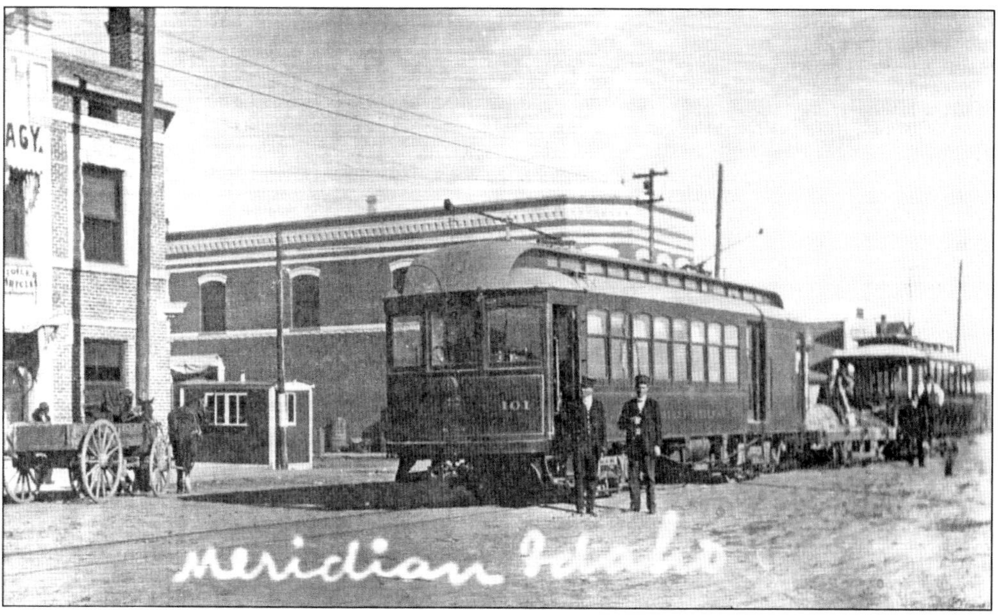

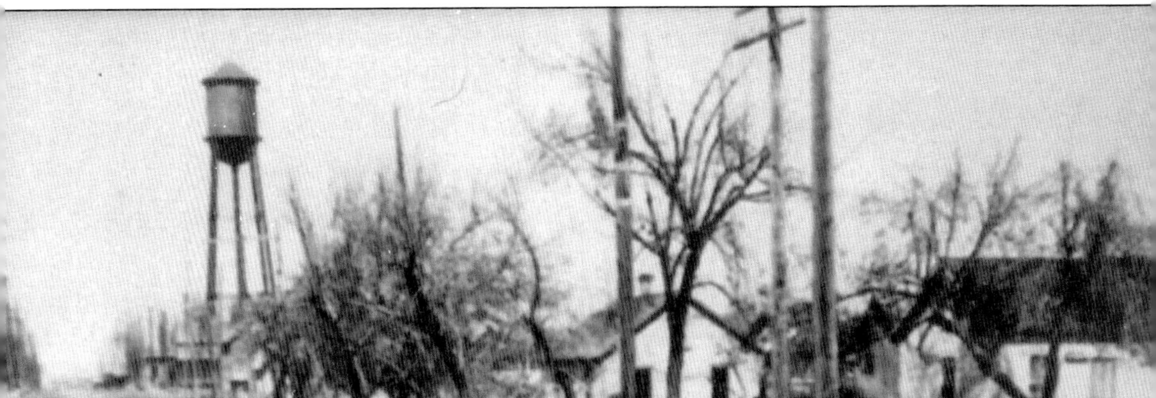

The above photograph shows the interurban trolley tracks and the 1910 water tower on the east side of Meridian Road. Farther to the north on the west side of Meridian Road north of Pine Avenue was the 1904 Grade School. The electric railway system carried students to and from school as well as produce and milk cans to and from the railroad tracks and the creamery. The late Clysta Gray recalled, "An electric streetcar line was built through Meridian in 1907. At first, it came to the corner of Meridian and Broadway, then turned east and went as far as East Second Street and Broadway. Prior to the automobile's arrival, there was heavy traffic between Meridian and Boise in the interurban. It was much faster than traveling in a buggy or a wagon or on horseback, and many were sorry to see the mass transit go in 1928."

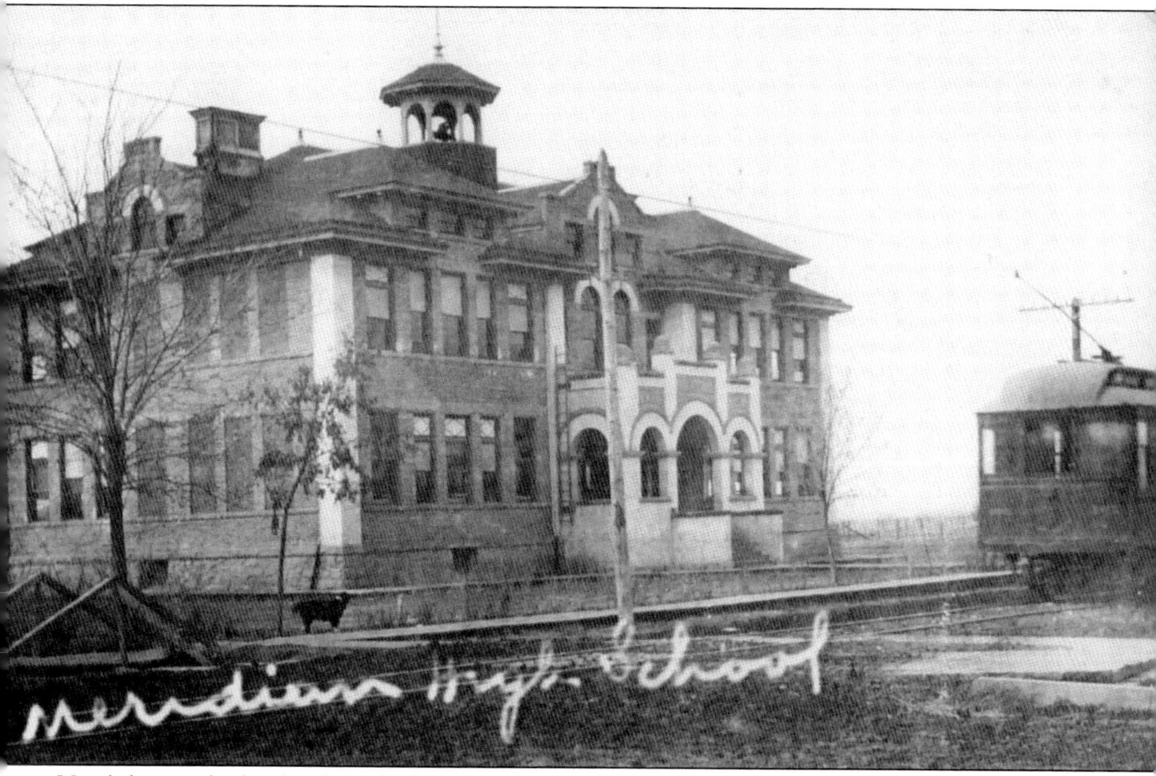

Until the new high school was built at 200 East Carlton Avenue in 1911–1912, seniors and lower classmen convened in the 1904 building known as the Meridian Grade School. In the above photograph, an interurban railcar is proceeding south on Meridian Road to its nearby station on the northeast corner of Idaho Avenue. Meridian's trolley service began in 1908, coincident with the last attendance of high school students in this building. According to the *Meridian News-Times*, on July 16, 1959, the school board announced the sale of the building and music room to Fred Bower for $20,000. Cullen and Sons of Eagle bought the old fire escape. Terms of the sale included removal of the building and within six months, it was torn down. But it lasted longer than the interurban, which was forced out of business back in 1928.

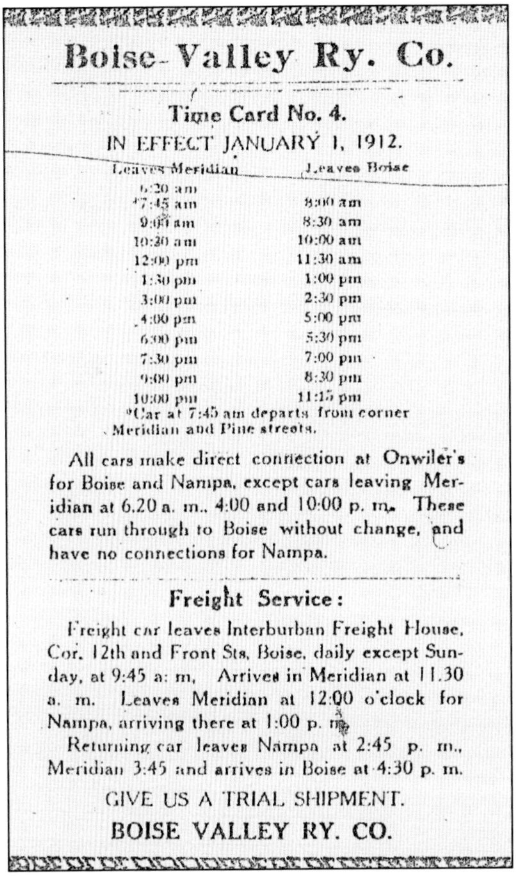

Boise-Valley Ry. Co.

Time Card No. 4.

IN EFFECT JANUARY 1, 1912.

Leaves Meridian	Leaves Boise
6:20 am	
*7:45 am	8:00 am
9:00 am	8:30 am
10:30 am	10:00 am
12:00 pm	11:30 am
1:30 pm	1:00 pm
3:00 pm	2:30 pm
4:00 pm	5:00 pm
6:00 pm	5:30 pm
7:30 pm	7:00 pm
9:00 pm	8:30 pm
10:00 pm	11:15 pm

*Car at 7:45 am departs from corner Meridian and Pine streets.

All cars make direct connection at Onwiler's for Boise and Nampa, except cars leaving Meridian at 6.20 a. m., 4:00 and 10:00 p. m. These cars run through to Boise without change, and have no connections for Nampa.

Freight Service:

Freight car leaves Interburban Freight House, Cor. 12th and Front Sts. Boise, daily except Sunday, at 9:45 a. m, Arrives in Meridian at 11.30 a. m. Leaves Meridian at 12:00 o'clock for Nampa, arriving there at 1:00 p. m.

Returning car leaves Nampa at 2:45 p. m., Meridian 3:45 and arrives in Boise at 4:30 p. m.

GIVE US A TRIAL SHIPMENT.

BOISE VALLEY RY. CO.

Left, a posted Boise Valley Railway Company schedule, called a "time card," took affect January 1, 1912. It shows that the interurban trolley cars left Meridian starting at 6:20 a.m., continuing at intervals of an hour or more for a dozen runs, with the last one leaving Meridian at 10:00 p.m. The adjacent column tells passengers when their returning cars were slated to depart from Boise. Most cars made a direct connection at Meridian and Ustick Roads for Boise and Nampa. The bottom half of the flyer contains Interurban Freight House shipping information. Below, an express bill of lading of the other interurban firm, Idaho Traction Company, is pictured, showing a 20-pound box of butter consigned to G. H. Wayman of Boise from Meridian grocer Sam Webb on June 18, 1915, at a shipping cost of 25¢.

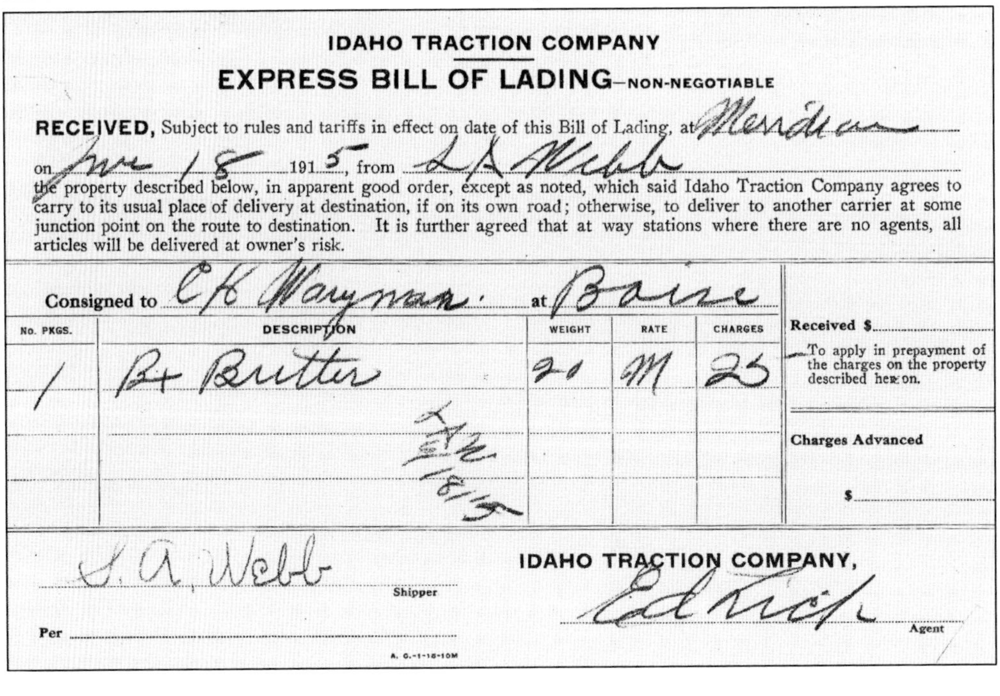

IDAHO TRACTION COMPANY

EXPRESS BILL OF LADING—NON-NEGOTIABLE

RECEIVED, Subject to rules and tariffs in effect on date of this Bill of Lading, at Meridian on June 18 1915, from S A Webb the property described below, in apparent good order, except as noted, which said Idaho Traction Company agrees to carry to its usual place of delivery at destination, if on its own road; otherwise, to deliver to another carrier at some junction point on the route to destination. It is further agreed that at way stations where there are no agents, all articles will be delivered at owner's risk.

Consigned to G H Wayman **at** Boise

No. PKGS.	DESCRIPTION	WEIGHT	RATE	CHARGES
1	Bx Butter	20	M	25

Received $ ..... To apply in prepayment of the charges on the property described hereon.

Charges Advanced

$

S. A. Webb — Shipper

Per

IDAHO TRACTION COMPANY, Ed Rich — Agent

A. C.-1-15-10M

Three

Education in Early Meridian

Arable land, salvaged or reclaimed, from sagebrush and village rooftops symbolize an age-old social dichotomy. When settlers arrived and cleared the brush away for buildings, they constructed houses and established a bank, postal service, and firms to supply the needs of residents and business people. Then the foremost need of area families was public education. But what is taught and who is paying for it continue to be subjects of community and public debate.

Generational differences emerged later and in the case of Meridian persisted as late as the 1940s and 1950s, when consolidation produced Joint School District No. 2, also known as the Meridian School District, from several dozen disparate common districts. Parents of students at former country schools, such as Locust Grove and Hillsdale, were often residents from Oklahoma, Arkansas, and elsewhere whose formal schooling went only as far as the eighth grade.

These differences came to the fore in areas of concern over education with respect to taxation and money issues and local control over school boards and curricula. Perhaps ironically, as population growth produced a village called Meridian, educational values and concerns began to shift from a rural landscape completely dependent upon hard work and irrigation to wrest a living from the land, to an urban set of values divorced from its rural roots. This is the genesis of the rural-urban social and economic divergence, the classic farm-versus-town clash of mentality and values.

One critical value is the notion of shared responsibility within a democracy. While the principals and school district board members promoted growth, they contended with a population characterized by persistent sentiments of opposition to government in general and to taxation and local control in particular. That is why the common school districts initially gave verbal support to and even voted for the Rural High School District but withdrew when it came to funding. In 1924, Supt. S. L. Hughell wrote in the school annual, *Mana Hasa*, that the Rural High School filled a need for more education than offered in the old, common country districts. But the social and economic divisions of that era persist to this day. The Meridian School District has evolved from a one-room schoolhouse along Five Mile Creek in the 1880s into the largest district in the state, with over 50 school buildings and more than 30,000 students.

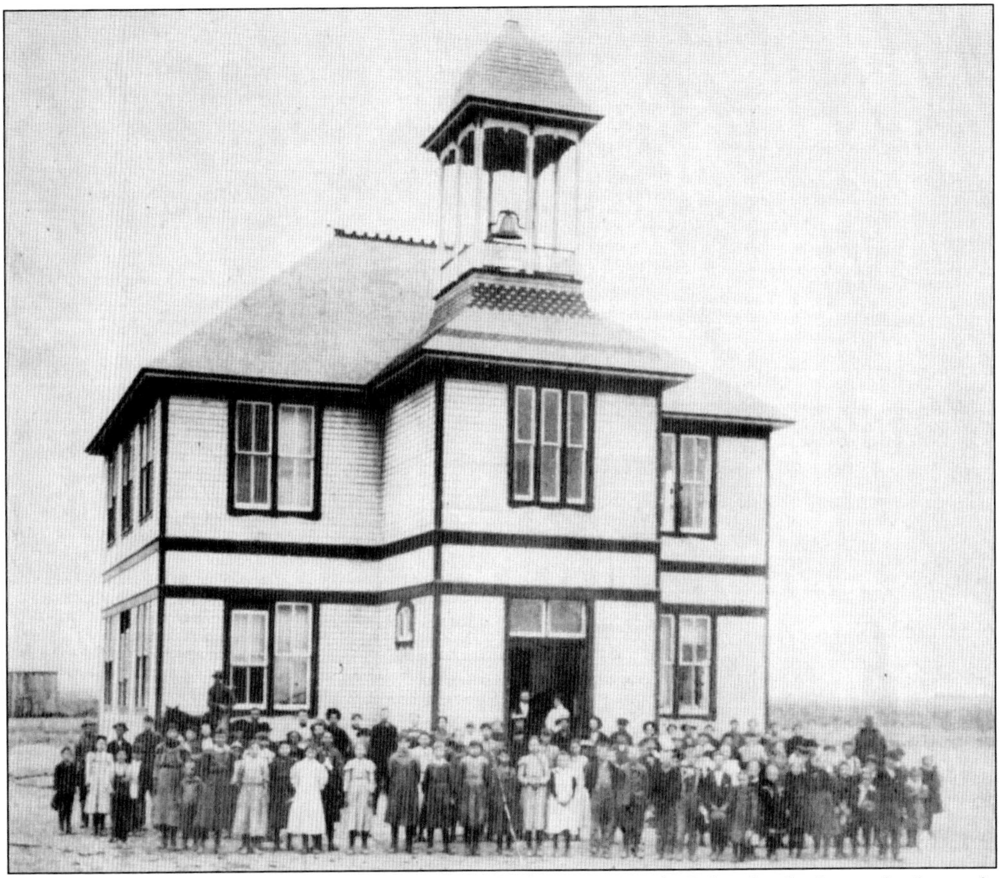

Above, students are pictured around 1900 outside the 1894 Grade School, which was built inside the village on the east side of East Second Street between Idaho and Pine Avenues. It succeeded the first schoolhouse in Meridian, a 16-foot-by-20-foot building of rough lumber north of Fairview Avenue along Five Mile Creek. The new structure boasted two stories and four rooms and was the first school in the area to feature indoor plumbing.

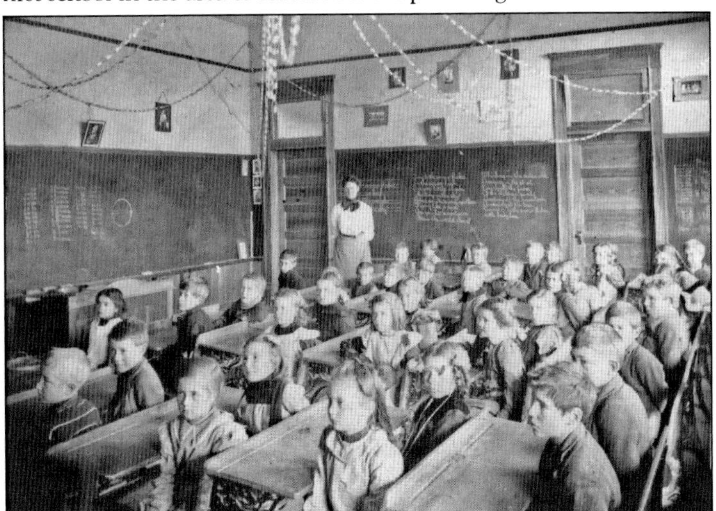

At left, about 40 students and the schoolmarm are pictured in the classroom of the 1894 building, which reflects a rapid growth in population in the area. Many families from Nebraska and elsewhere relocated to Meridian, where they took up residence and engaged in commerce. Overcrowding led to construction of a new school building in 1904.

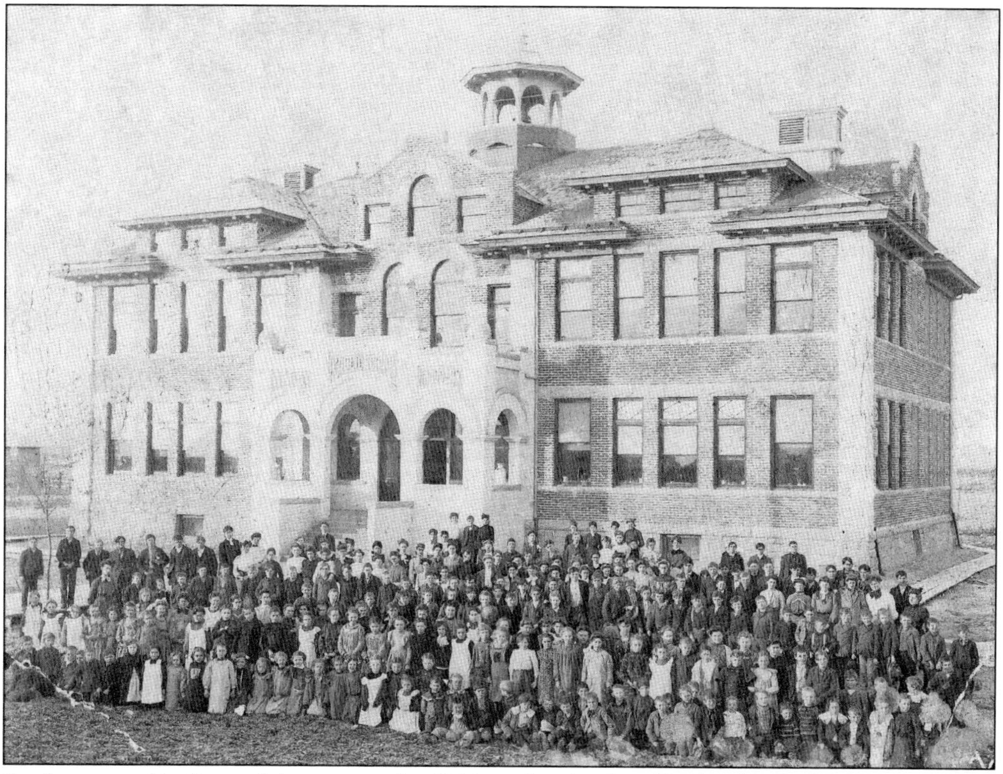

Students stand in front of the spectacular 1904 grade school and high school, which was designed by Tourtellotte and Hummel and built by Michel and Webber on the west side of Meridian Road between Pine and State Avenues. Clysta Gray wrote, "In 1904, a new school was constructed to accommodate the growing population and an influx of pupils. The old (1894) school was later reopened to hold an overflow of pupils and continued in use until a new high school was erected (1911). The 1904 building was torn down when the new elementary school was built (early 1960s) and stood where the district school offices are now (1990s)." Below, a later photograph shows mature trees in front of the school. (Above, RN; below, ISHS.)

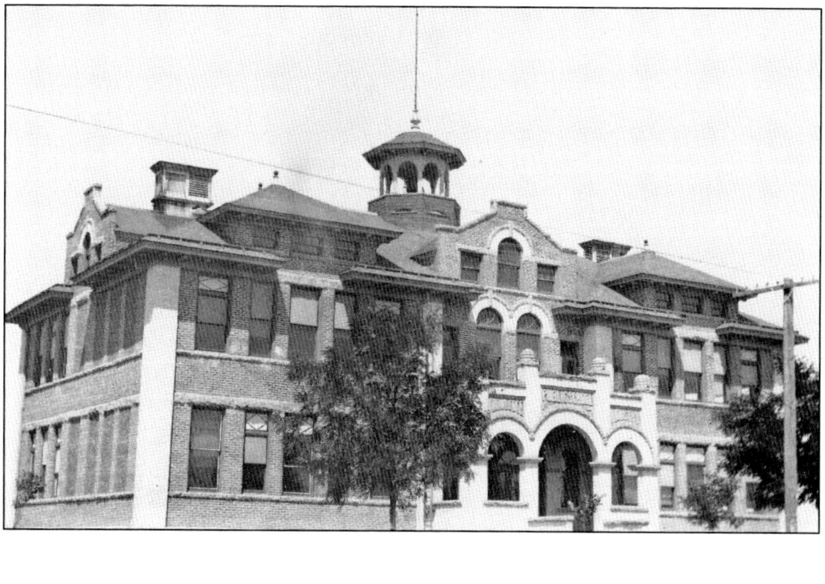

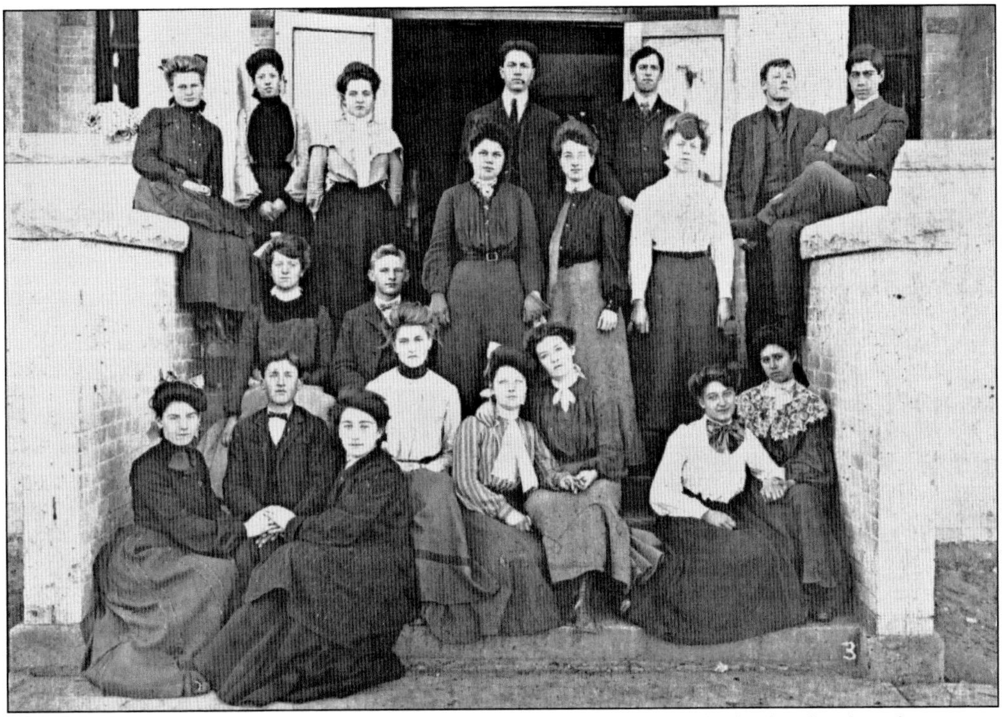

Above, 20 members of the 1906 sophomore class are pictured when the high school students were still grouped with other classes in the 1904 grade school building. In 1907, J. J. Caldwell succeeded J. F. Lawwill as principal of the 40-student high school. Students who wished to obtain a diploma were required to enroll in Boise for their senior year. The 12-man high school football team of 1907 is pictured below. They are, in no particular order, Billie Madden, Ray Seatt, Chad Clark, Henry Compton, Guy "Doe" Barker, Marion Rose, Guy McIntosh, Art Frazier, Lou Stokesbury, Don Barker, Harry Opie, and Jess Hedges. Hazel Ryska donated this photograph to the Idaho Historical Society. (Above, MHC; below, ISHS.)

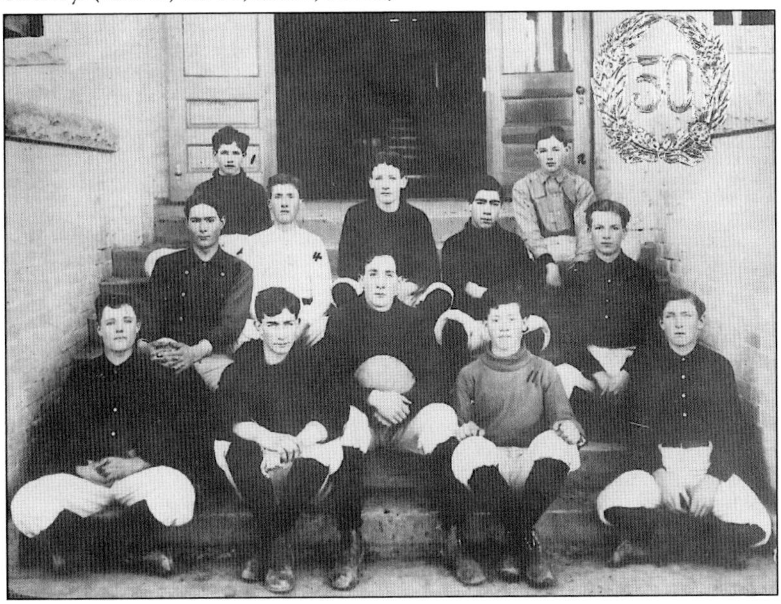

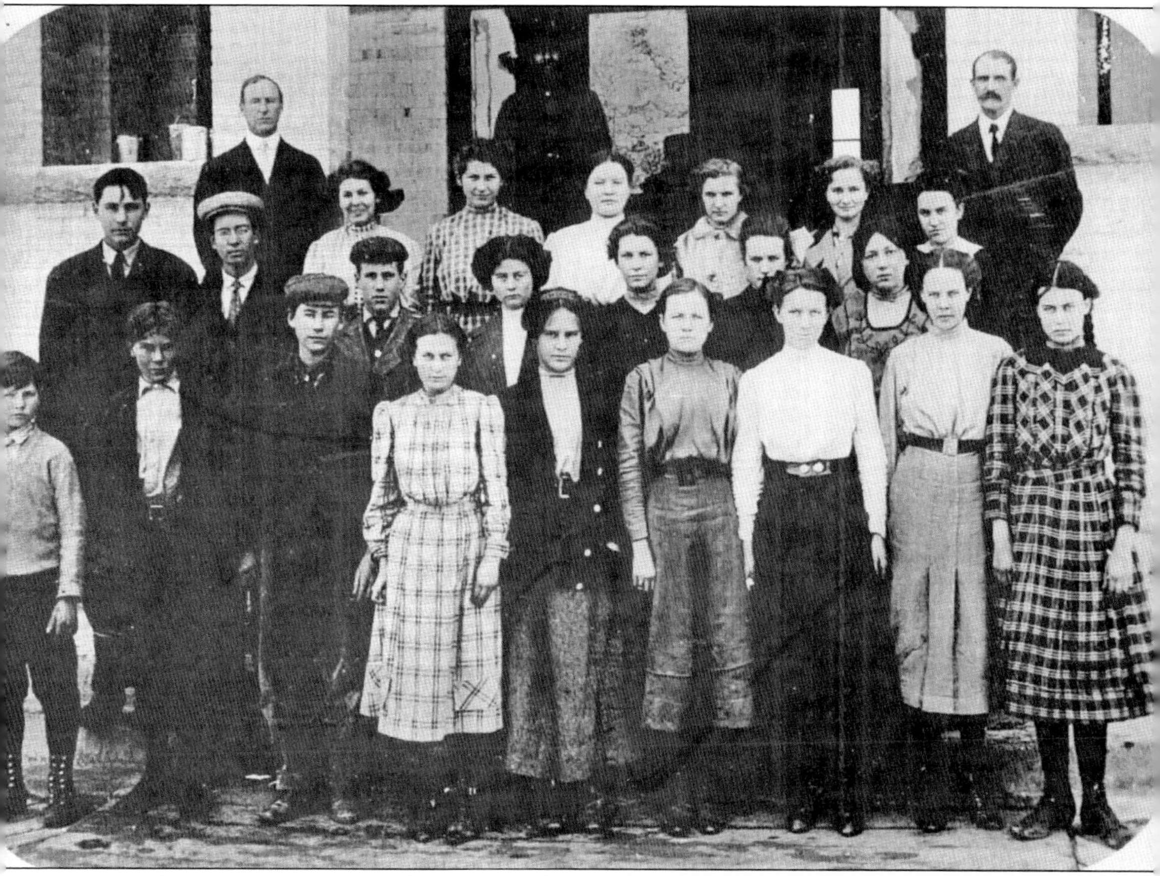

Donated by the Fenton and Hardin families, this photograph shows the entire Meridian High School student body in 1908. Depicted in no particular order are Carrol Hadley, James Woods, Gayle Shook, Ahmo Deck, Marie Millspaugh, Jennie McKennie, Jewel Beasley, Nellie Stalker, Bertha McKie, Fred Smith, Walter Smith, Fred Fenton, Alice Helm, Marie Palmer, Albert Daly, Thelma Jones, Naomi Starr, Vera Watts, Viola Clark, Estella Jameson, Lillian King, and Leda Tucker. Also pictured are Principal J. J. Caldwell, teacher W. P. Fuller, and janitor A. Picher.

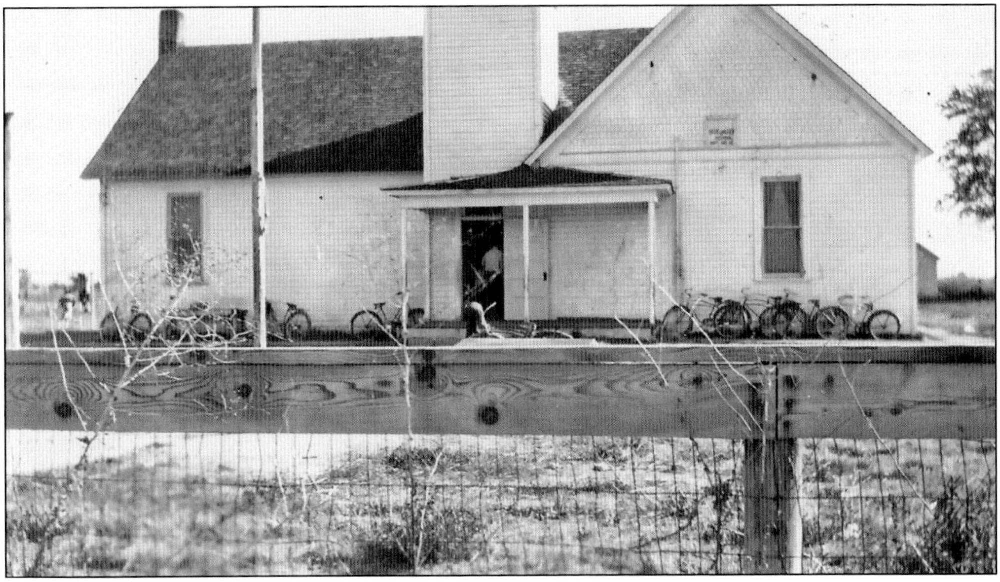

Blue Valley Schoolhouse, pictured above, was 3 miles north of the village and similar to other common school districts as it accommodated all 12 grades in the early part of the 19th century. In those days, students brought their own lunches, usually packed inside a container with a tight-fitting lid that was often a lard bucket. Boys wore overalls and girls wore dresses and, in the wintertime, long stockings for warmth. Inside the schoolhouse, pupils often had to share textbooks, and lessons involved memorization of words and numbers. Below, students gather outside the building for possibly a picnic or other special occasion. Note the wildflowers in the foreground.

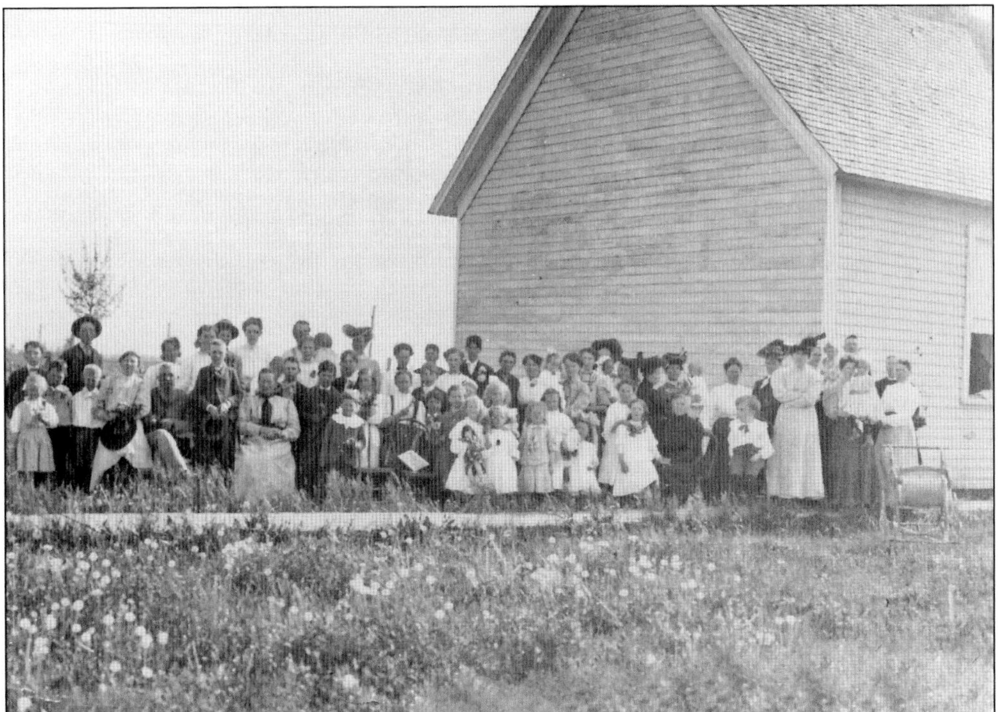

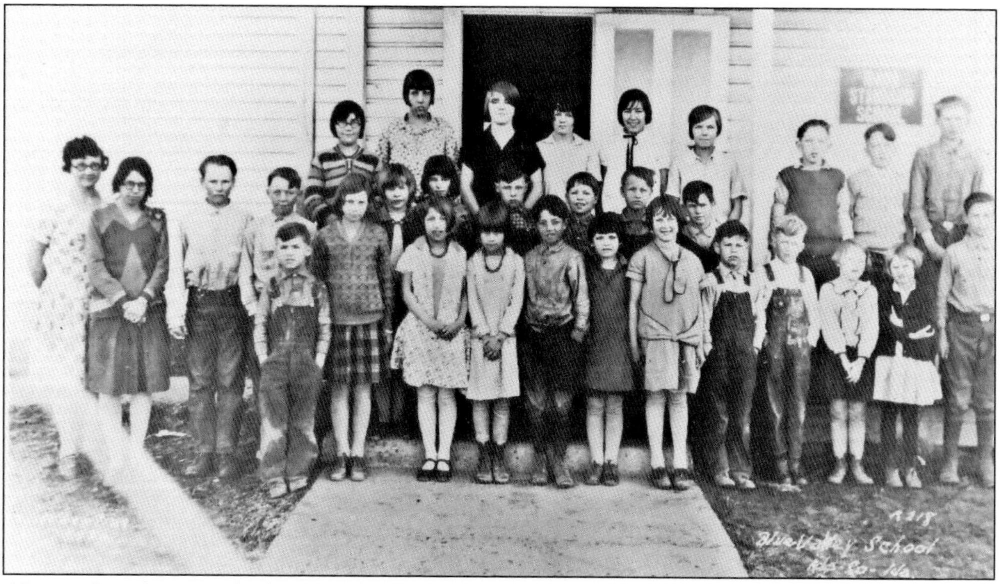

Above, this photograph shows a Blue Valley School class of 30 pupils and teacher Addie Powell on the left. From left to right are (first row) unidentified, Fern Adams, Edna Maw, unidentified, Donald Gish (son of Alice Gish, who turned 100 in 1993), Joyce Ulmer, Floydean Starkey, Eldon Adams, Al Butler, Ellen Cox, Ellen Gish, and Frankie Gish; (second row) teacher Addie Powell, unidentified teacher, Clifford Mathews, Leslie Cox, Vivian Gish, unidentified, Freddie Gish, unidentified, Leonard Starkey, and unidentified; (third row) Dorothy Bower, Bernice Getz, Dorothy Bentzinger, Louise Caster, unidentified, Alma Mathews, Eddie Maw, Wayne Bower, and Bill Gish. The Roosevelt School, pictured below around 1904–1905, was west of Meridian on Black Cat Road. There were nearly 50 "common schools" in what is now Joint School District No. 2. Other schools included Amity, Locust Grove, Linder, Hillsdale, Upper Fairview, Victory, Eagle, Star, and Dry Creek. (Above, MHC; below, ISHS.)

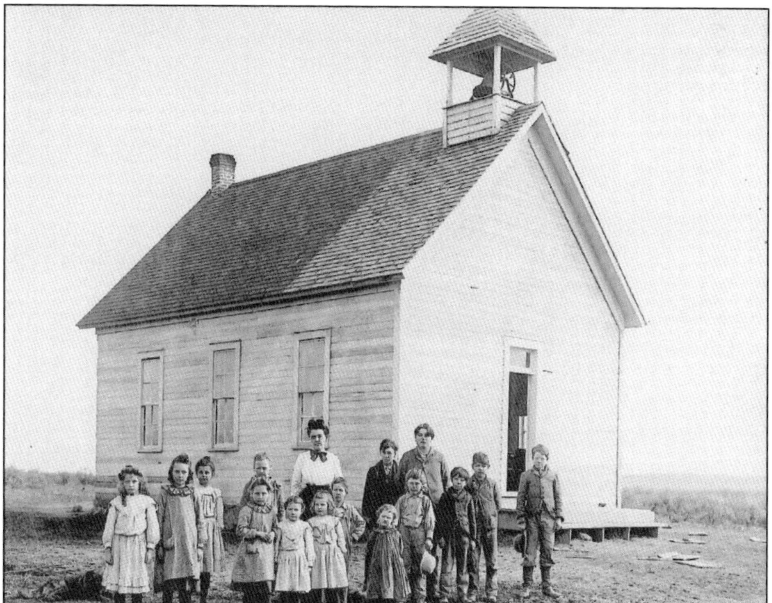

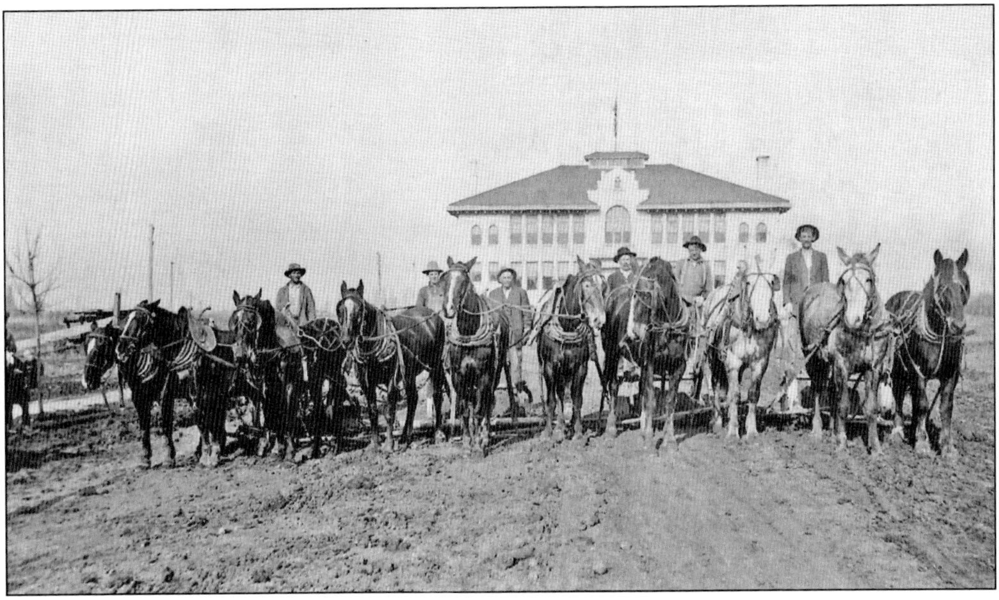

Above, teams of horses level the area in front of the high school. Local, taxpaying citizens submitted a petition to Ada County commissioners for a rural high school district. The latter authorized an election on August 10, 1910, when a majority of those casting ballots were in favor of the measure. However, all except two of the surrounding common districts balked at paying and withdrew from the project, causing financial problems for the new district that continued for many years. In 1920, six districts decided to pay taxes for the high school, raising the number to eight districts in support. Below is a close-up of the Rural High School that was built in 1912 on East Carlton Avenue. (Above, ISHS; below, MHC.)

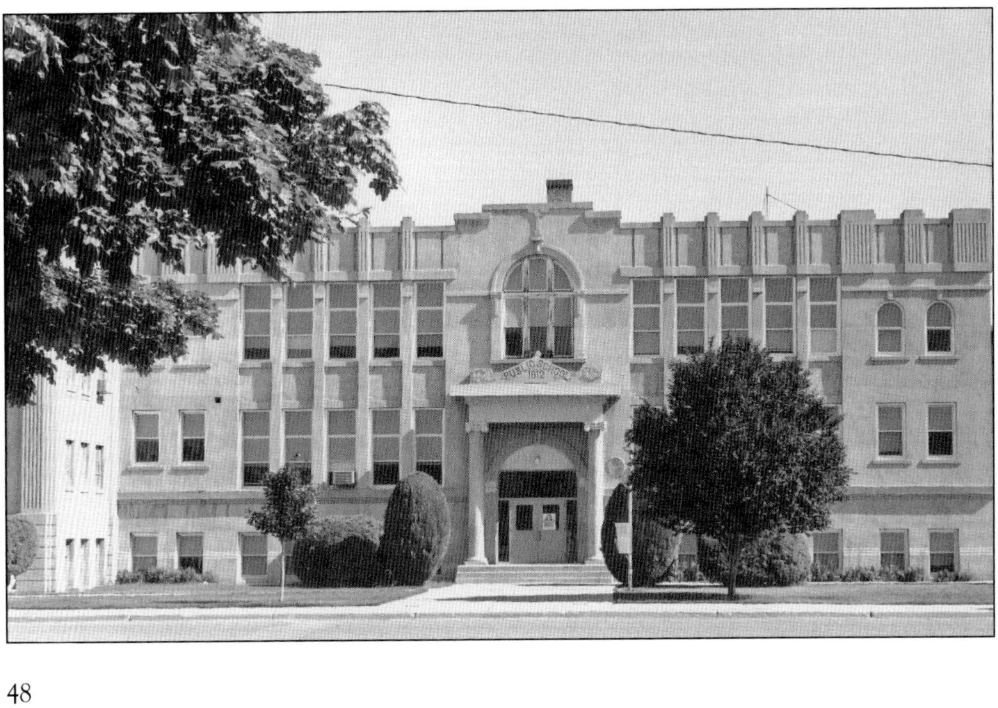

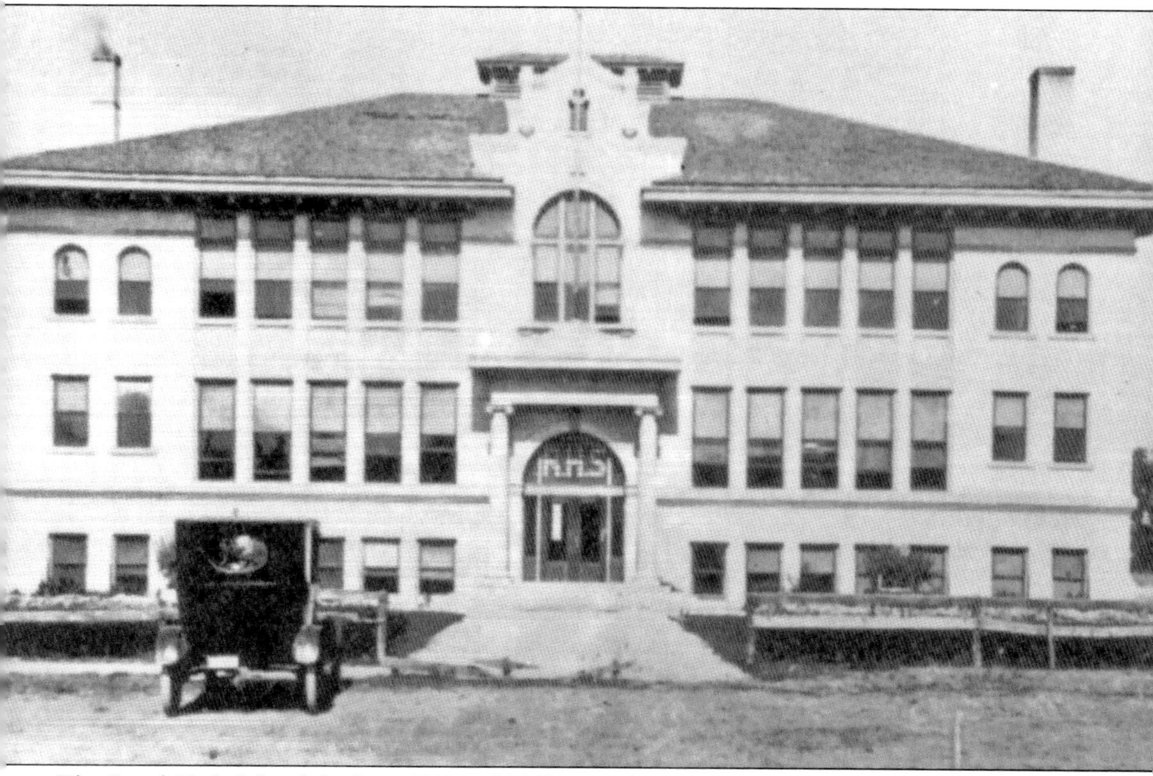

The Rural High School, built in 1912 at 200 East Carlton Avenue, was the first building west of Denver, Colorado, "to have cement to the level of the first floor," according to Lila Hill. The building cost $32,000 and admitted students from common districts and boasted an enrollment of 100 students by the end of 1917. Local students could now attend their senior year in Meridian, rather than riding on the interurban to Boise High School or living with a family in Boise. In the fall of 1919, officials organized a junior high school inside the building. In 1932, Pres. Franklin Delano Roosevelt began the New Deal, and the auditorium was added to the west side of the original building as a Works Project Administration solution to overflowing classes. The new expansive gym replaced the small basement facility in the original building, the first gym in the district where the red bricks and scrawled names can still be seen.

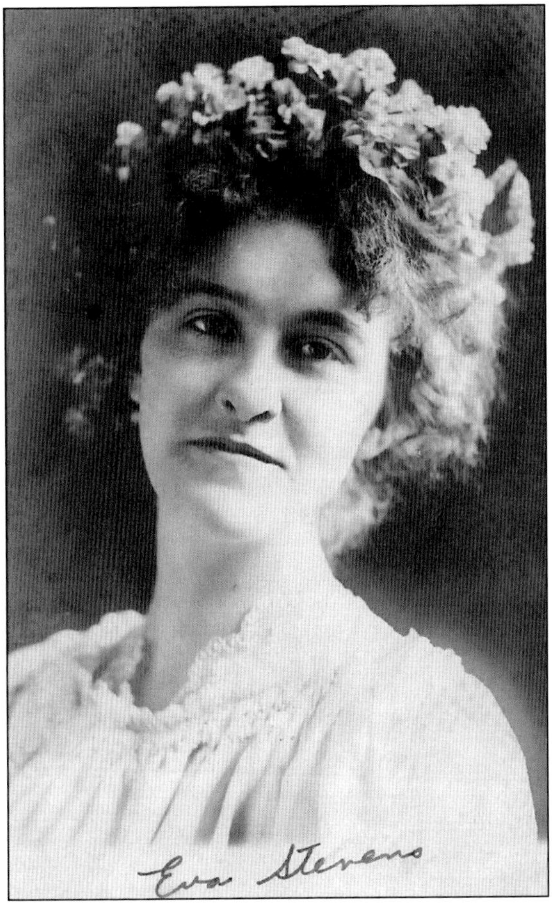

Left is Eva Stevens, principal of Meridian High School in 1915 and a longtime teacher. The late Clysta Gray remembered how Stevens taught her "a great appreciation of good literature, both poetry and prose," during her last two years of high school. Clysta said there might have been excessive emphasis on memorization but that its complete absence from modern education is regrettable, "and a mistake, I think. Incidentally, memorizing the poem 'Thanatopsis' was a very popular method of punishment by some of our teachers." Clysta added, "Eva Stevens taught me to say, 'a gentleman or lady will not insult me, and no one else can.' That, coupled with 'Nothing can separate me from the love of God,' has been a great stabilizer." Below, the 1912 Meridian High School girls' basketball team is pictured.

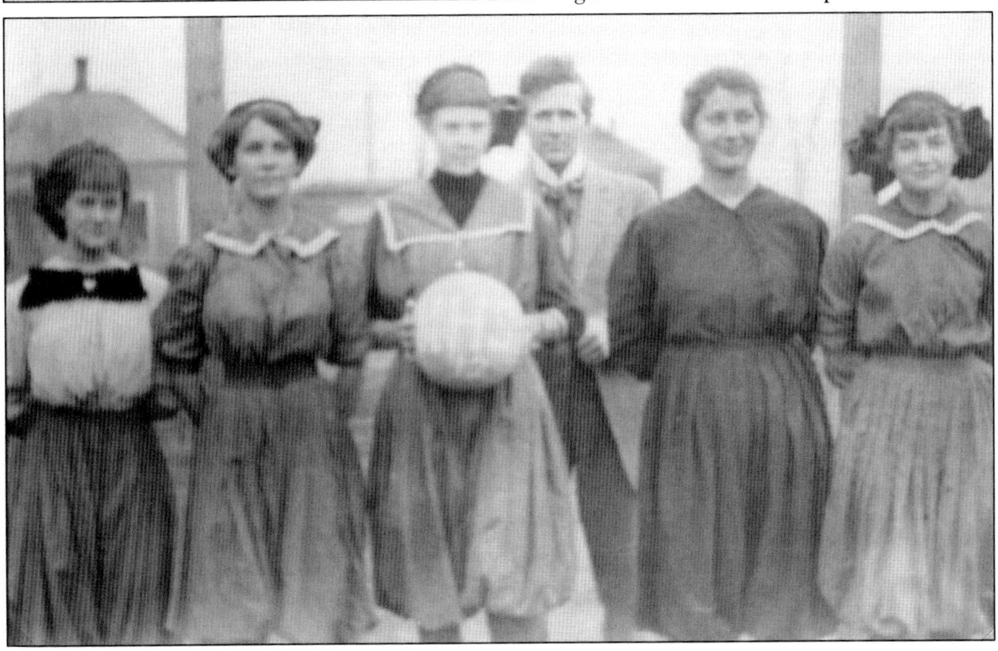

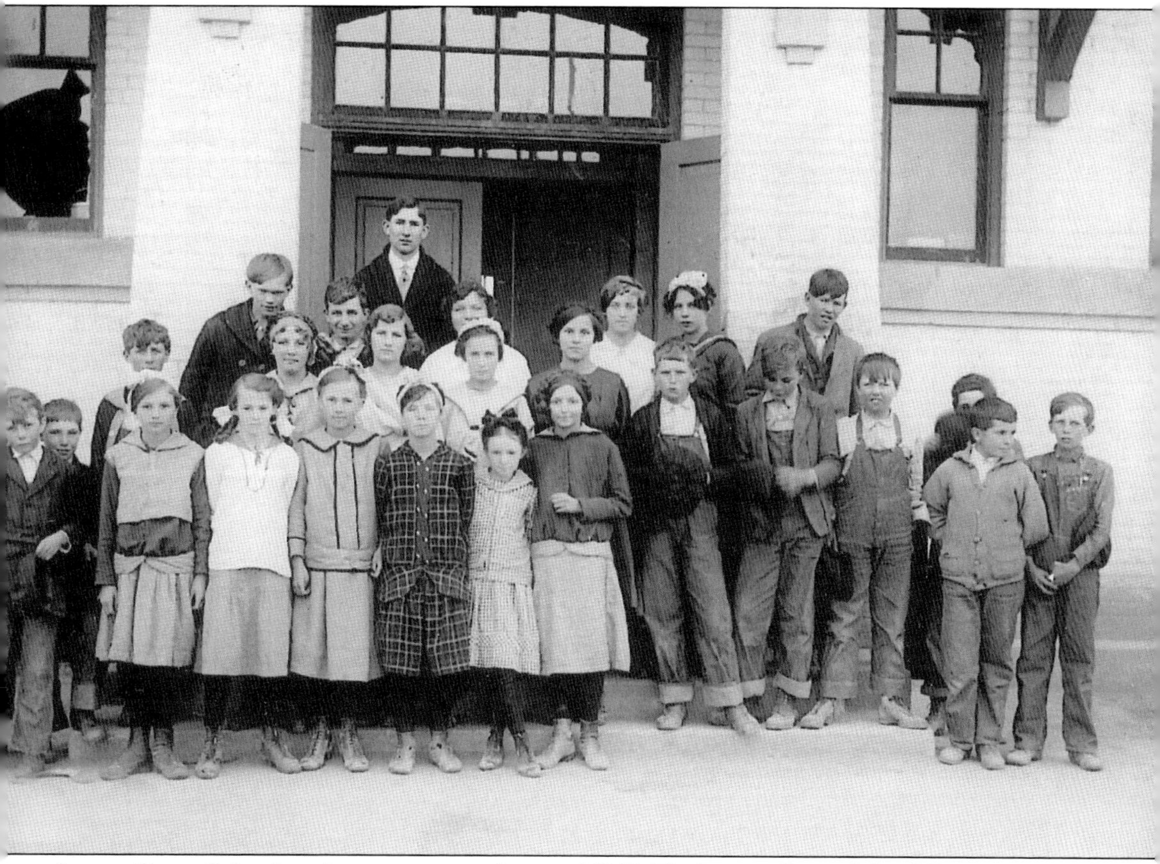

Locust Grove School students are pictured around 1917. The Locust Grove School District was organized in 1902. The first school board members were James Cato, Walter Evans, and M. Z. Davidson. The district purchased an acre from a man named Redman for a "good-sized one-room school building," wrote Frances Ellis. The first teacher, Maude Cornish, was charged with educating a class of 14 pupils. A new red and white brick building was constructed in 1911 with two stories and a basement. The two-room upper story, finished in 1917, was used as a community center, and the Grange organized and helped furnish the school with chairs and a piano. That building burned and was replaced in September 1929 with an external red brick one. Above, teacher Verne Caldwell is pictured with students (no row number listed): Claude Hedgecock, Lawson and Ernest Elliott, Carl Egbert, Wesley Able, Nola Finch, Fay Ross, Hazel Sundell, Helen H., Edna Finch, Earl Evans, Edward Finch, Richard Thielke, Acie Rutledge, Rolla Lauderbaugh, Bertha Able, Ida and Violet Callisen, Jesse and Eura Maden, Edith Wright, Edna Evans, Alma Cox, Oliver Kelly, and Oran Evans. (ISHS.)

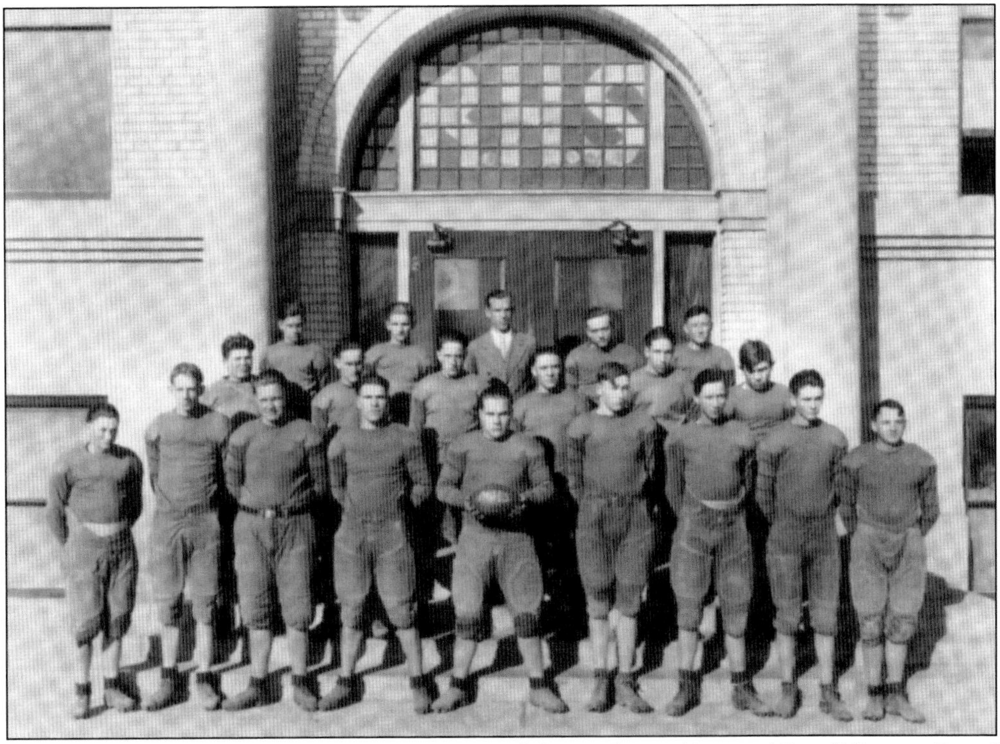

Above is the 1929–1930 MHS football team. From left to right are (first row) Jerrell Bowers, David Frost, Jim Stone, Orris Shelby, George Stone, Elwood White, Leo Marsters, Conrad McClure, and Carl Van Houten; (second row) unidentified, Jack McGuire, Harold Bales (nicknamed "Skinny," he later served as postmaster), Harold Wallace, unidentified, and Carl Lund; (third row) Lloyd Fogerson, Carlton Fogerson, coach Harry Durall, Gerald Voorhees, and Harold Doan. Below, the 1932 MHS orchestra members from left to right are (first row) Marguerite Atwater, Evelyn Dodds, Margaret Haskins, Mary Burnham, Blaine Headrick, Frances Jackomeit, Pansy Stalker, Dorothy Dodds, Maureen Voorhees, Beth Biddick, and Vina Jasper, director; (second row) Kathleen Walt, Lowdema King, Eloise Hyde, Clarence Aldrich, Howard Scott, Merle Estes, Johnny Anderson, Clarence Helm, and Kai Hansen; (third row) Emily Aldrich, Ethel Keller, Cleora Webb, Wayne Bower, and Bill Everett. (Above, ISHS; below, MHC.)

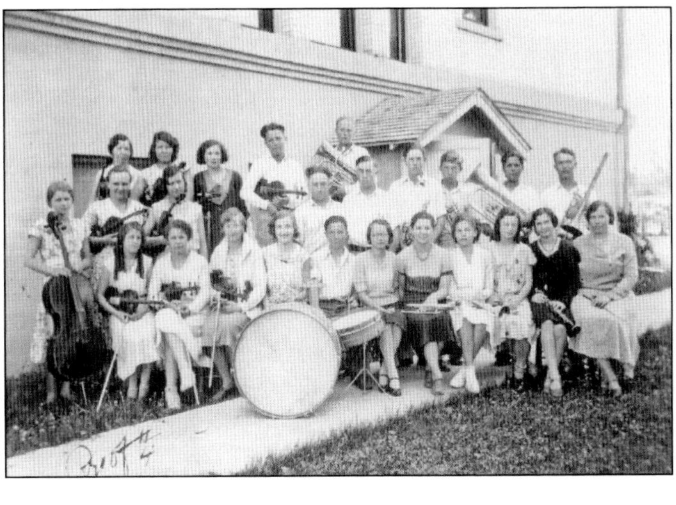

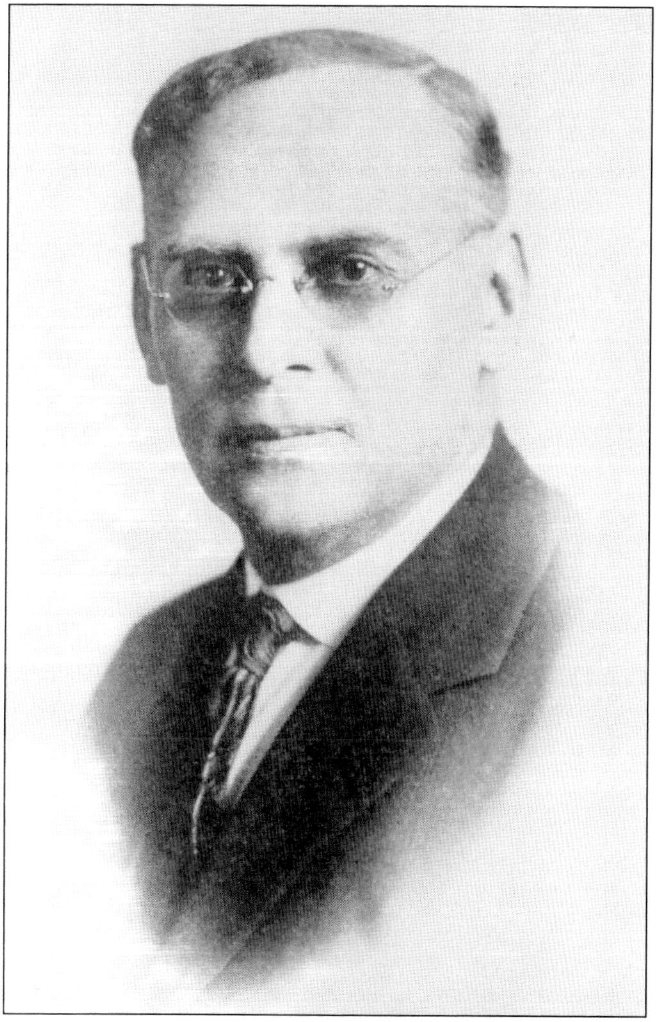

Right is Samuel L. Hughell, superintendent of Meridian High School, around 1930. His predecessors included J. J. Caldwell, C. W. Holt, George W. Gould, and Harvey B. Powers. Hughell's wife, Mary, taught at the Meridian Grade School. Their daughter, Martha Hughell, served as a missionary to Africa. Samuel L. was a lay church leader. In 1925, he was a member of the official board of the Meridian Library. Below, Meridian's first library was a small collection located at various times in Songer's Drugstore, city hall, and the Neal Pharmacy. The 1926 Occident Club promoted the library, raised funds, and bought the Interurban Depot when the trolley ceased to operate on May 17, 1928. The building became the first public library, but the club still met there after September 1983, when they transferred ownership to the Meridian Free Library District.

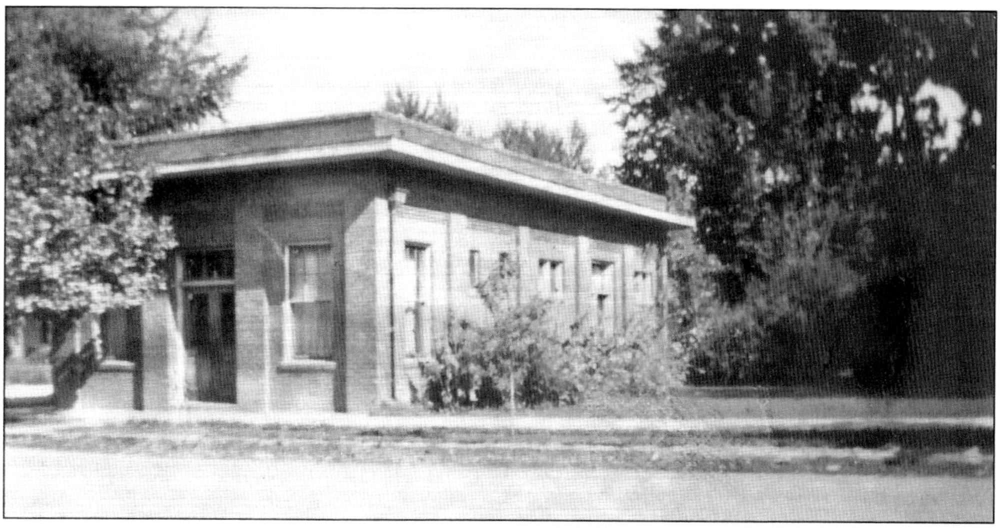

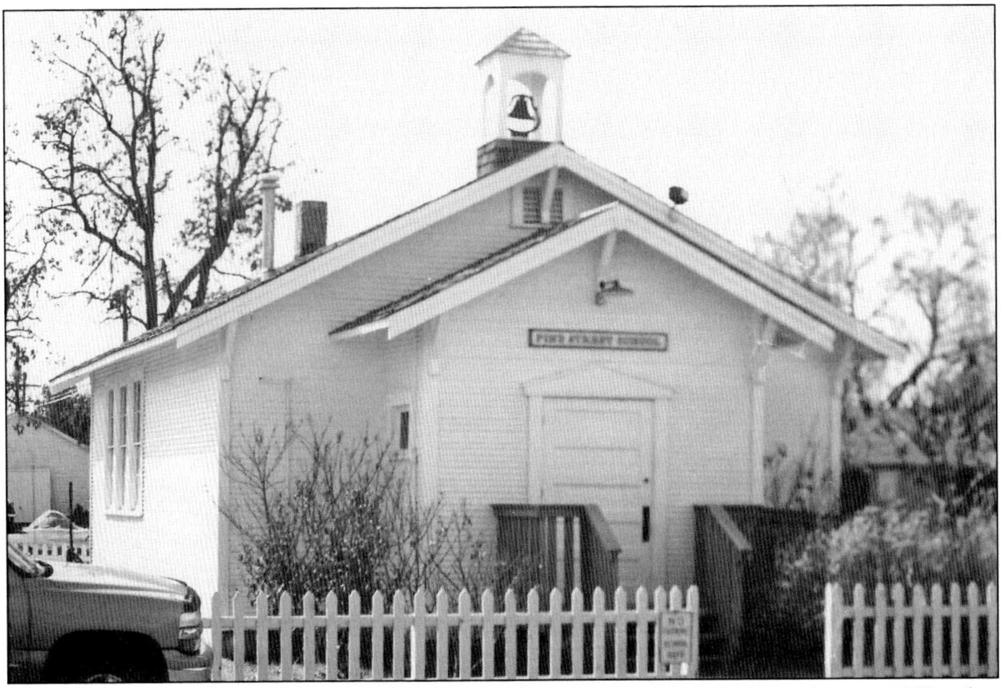

The Pine Street School, pictured above, officially opened as a museum in August 1993, after winning a governor's award as a "lasting legacy" project of the Meridian Centennial Bureau. The building was constructed behind the old Meridian Rural High School in 1920. The elementary school district purchased it at an auction in 1937 and moved it to the old Meridian Grade School for second-grade and music classes. In 1959, the new Meridian Primary opened and the old school was torn down, but the classroom was spared and used for maintenance and storage for the next 30 years. Below, curator Betty Kusler is seen with photographs of 10 years of her second-grade classes she taught in the one-room school. Doug Rutan spearheaded the centennial project involving many volunteers and former students, such as Brent Alger. The Boy Scouts restored the schoolroom and added original desks and other materials. (Above, MHC; below, PAP.)

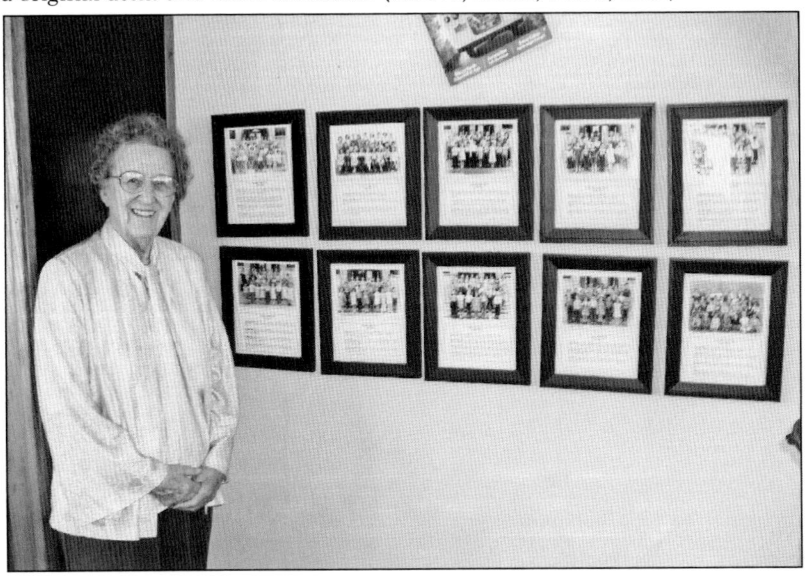

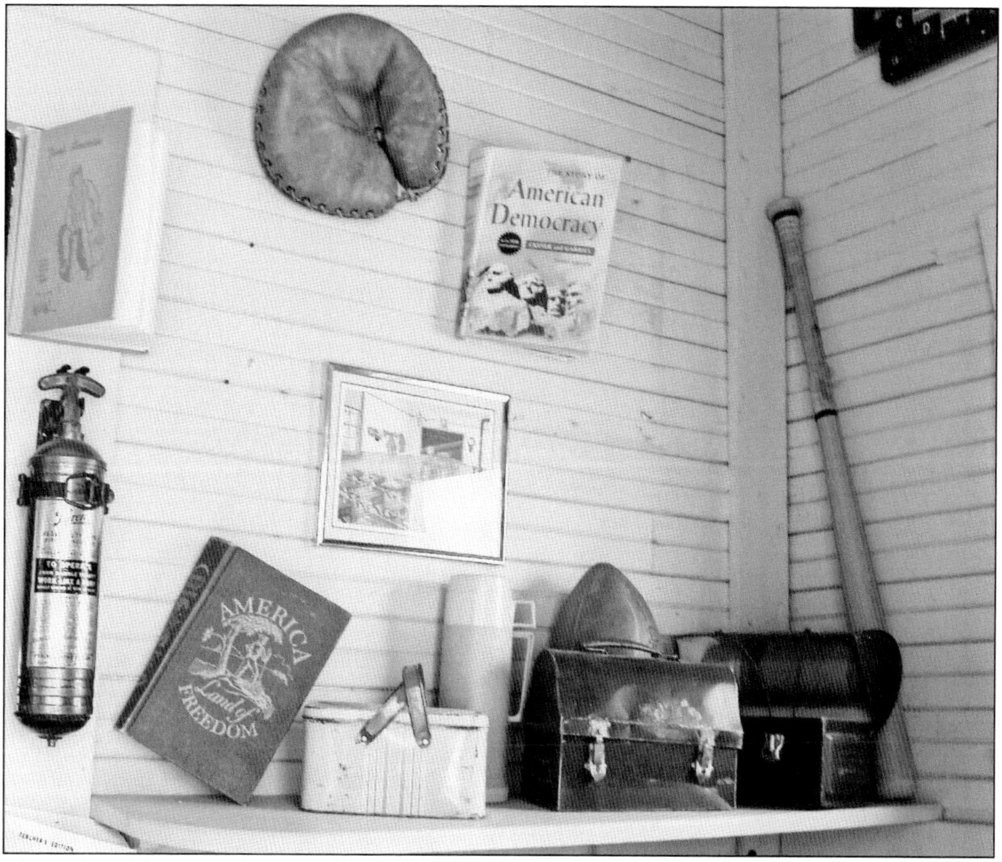

Above, lunchboxes, a thermos, baseball bat, catcher's glove, and textbooks adorn a corner in the Pine Street School. For the hundreds of students who visit the museum, it is a virtual classroom where they experience what it was like to learn, study, and play in an old, one-room, country school as they sit at desks and read from books as their grandparents did many years ago. For adults, and especially former students, it is an opportunity to revisit the educational era of their youth. For the community, the building is a gathering place for clubs and Scout troops, who use the schoolhouse for special occasions and meetings. At right, a vintage Cole's coal and wood stove sits next to a bucket filled with pieces of coal, a small shovel, and a box of kindling. (Both PAP.)

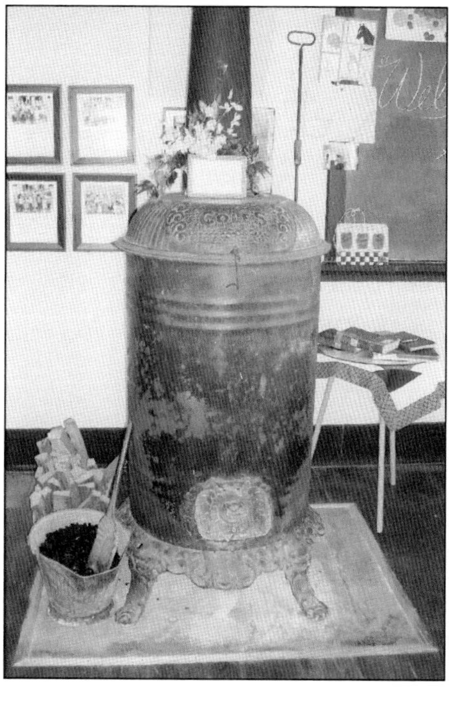

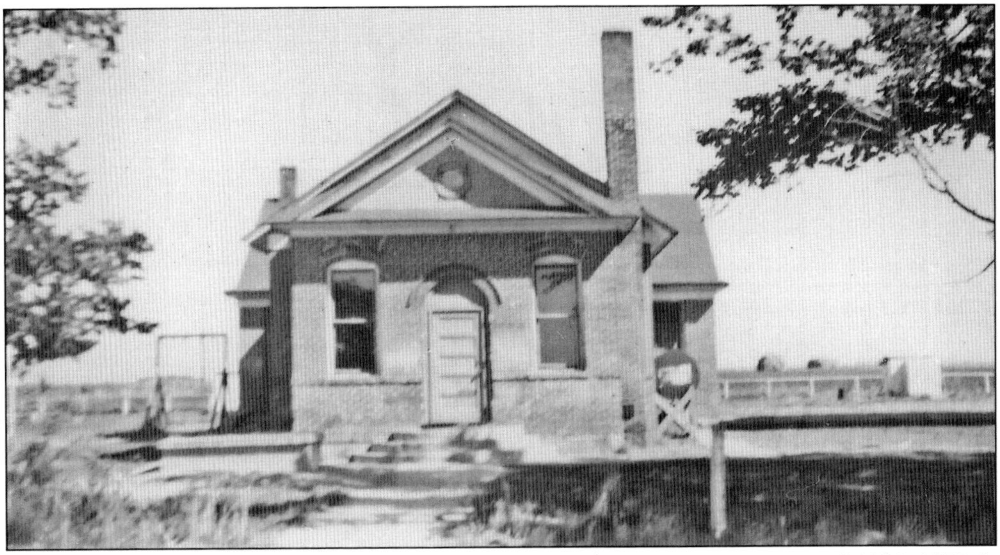

Hillsdale School, pictured above, was built in 1908 and was in operation until 1958–1959. It originally sat on 1 acre and then 2 acres donated by Angus Hill to the district for a schoolhouse. Over the years, the number of classes inside its two rooms gradually shrank from 12 to eight and, finally, two. Note the oil barrel for heating on the right side of the building and the boys' outhouse in the distance to the right. The fourth-grade 1957–1958 Hillsdale class is pictured below. From left to right are (first row) Dale Owens, Frank Thomason, and Clarence Bolen; (second row) Peggy Moser, Susan Tenney, Janet Fairbanks, Marcine Quenzer, Sue Randolph, Margie Flynn, and Carol Boyack; (third row) Barbara Griffiths, teacher Christine Pullin, Clyne Hodges, Linda Tompkins, Frank Trowbridge, Louise Hill, Gordon DeWaard, Janice Shaul, and Wayne Shuyler. (Above, MHC; below, FT.)

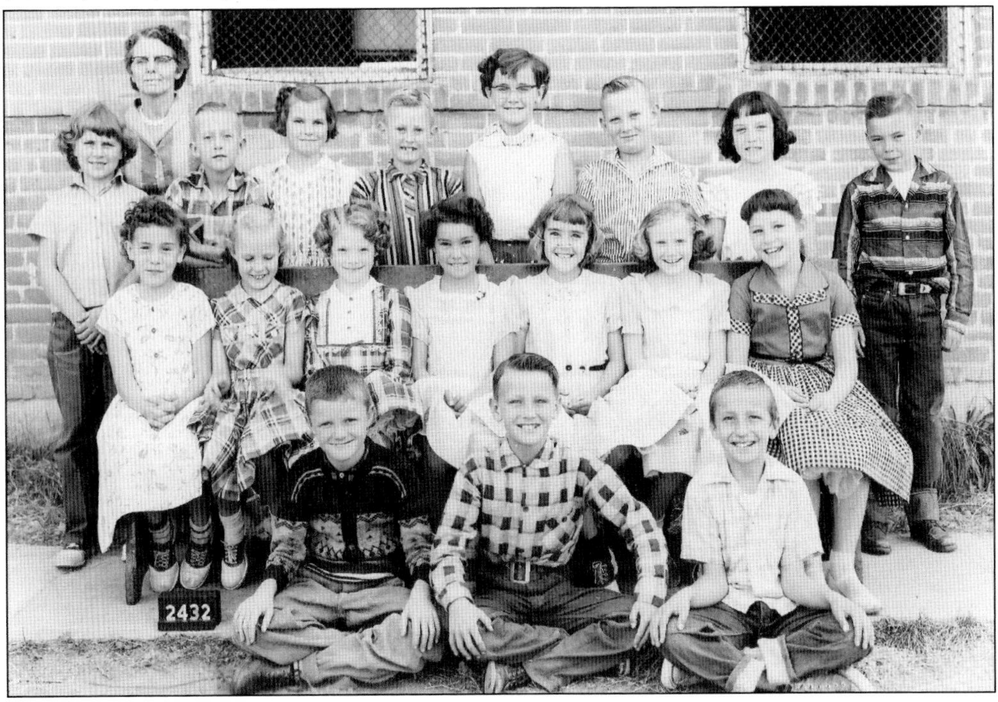

Four

People and Places in Meridian Village

The greatest change in Meridian over the past century has been from migration of settlers from the East and South (Iowa, Kansas, Missouri, Nebraska, Arkansas, Oklahoma, and elsewhere) relocating to the West and Northwest, including this area. A later movement brought even larger numbers of residents from California, Oregon, and Washington.

Frederick Jackson Turner presented his thesis of western development to the American Historical Association at a convention in Chicago in 1893, the year Meridian came into existence. Turner observed that "Montana and Idaho were receiving settlers" by 1880 in a pattern familiar elsewhere involving "a distinct series of waves" or classes. First came the pioneers, then the clearers and buyers of land, and finally "men of capital and enterprise."

Meridian's town site was platted by men as well as hardy women, including Eliza Zenger, wife of a Mormon and mother of three children. The family cleared the sagebrush and then plowed and planted alfalfa where the commercial portion of the village evolved. Christian Zenger was also a dairy farmer, so this one family symbolizes the row-cropping and dairy aspects of Meridian's agricultural development.

Those who settled Meridian were mostly religious people, including Methodists, Baptists, Catholics, and people of other faiths who believed in looking after themselves and their neighbors. This was the genesis of volunteerism that characterized a fiercely independent and dynamic community.

A visitor to Meridian in the 1890s would have noticed the IOOF Hall, also known as the Odd Fellows building, several stores and harness shops, the Methodist church, and other buildings, including the 1894 Grade School that stood near the site of the present-day Methodist church.

The Ridenbaugh's Hunter lateral provided irrigation water to Meridian and runs east of city hall from Pine Avenue and East Second Street south to the cemetery. The early settlers homesteaded in the area along Five Mile Creek that runs from Franklin and Locust Grove, across Pine Avenue near East Sixth crossing Fairview Avenue, and proceeding north to Meridian Road near its intersection with Ustick Road. The original schoolhouse sat on the west bank of the creek, north of the current Fairview Avenue.

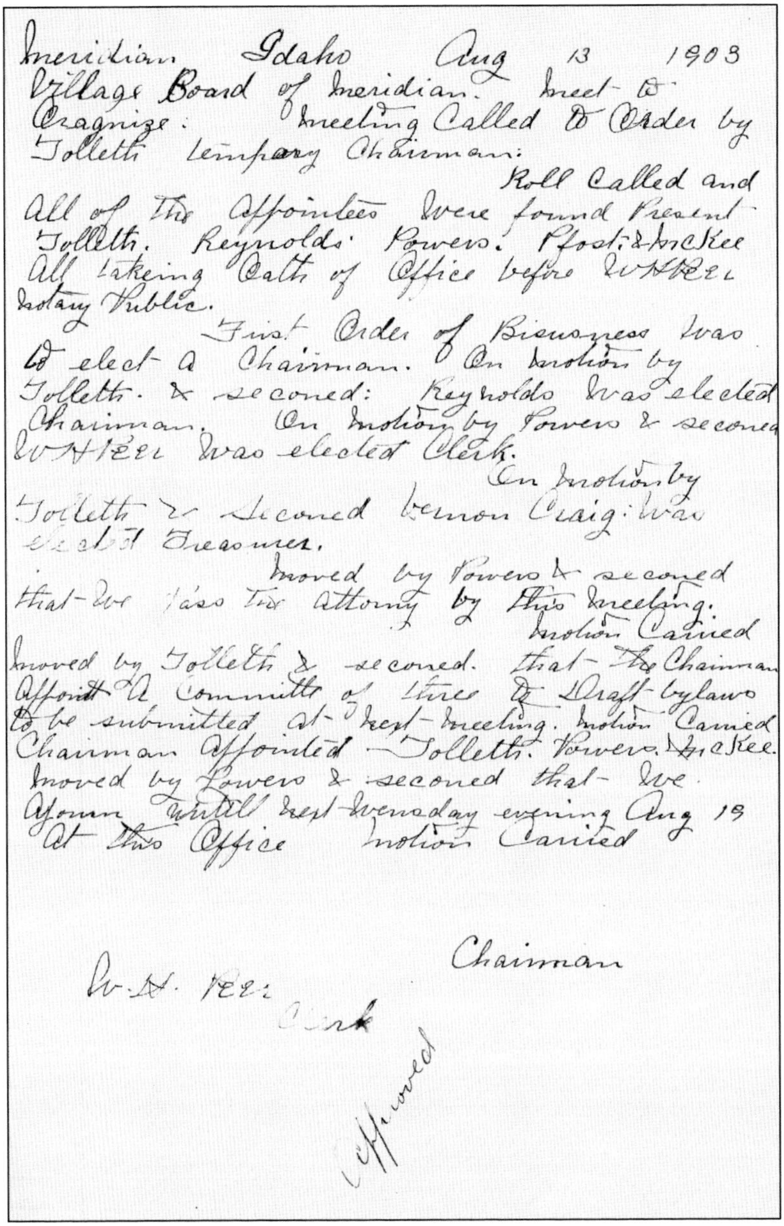
Meridian Idaho Aug 13 1903
Village Board of Meridian. Meet to Oragnize: Meeting Called to Order by Tolleth temporary Chairman:
Roll Called and All of the Appointees were found Present Tolleth. Reynolds. Powers. Pfost. & McKee All takeing Oath of Office before W H Peer Notary Public.
First Order of Bisuness was to elect a Chairman. On Motion by Tolleth. & seconed: Reynolds was elected Chairman. On Motion by Powers & seconed W H Peer was elected Clerk.
On Motion by Tolleth & Seconed Vernon Craig: was elected Treasurer.
Moved by Powers & seconed that we pass the attorny by this Meeting.
Motion Carried
Moved by Tolleth & seconed. that the Chairman Appoint a Committe of three to Draft bylaws to be submitted at next Meeting. Motion Carried
Chairman Appointed Tolleth. Powers. McKee.
Moved by Powers & seconed that we Ajourn until next Wensday evening Aug 19 At this Office Motion Caried

Chairman

W. H. Peer
Clerk

Approved

Upon application to the Board of Ada County Commissioners, Meridian incorporated as a village in the summer of 1903. The minutes of the first meeting, organizing the village Board of Trustees, are pictured above. Temporary chairman Homer Tolleth called the meeting to order on August 13. Other members appointed to the board included Dr. S. M. C. Reynolds, Harvey B. Powers, T. J. McKee, and Isaac Pfost. All took the oath of office before W. H. Peer, notary public. The first order of business was election of a chairman. Dr. Reynolds assumed that position, while Peer was elected clerk and Vernon Craig, treasurer. The new officials authorized the chairman to appoint a committee of three to draft bylaws for submission at the next meeting on August 19. Committee members were Tolleth, Power, and McKee. Since that order of business concluded this initial meeting of trustees, it may be presumed that the entire meeting lasted only a few minutes. (MHPC.)

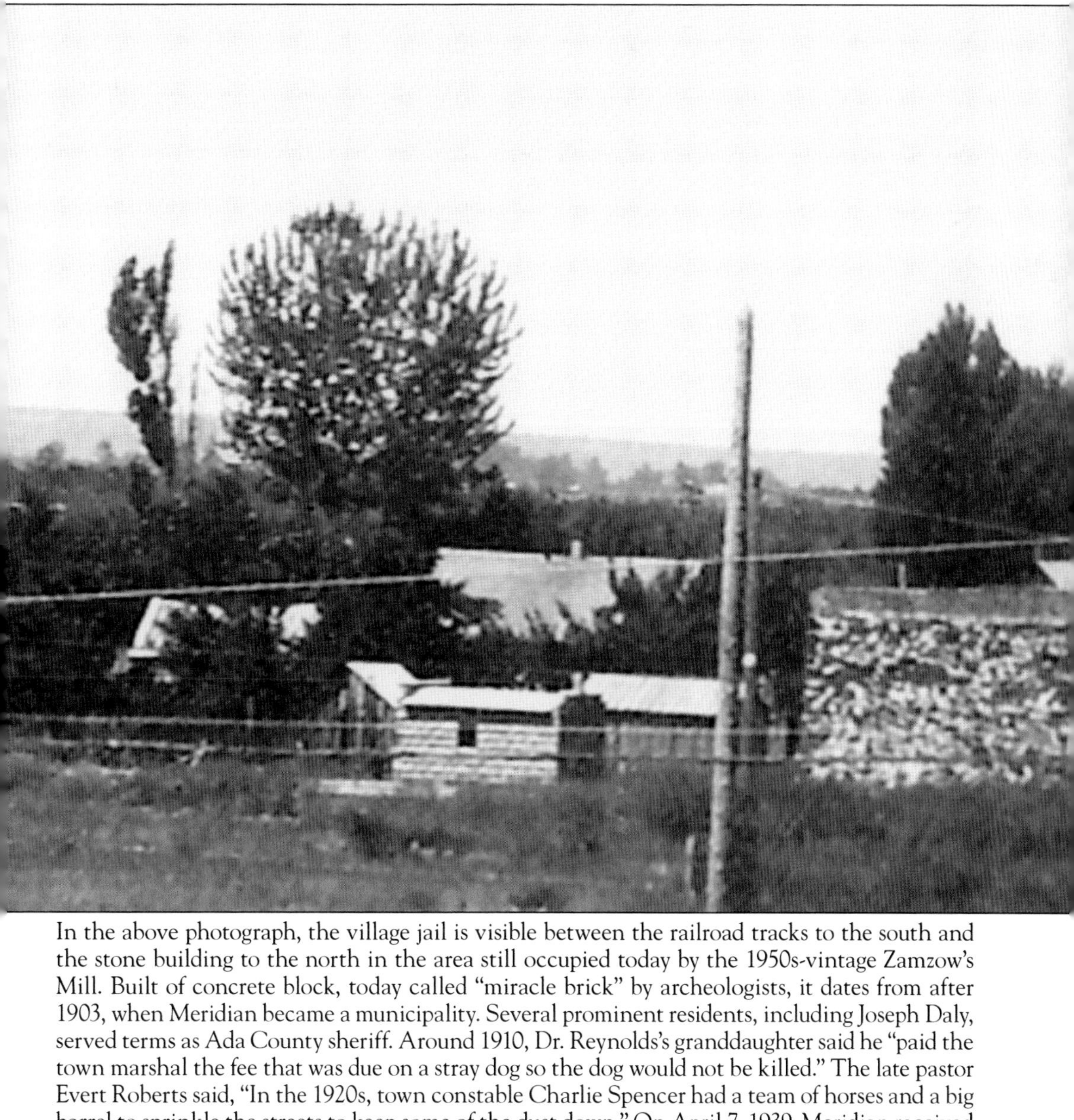

In the above photograph, the village jail is visible between the railroad tracks to the south and the stone building to the north in the area still occupied today by the 1950s-vintage Zamzow's Mill. Built of concrete block, today called "miracle brick" by archeologists, it dates from after 1903, when Meridian became a municipality. Several prominent residents, including Joseph Daly, served terms as Ada County sheriff. Around 1910, Dr. Reynolds's granddaughter said he "paid the town marshal the fee that was due on a stray dog so the dog would not be killed." The late pastor Evert Roberts said, "In the 1920s, town constable Charlie Spencer had a team of horses and a big barrel to sprinkle the streets to keep some of the dust down." On April 7, 1939, Meridian received four jail cells from the Ada County Courthouse. Clysta Gray contributed to the ongoing battle against alcoholism by tossing pebbles atop the jail's tin roof to awaken the sleeping drunks. In August 1953, when Steve McGill was named chief of police, Meridian still had a one-man force. Three years later, a deputy was hired. Today there are 80 sworn officers.

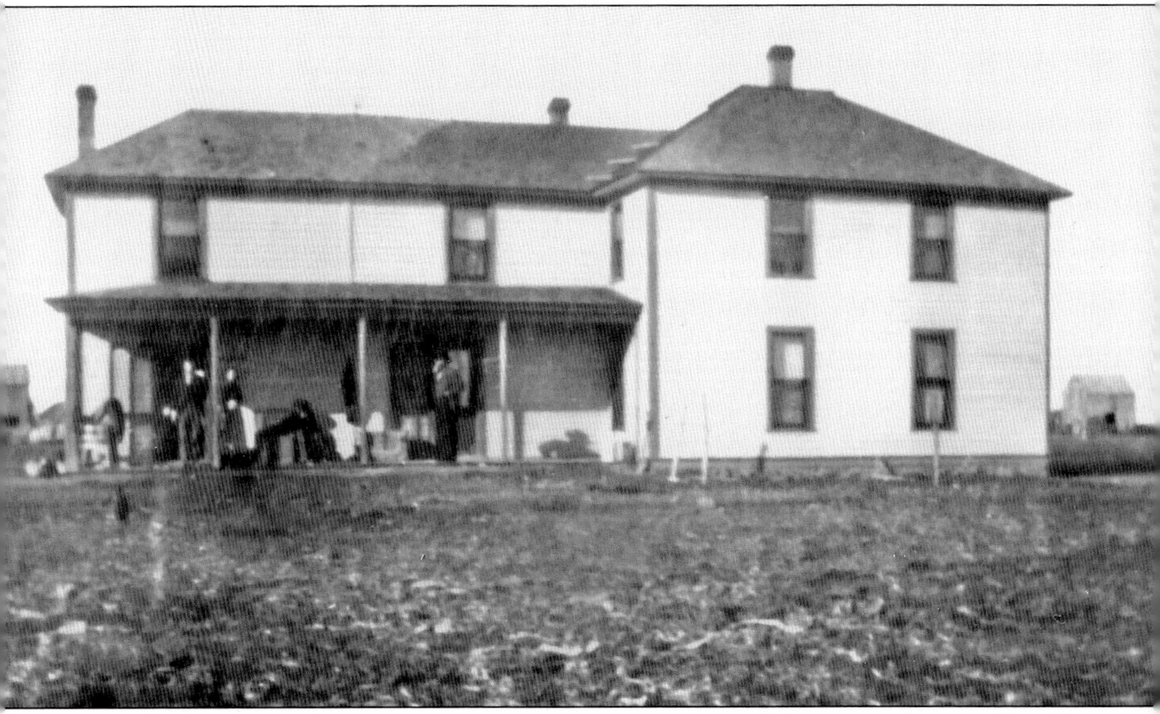

The Meridian Hotel, pictured above in 1900, was at 113 East Idaho Avenue between East First (Main) and East Second Streets. In a 1904 article published in the *Idaho Magazine*, F. W. Ellis wrote there were two hotels in Meridian. The one pictured above underwent various ownership over the decades. In 1908, the proprietor of the hotel and of the Meridian Bakery was Homer N. Champlin, son of S. L. and the late H. C. Champlin. Homer Champlin came to Meridian from Chicago with his parents in 1905. In June 1908, he married Anna Powers, daughter of Harvey B. and Maria Powers. In September 1909, the *Meridian Times* reported, "Mr. and Mrs. Frank Wilcox have rented the Meridian Hotel of Mrs. E. C. Onwiler, and will take charge next week." The late Pastor Roberts said that in the 1920s, "Mrs. Pfortner had the hotel." The hotel was reportedly popular with Boise men, who brought their girlfriends to Meridian because they were not required to sign a register at the hotel. The hotel was later torn down.

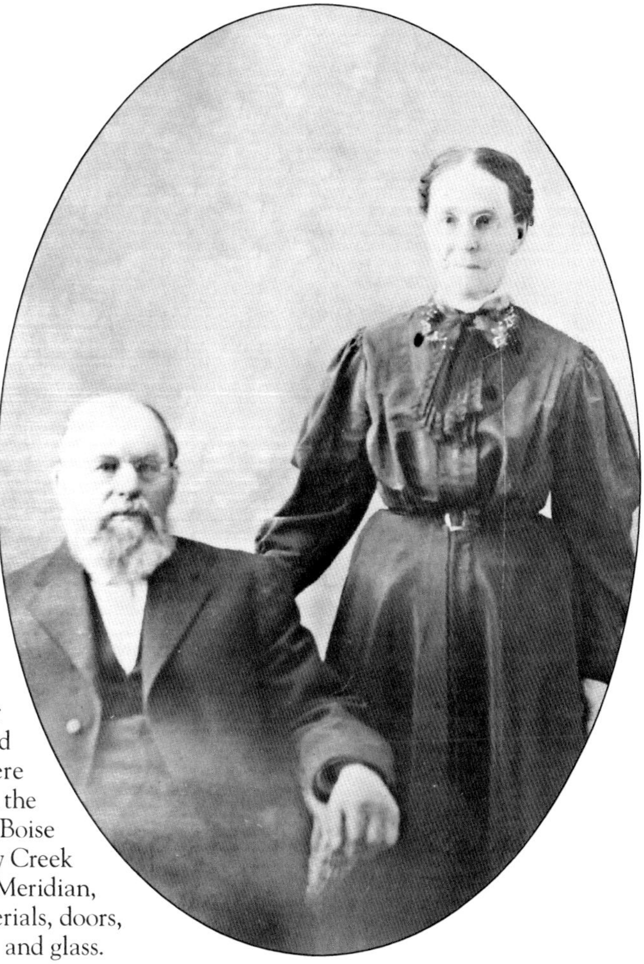

Early settler and businessman, Peter Taylor, and his wife, Laura, are pictured at right in a photograph donated by Vernon Taylor. Peter was a half-brother of William, Isaac, and James Daly, who were part of a wagon train led by William Daly Sr., which left Missouri for Oregon in 1876. They wintered a half-mile east of the settlement of Star along Old Valley Road and resumed their westward trek to the Willamette Valley the next spring. But after stopping in Enterprise, Oregon, and encountering an extremely severe winter storm, they turned around in the spring of 1878 and returned to the Boise area, where they settled in the Dry Creek area. Taylor Lumber Company in Meridian, pictured below, sold building materials, doors, windows, lime, cement, paint, oil, and glass.

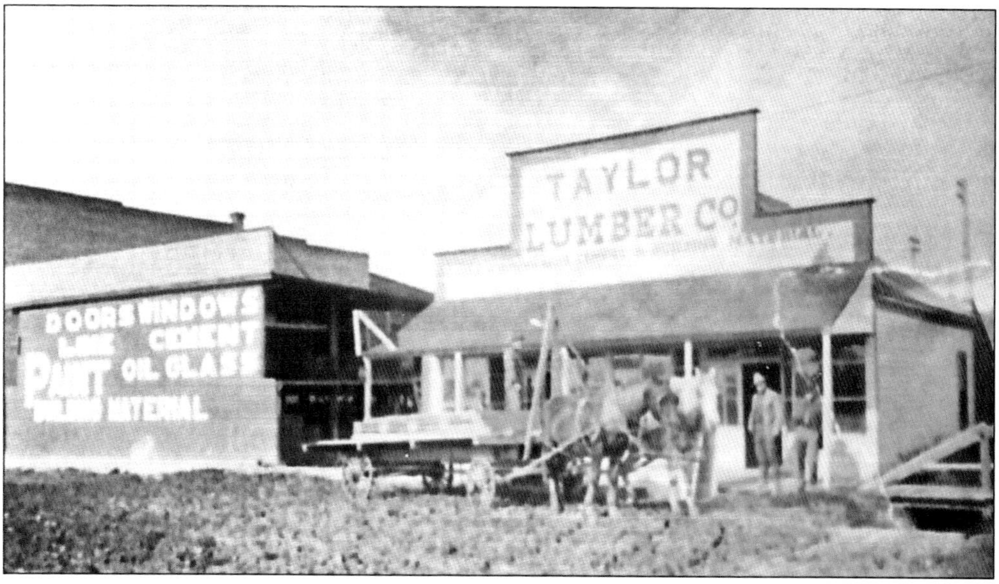

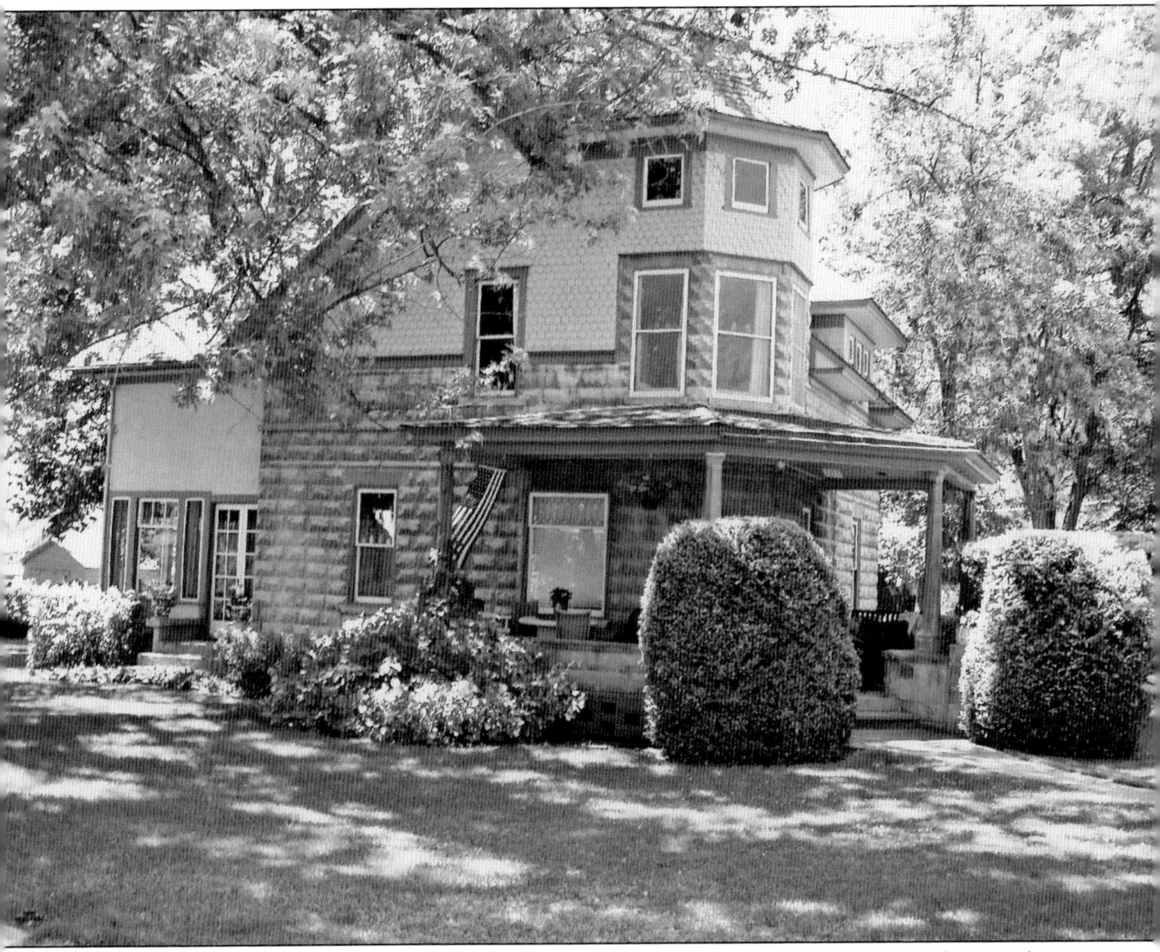

Built in 1905, the Halbert Fletcher Neal House at 101 West Pine Avenue was in what was known then as the "suburbs." It was two-story building, rectangular in shape, and constructed of "cast stone" or concrete blocks up to the eaves line, with shaped shingle work that covered the surfaces of the upper wall. A corner turret and hipped roof with flared eaves and double-hung sash windows recall the Queen Anne style, while the entryway's corner position and turret evoke the earlier Victorian era. Halbert Fletcher Neal and Grace Andrews were married in 1904 and moved from Indianola, Nebraska, to Meridian in 1905. They set up one of Idaho's first pharmacies and drugstores, with Grace as pharmacist. However, within a year, they abandoned the pharmacy, and Dr. Neal devoted himself full time to his country practice. He was Meridian's only resident physician for 28 years, was a charter member of the Meridian Masonic Lodge, and helped build the Methodist church. He also served on the school board and city council. (PAP.)

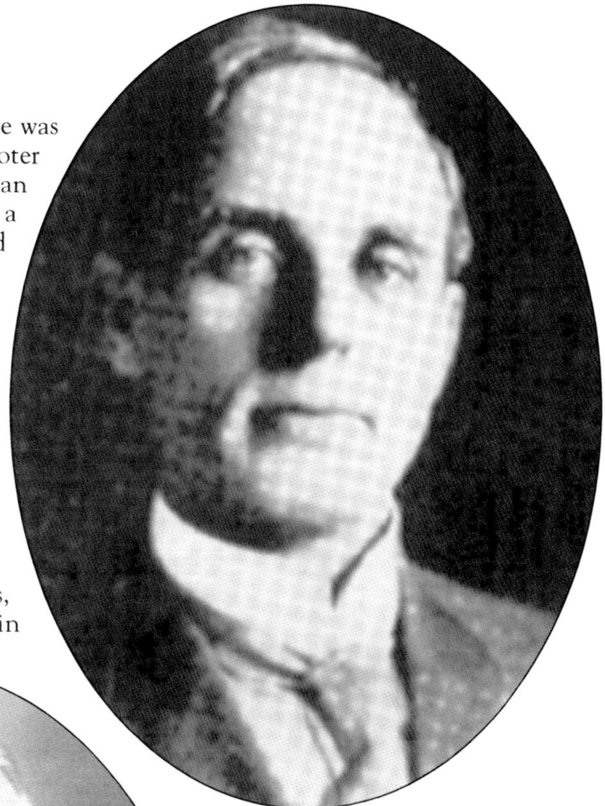

Connecticut native John Tourtellotte was a self-educated architect and promoter who arrived in Idaho in 1890. German native Charles Frederick Hummel was a formally trained architect who arrived in Idaho in 1895. Five years later, Tourtellotte opened his own office, and in 1910, Tourtellotte and Hummel was formed. The firm developed extensive residential and commercial client lists in Idaho and neighboring states, but their strongest institutional base remained in the Boise area. The firm designed many buildings for the Catholic Diocese, state-funded institutions in Boise, and several residential and commercial buildings, as well as the 1904 Grade School in Meridian. (Right, ISHS; below, HA.)

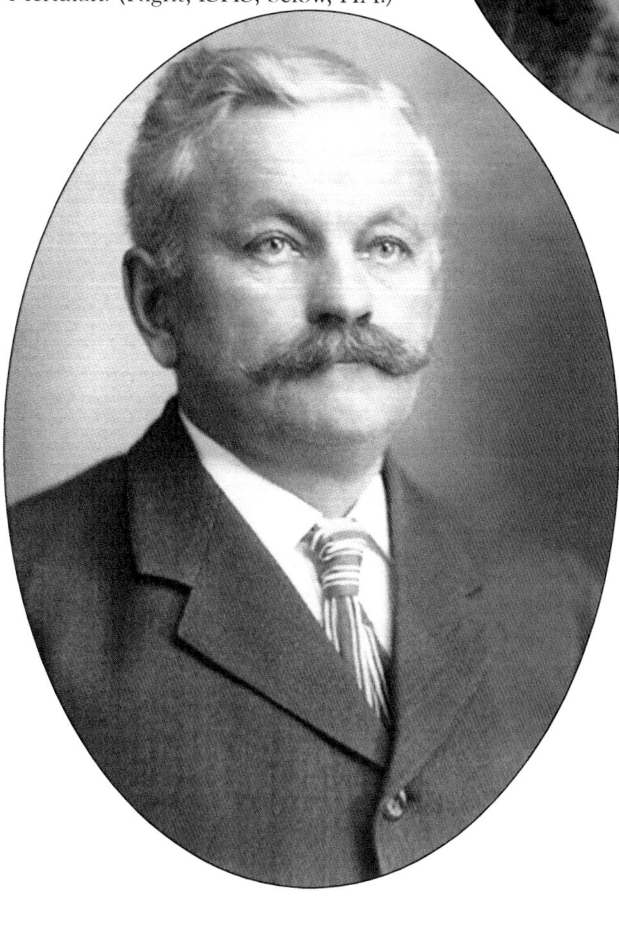

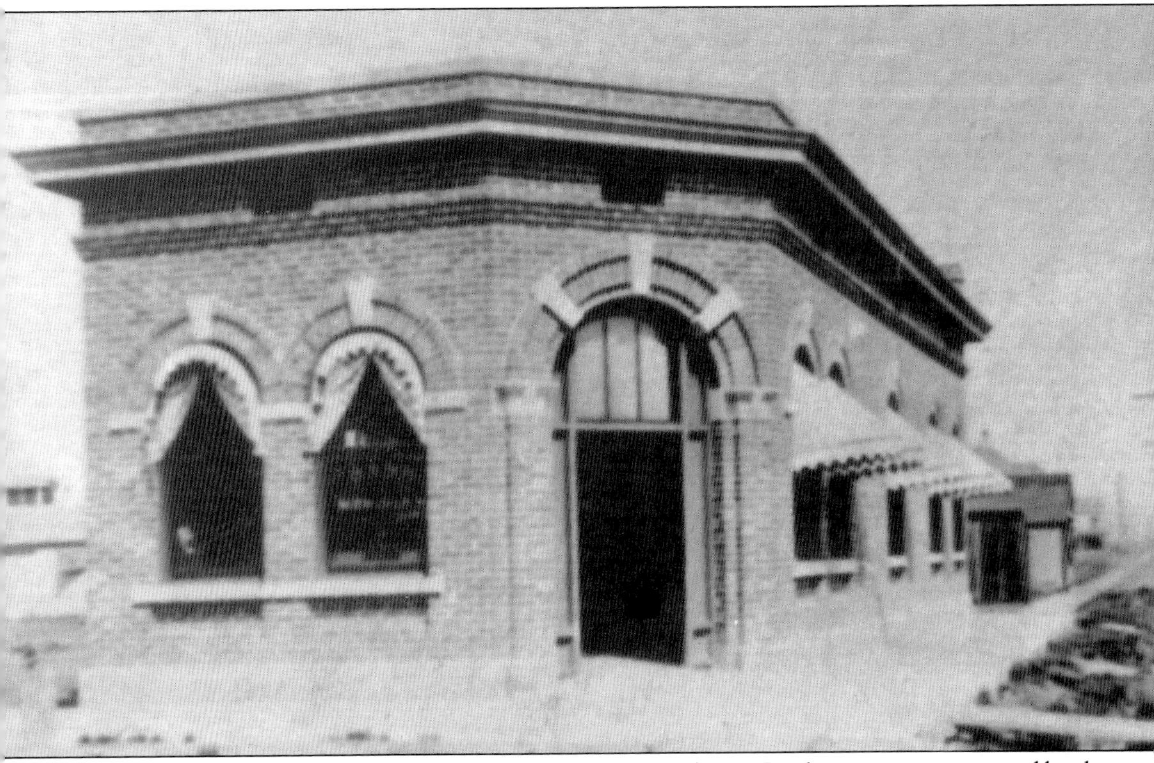

Built in 1906 at 109 East Second Street, the Meridian Exchange Bank is a two-story pressed brick and stone Renaissance Revival structure with a classical corner entryway on the northwest corner of Second and Broadway Avenues. Like the Boise Turnverein building, it employs contrasting colors of brick and was designed by Tourtellotte and Hummel of Boise. The Meridian Exchange Bank commission actually resulted from the firm's Boise contacts. Horace Neal of Boise's Capital State Bank became president of the Meridian bank, founded in 1903, when it was reorganized and incorporated two years later. The first story was to accommodate the banking area and three stores. Only one store was ever built. The second floor housed the offices of the Independent Telephone Company. The building's projected cost was $9,000, and the contractors were Allen and Barber.

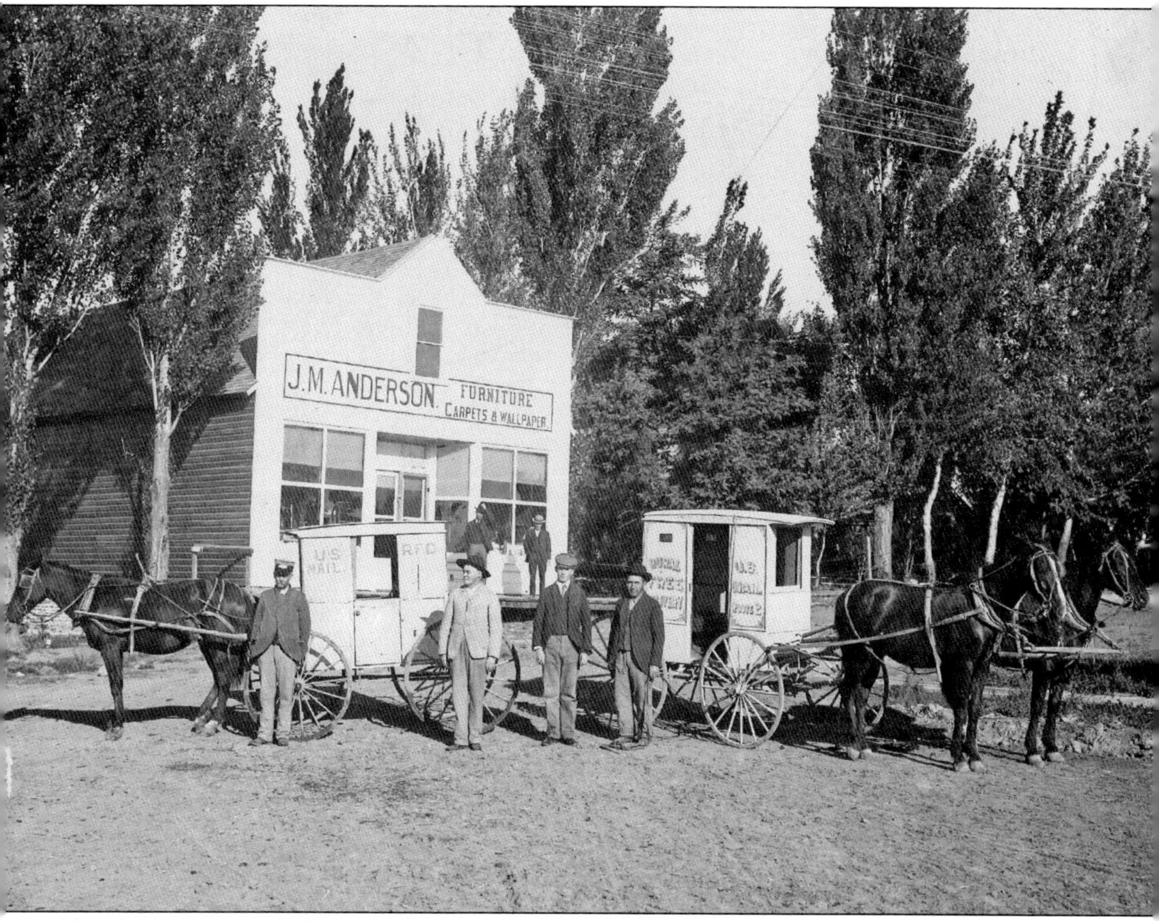

The above photograph shows two horse-drawn mail wagons in front of J. M. Anderson's furniture business on Meridian Road. "Pa" Anderson was a hardworking, civic-minded carpenter who homesteaded and worked the land in addition to running a business with his wife, Hulda. His granddaughter, Jessie, said when she was in the fourth grade, that he visited her class to talk about the early days, when family members perished as the wagon train crossed the Oregon Trail. "It was too much for him, and he broke down weeping in the middle of his presentation." For many years, James Madison Anderson was the Ada County treasurer. He also served on the village board and was part of the processes whereby electricity came to town, city water was provided, and schools and a cemetery were established. In his store's back room, a half-dozen coffins were stored upright in wooden boxes. His grandchildren loved to be left alone there, "hoping a ghost would jump right out at them."

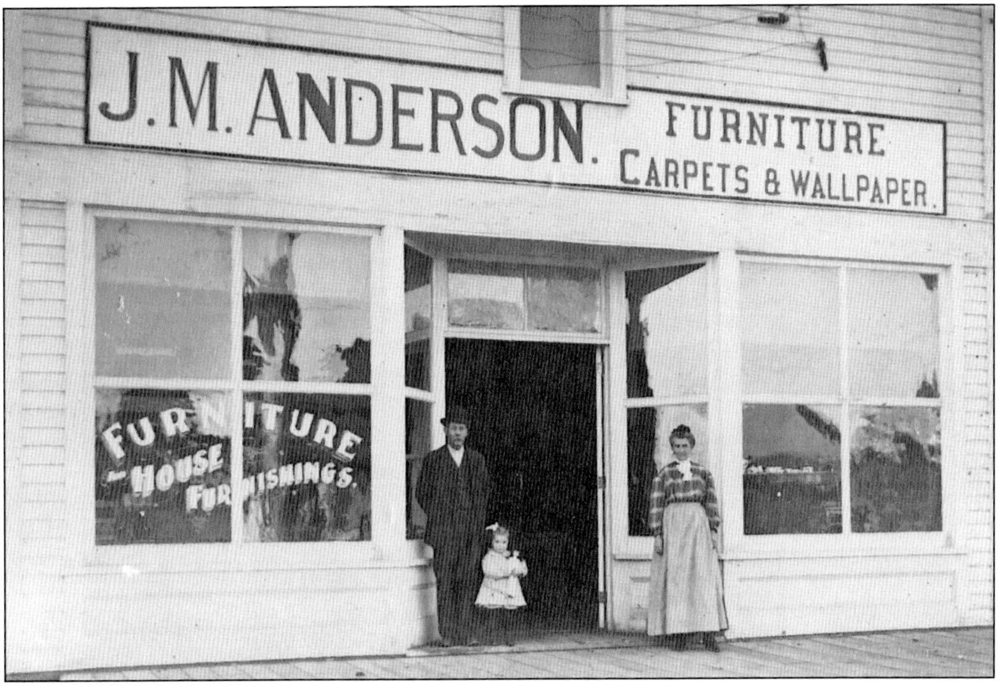

James Madison Anderson, pictured above, was one of nine prominent Methodists who served as mayor of Meridian in the early 20th century. He was also a prominent businessman whose furniture, carpet, and wallpaper store was on the west side of Meridian Road near the present-day American Legion Hall. James and his wife, Hulda, were known as "Ma and Pa Anderson." The couple and their two small children were part of a caravan of covered wagons that traveled west in 1876, starting in Harrison, Arkansas. He sold coffins as well as home furnishings, and his wife operated a millinery shop inside the store. The Andersons had homes in Boise, Star, and Meridian. Ma and Pa Anderson are pictured below inside their store.

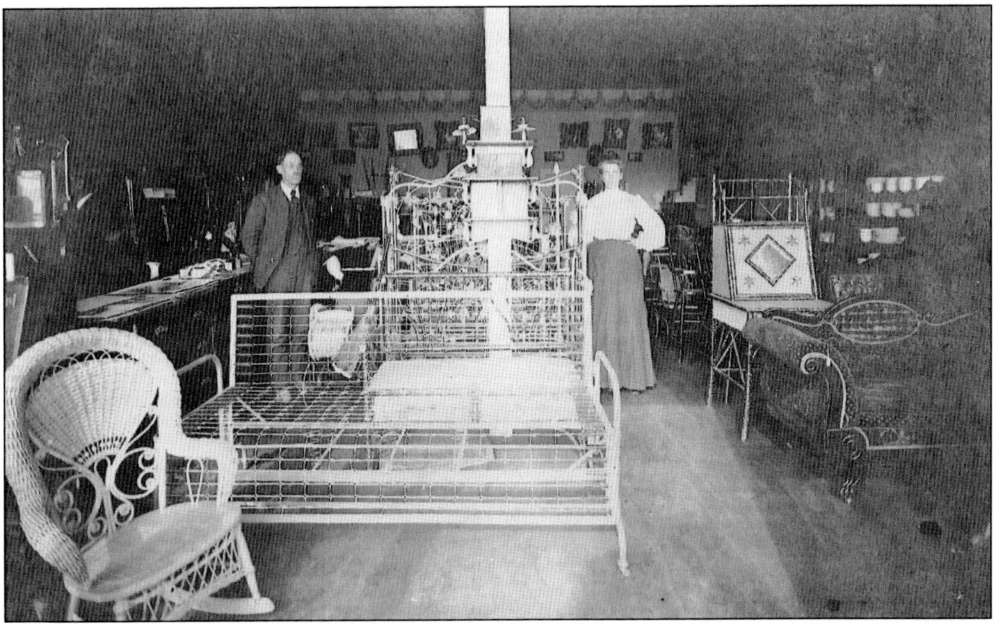

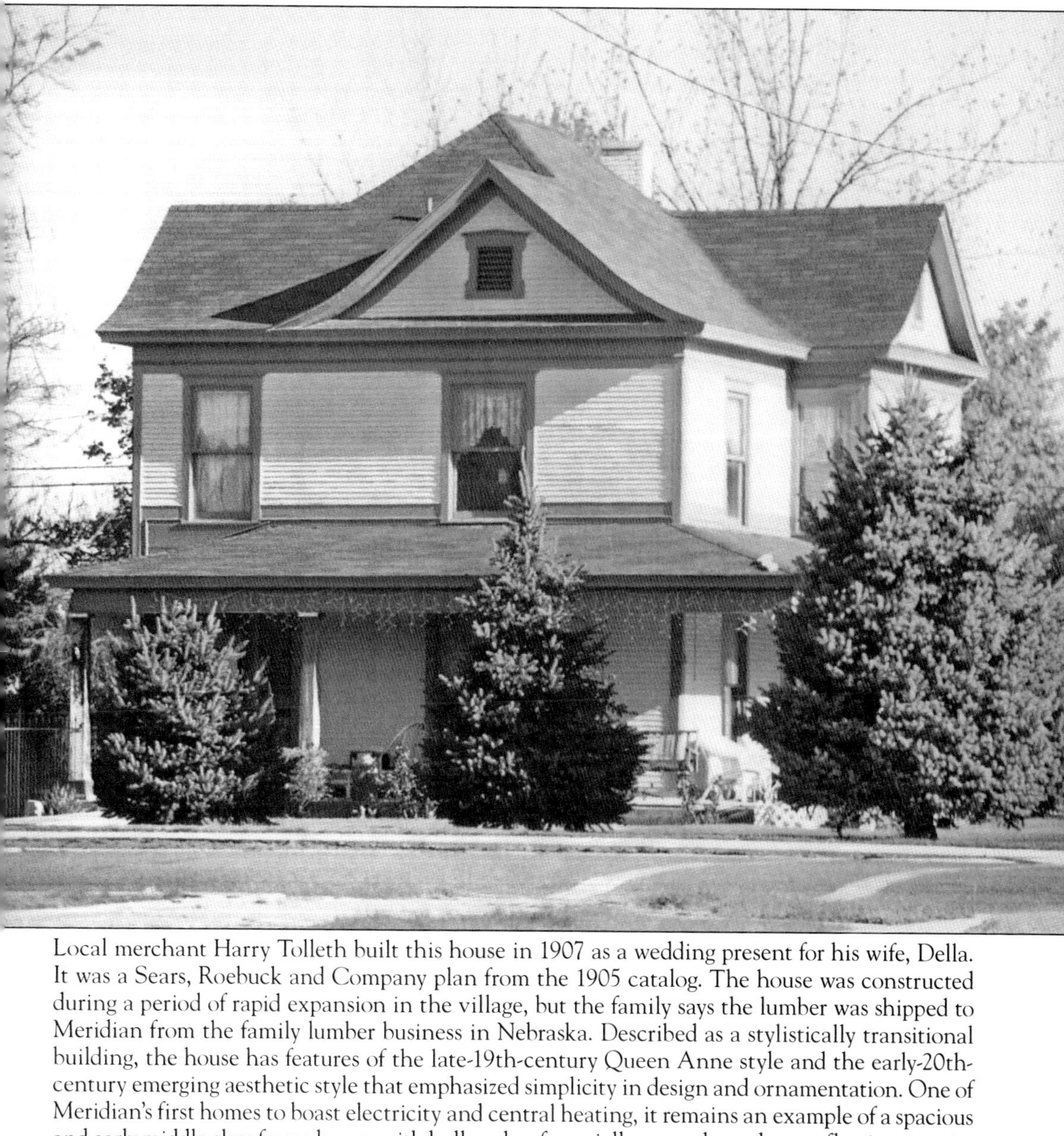

Local merchant Harry Tolleth built this house in 1907 as a wedding present for his wife, Della. It was a Sears, Roebuck and Company plan from the 1905 catalog. The house was constructed during a period of rapid expansion in the village, but the family says the lumber was shipped to Meridian from the family lumber business in Nebraska. Described as a stylistically transitional building, the house has features of the late-19th-century Queen Anne style and the early-20th-century emerging aesthetic style that emphasized simplicity in design and ornamentation. One of Meridian's first homes to boast electricity and central heating, it remains an example of a spacious and early middle class frame house, with hallmarks of a socially upward merchant reflecting security and stability to his clients and the community. Listed on the National Register of Historic Places in 1997, it is located at 134 East State Avenue on the northwest corner of State and East Second Street, one block south of the 1911–1912 Rural High School.

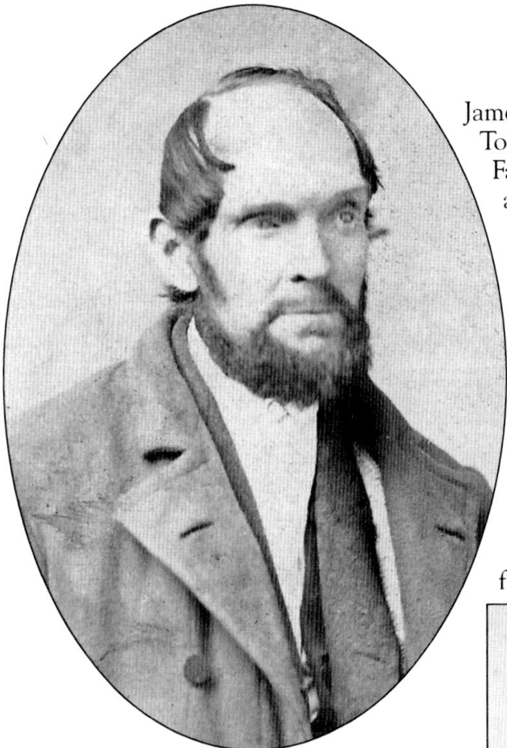

James Tolleth, grandfather of Homer and George Tolleth, is pictured at left. The Tolleth family, from Fairbury in Jefferson County, Nebraska, was part of an early group of immigrants who attained success and prominence in a new and barren land, where hard work was the norm. Homer Tolleth brought livestock on a train to Idaho. He built the first telephone line in Meridian in 1900 for eight families, and in 1902, he organized an independent telephone service for the entire Meridian area. In 1903, he was an original trustee of the village incorporation along with Harvey Powers, T. J. McKee, and Dr. S. M. C. Reynolds. Below is George Tolleth, father of Harry, who became a prominent merchant and in later years helped Ed Hartman dismantle the first school building erected in 1895.

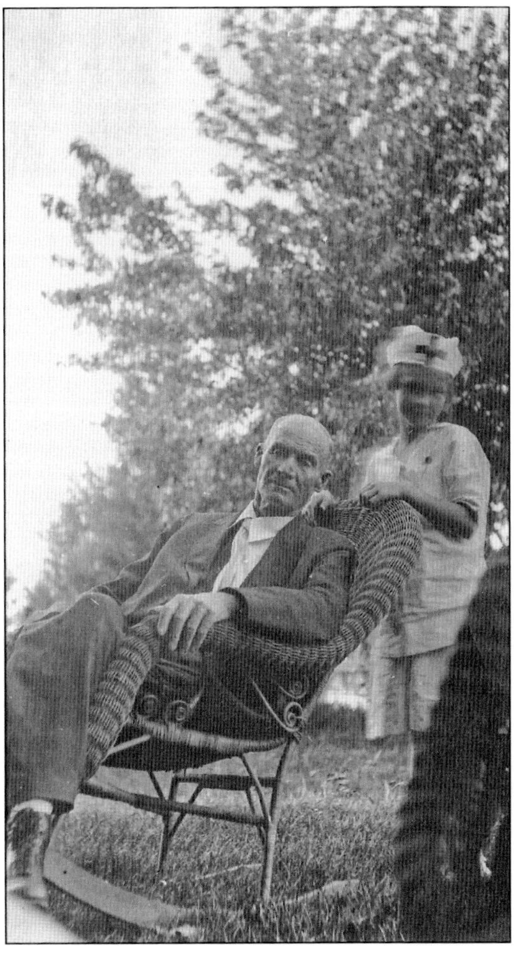

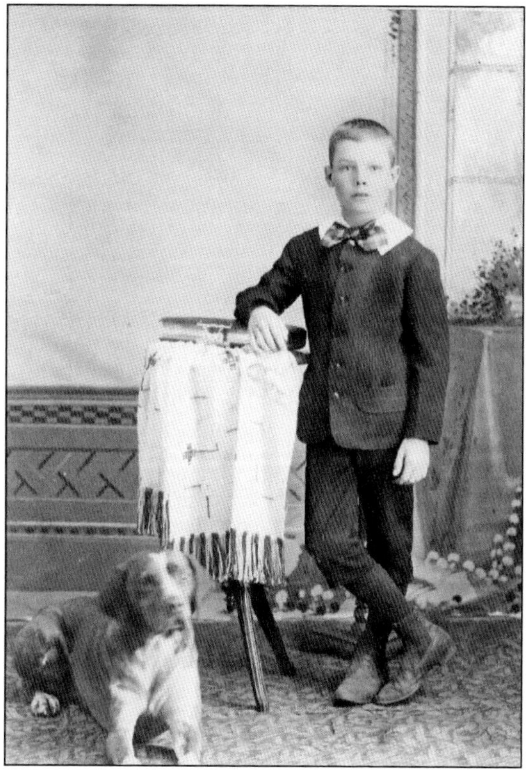

Young Harry Tolleth is photographed right around age eight. His right forearm is resting on what appears to be a clasped book atop a shawl on a plant stand that is partially obscured by the large family dog lying to his right. Sisters Dorothy and Charlotte Tolleth, daughters of Harry and Della, are pictured below. The sisters grew up in the historic Tolleth House near the old Rural High School. They are leafing through a picture book with a piano and songbooks in the background and a Norfolk Island Pine houseplant to their left. The house today is an antique and gift shop. Their father was a merchant and their Uncle Homer was a promoter of a spray and vinegar manufacturing plant, prune dryers, and other fledging enterprises.

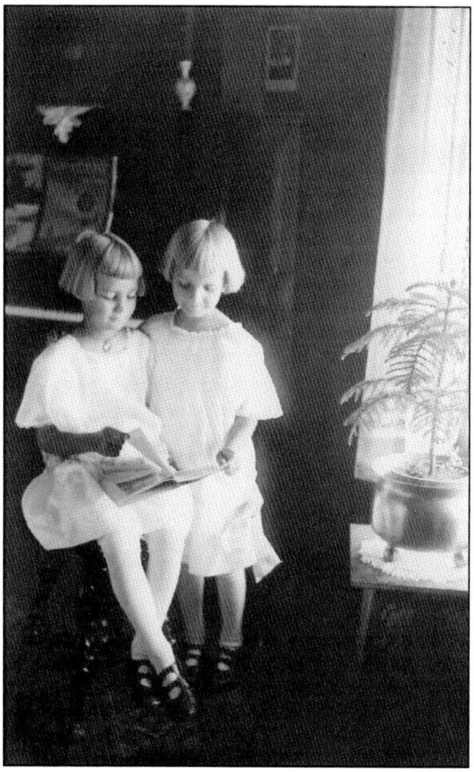

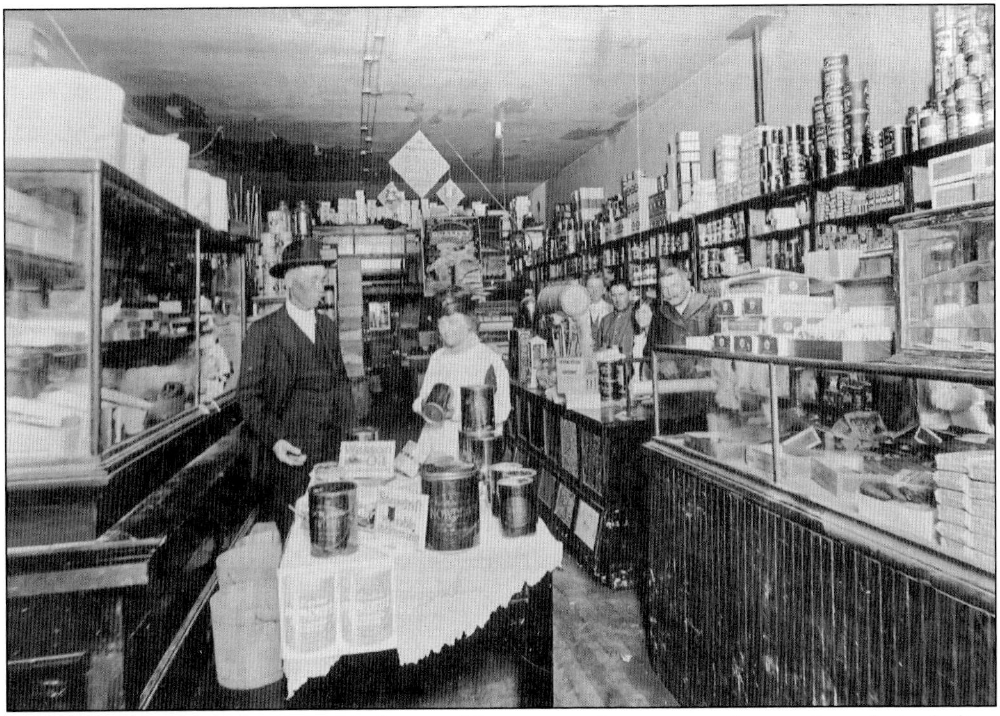

Sam Webb's Commissary, pictured above, sold a variety of counter and canned goods, including large containers. The customers in the middle of the store are examining Wesson Oil and Snowball Vegetable Shortening, which are displayed on a cloth-covered table. Note the glass-enclosed cases and walls lined with shelves packed full of assorted dry goods. Behind the counter, at right, are a man named Adams, Sam Webb, and W. S. Mateer. The interior of the Meridian Commissary, which later became McFaddens' Market, is pictured below. At the left is W. S. Mateer, and at the right is store owner Sam Webb, whose daughter Cleora later married Leonard McFadden. Cleora and Leonard operated the market until the early 1980s.

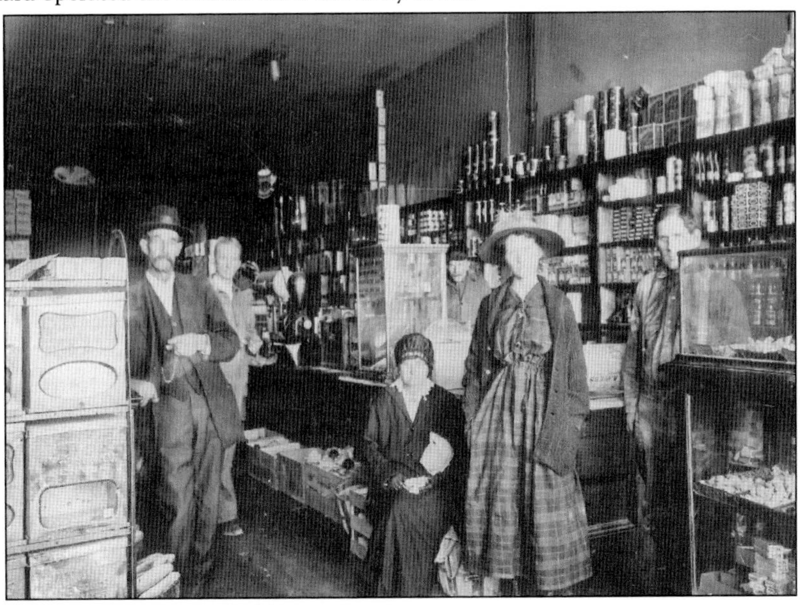

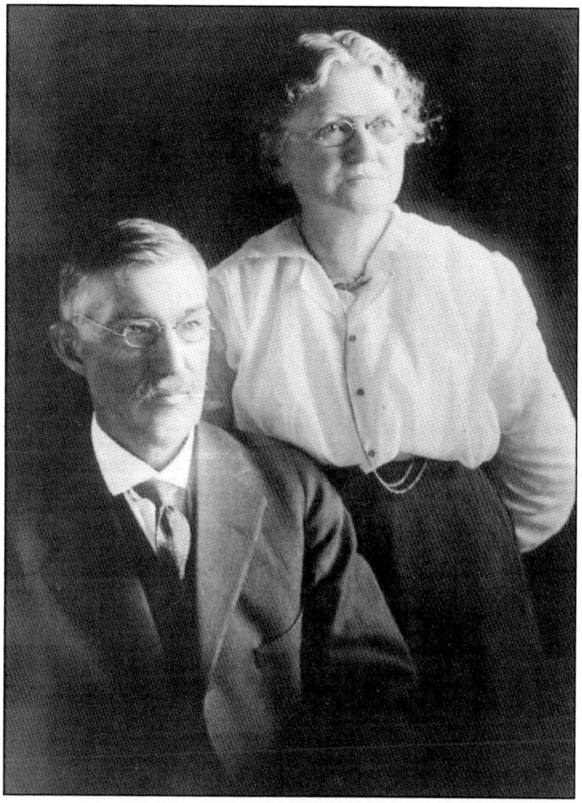

Clement "Clem" and Julia Hedges are pictured at right in an undated photograph. The Hedges family was active in business and church affairs. Hedges Mercantile is pictured below around 1910. The store sold clothing as well as White House and Brown's brand of shoes. In 1909, Emma C. Hedges and Georgia Vaughn completed their junior year and were the first graduates of the 1894 Grade School. Until the Rural High School was built several years later, Meridian students had to commute to Boise for their senior year. In mid-November 1911, Emma and six other village residents represented Meridian at an Ada County Sunday school convention held locally. Jess Hedges was very active for many years in the Methodist church and community activities. (Right, MHC; below, ISHS.)

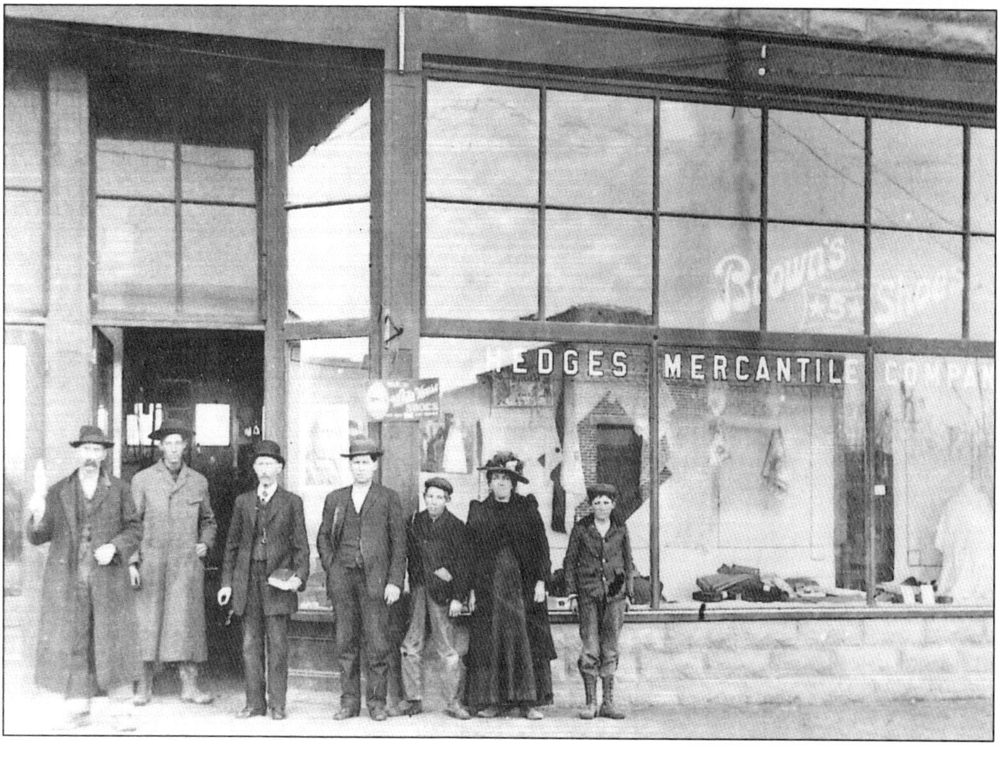

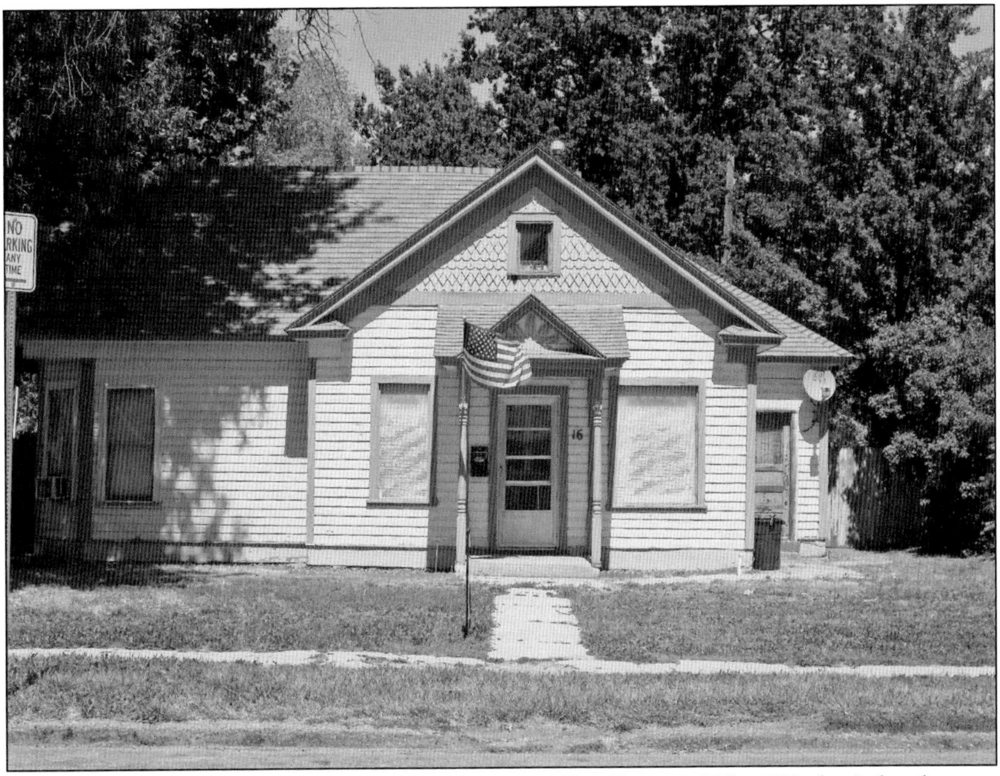

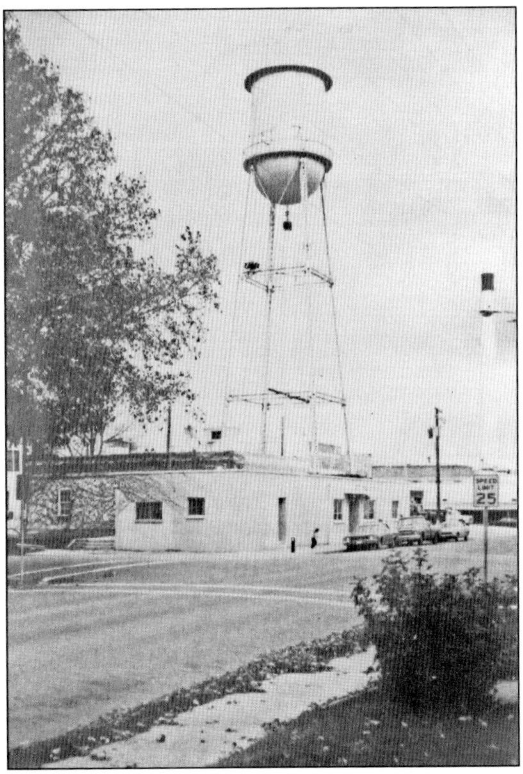

The Clement "Clem" Hedges's family home, pictured above, still stands on the northeast corner of Pine Avenue and Meridian Road. When an epidemic of typhoid fever struck Meridian in 1909, many shallow residential wells and school cisterns were pronounced dangerous. The Hedges's well was one of the few uncontaminated sources of drinking water in the area. Dr. Halbert F. Neal linked typhoid-causing germs to shallow sources of water, including ditch water. Church and community leaders led a successful bond election for a city well and municipal service that began in 1910. The 1910 water tower and waterworks are pictured left on the east side of Meridian Road between Broadway and Idaho Avenues. (Above, PAP; left, MHC.)

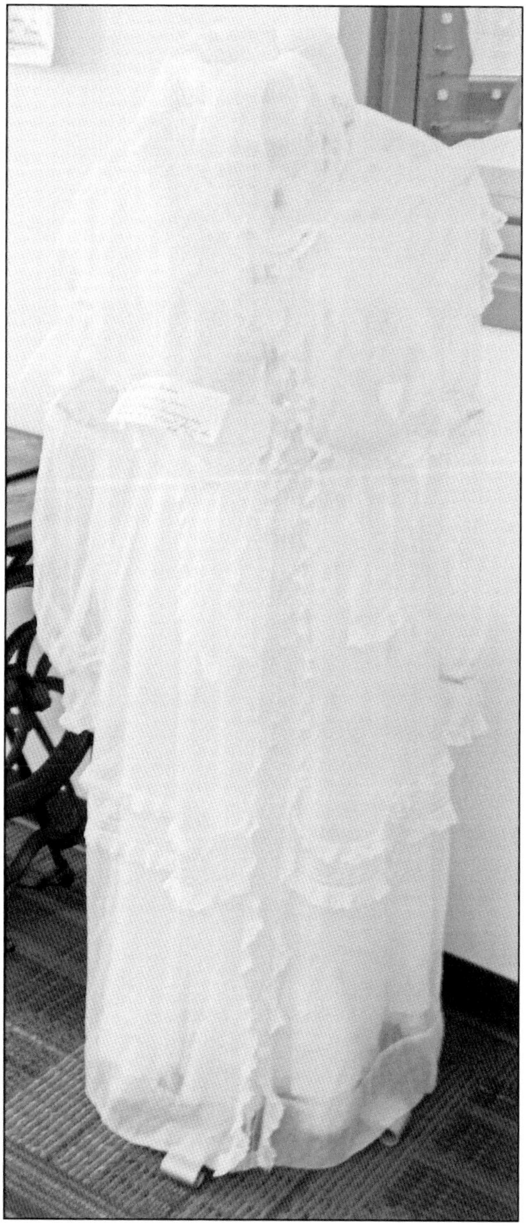

This beautiful wedding dress on display in the Meridian History Center is from the June 14, 1917, union of Minnie Minden of Moscow and Jess Hedges of Meridian. The Hedges' handsome residence was bedecked with vases of peonies and pink carnations. "The couple was preceded by two little ring bearers, Fern Lucile Burns and Clement Hedges, who carried the rings hidden in rosebuds on a large pink satin pillow. Portieres of honeysuckle and snowballs formed the archway under which the pillow was placed. The impressive double ring ceremony was solemnized by Rev. Charles McCoard, pastor of the Methodist Church of Meridian, and as the marriage vows were said, Harley and Blanche Hedges sang the duet 'Because You're You' by Harbert Spencer with J. G. Burns of Boise accompanying on the piano." The bride, a talented musician, graduated from the state university in Moscow, "while the groom is an enterprising young businessman," according to the *Meridian Times* on June 15, 1917. They went to Portland for a brief honeymoon. (PAP.)

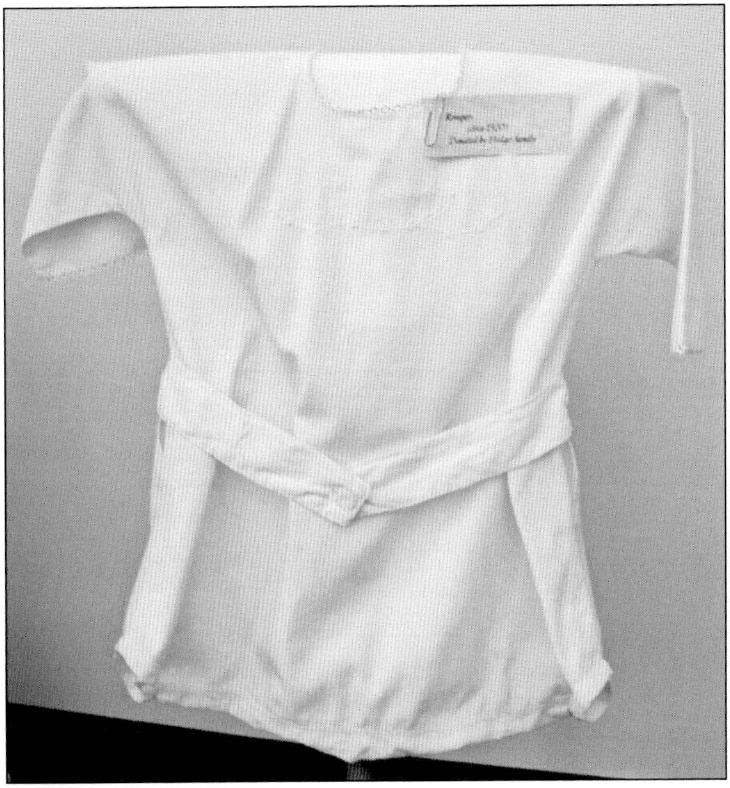

Rompers, a period item of children's clothing for playtime in the early 1920s, are pictured above. This article features tatting around the neckline and sleeves, an embroidered frontal area, and a belt of the same fabric that buttons in front. Rompers appeared in the 1910s and were very popular as playwear for younger children. Styles and conventions varied from country to country. Since 2006, rompers have enjoyed a minor renaissance as a fashionable garment for women. The young girl's dress pictured at right is embellished with lace, smocking, and embroidery features and was worn on special occasions. Like the above article, this dress dates from the early 1920s and was donated by the Hedges family. Both items are on display inside the Meridian History Center. (Both PAP.)

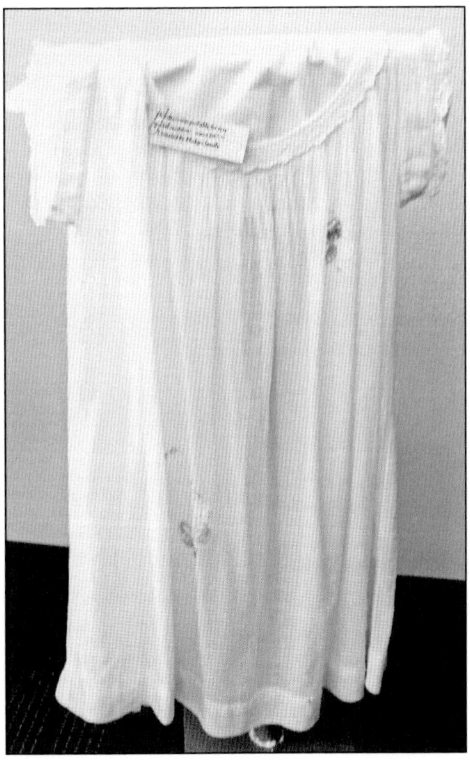

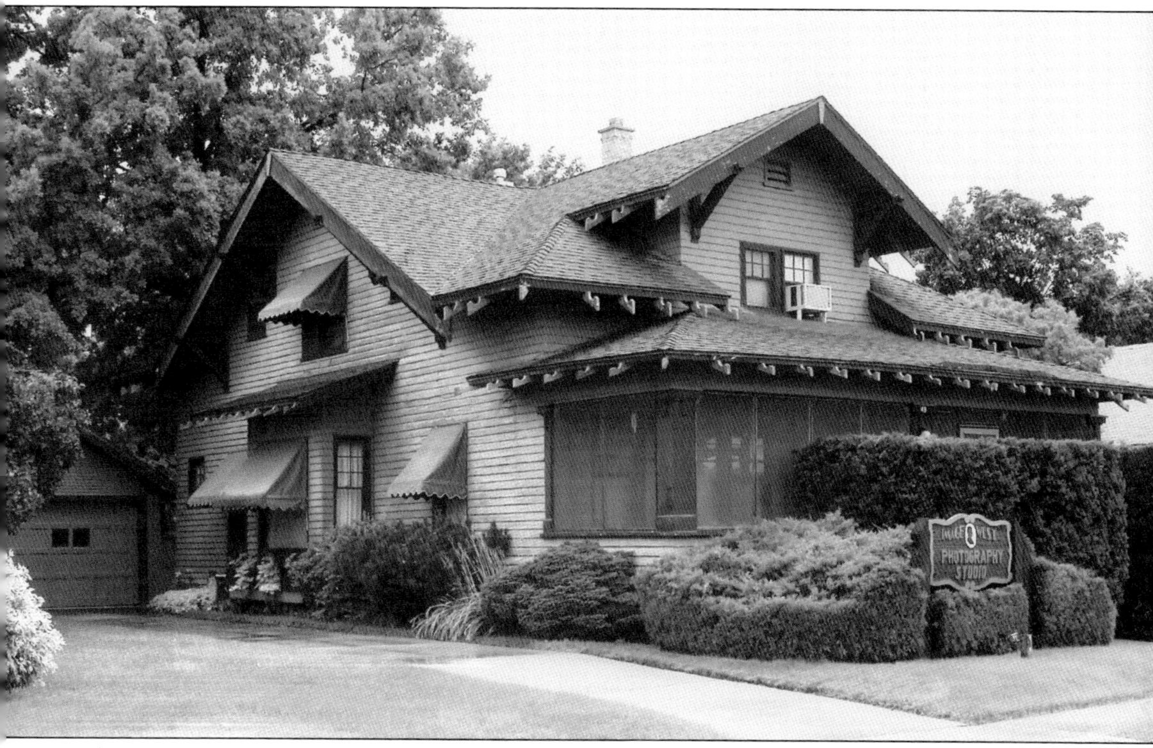

Built in 1913 by a Meridian farmer and businessman, the Ernest F. Hunt House is architecturally significant as the most handsome example of the residential bungalow style developed by the firm of Tourtellotte and Hummel of Boise. Located at 49 East State Avenue, this distinguished representative of pre-1920s architecture features extended rafters and elaborate gables as well as light cantilevered side bays and a roofline of interest, through a front slope around a large gabled dormer. These characteristics introduce a more formal overall appearance than is generally encountered in a bungalow. The arrangement of windows in the building includes double-hung sashes of various sizes. To the left of the entry is a traditional triple group with a wide central element, and the builder observed the traditional Victorian system of designating the lighted front room as the parlor, entered from a front entry hall. (PAP.)

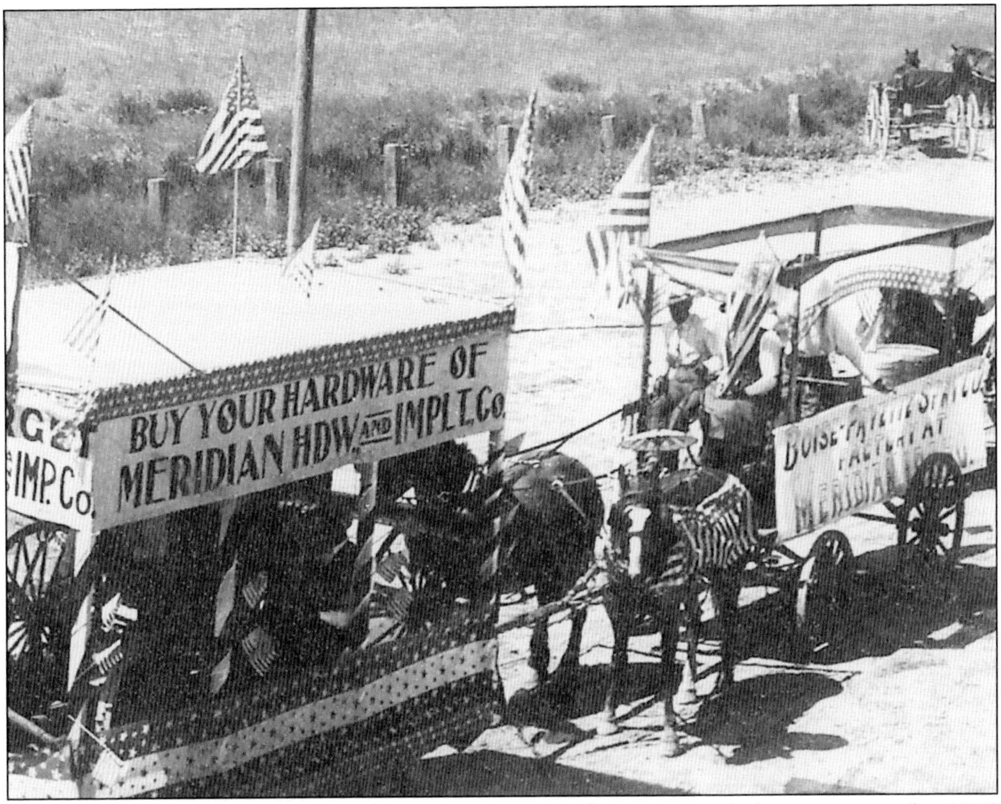

The Meridian Hardware and Implement Company's float, pictured above, was in the 1909 Independence Day parade along Broadway Avenue and featured flag-waving celebrants in a horse-drawn wagon. Below, the interior of the business on the first floor of Parkin Hall shows high ceilings and many shelves on both sides crammed with supplies of all types. The tall man in the center, J. J. "Jim" Jones, was the father of Veta Jones Hawkins. The photograph was taken prior to 1916, the year of his passing. Hardware stores as well as tack and harness shops carried the main staples of farm and domestic life in the village for early Meridian settlers. Note the several ornate stoves that occupy prime display space inside the hardware store.

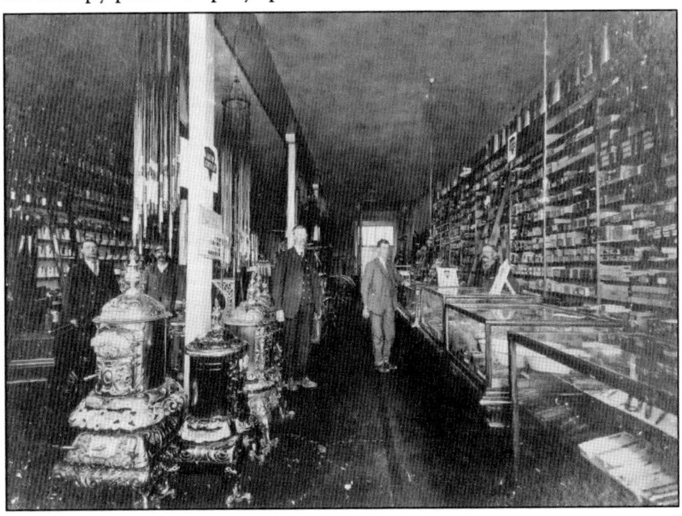

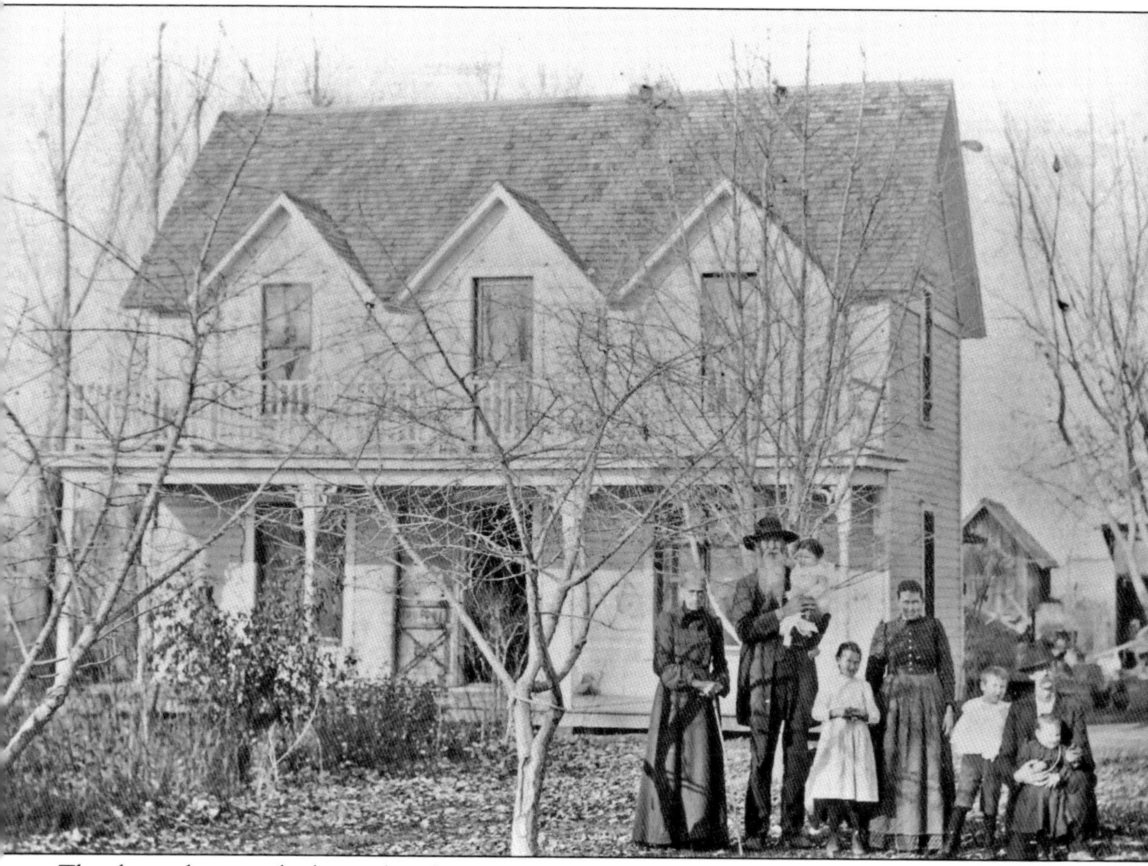

The above photograph, donated to the Meridian Historical Society by Arlene Merkel, shows the home of J. J. and Fanny Jones around the turn of the 20th century. Pictured in front of the spacious family house from left to right are Sarah Kyle Jones and her husband, Calvin Jones (holding Rebecca Jones), Veta Jones (Hawkins), Fanny Maloney Jones, Hike Jones, J. J. Jones, and Neal Jones in front of J. J. A tall man who was sometimes called Jim, J. J. was the grandfather of Arlene Hawkins Merkel and worked at Meridian Hardware and Implement Company in the Parkin Hall building on the northeast corner of East Second Street and Broadway Avenue. This area was the social and business heart of village life for several decades. Clysta Gray said that Broadway was known locally as "Gasoline Alley," after the popular comic strip. "Most of the underage town ruffians laid claim to that turf. It had more brats to the foot than any other area," said Gray.

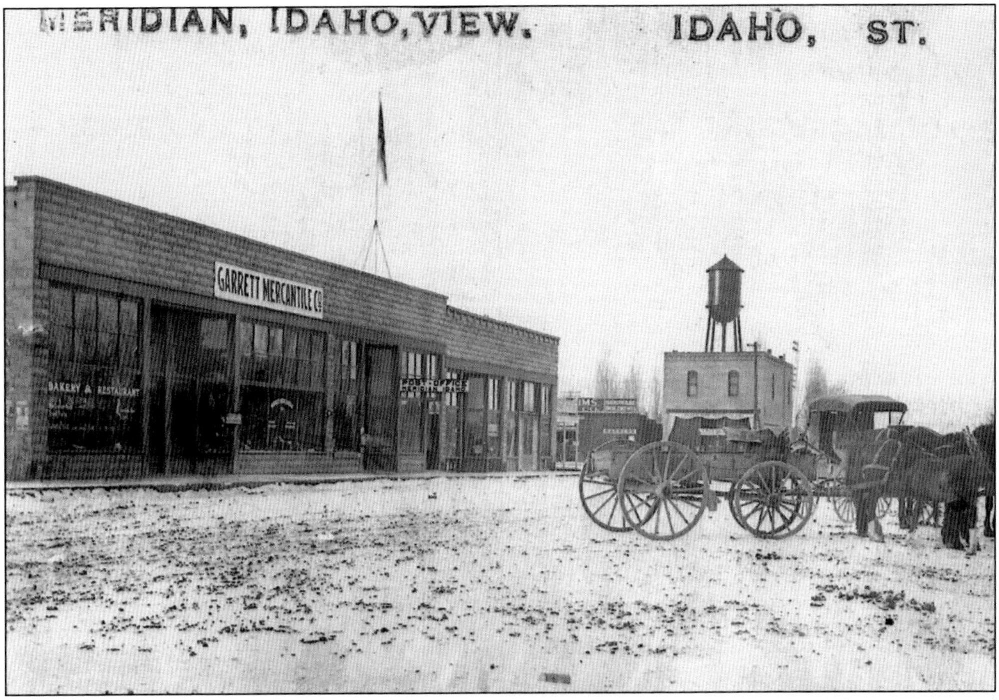

Above is the view looking west on East Idaho Avenue from its intersection with East Second Street. The 1910 water tower rises above the 1902 Modern Woodmen of America building and the horse-drawn conveyances in front. Note the post office inside the same block building with Garrett Mercantile Company and a bakery and restaurant business. Below, a later photograph of the same street scene shows the post office has zigzagged from the south side of Idaho to the northwest corner of its intersection with East Second Street, later the site of Elite Cleaners. The businesses formerly on the south side of Idaho have apparently vanished.

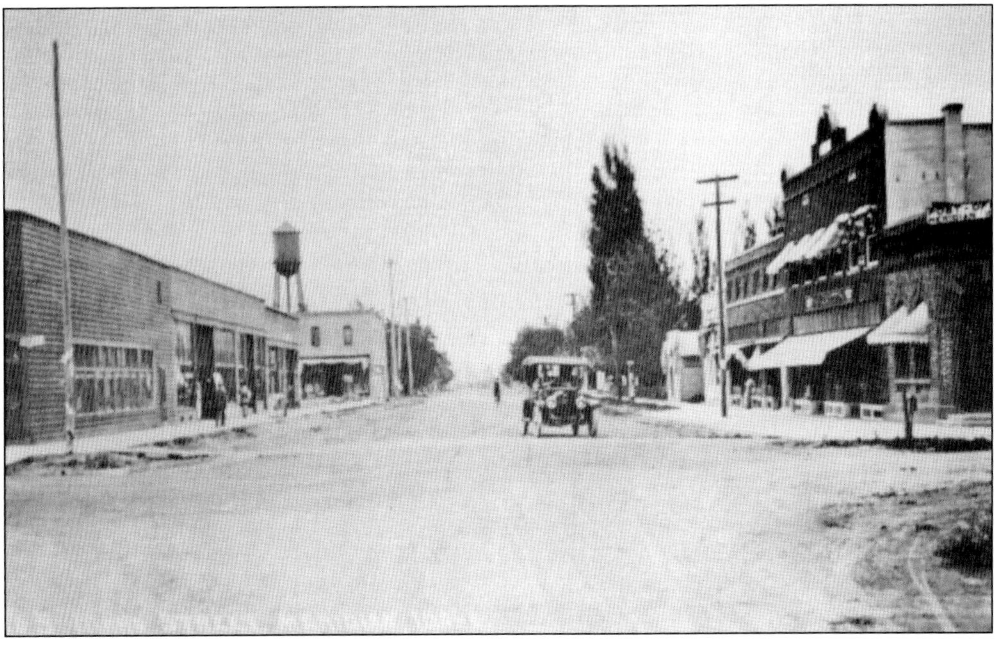

Five

Between the Wars and Beyond

Meridian settlers and residents have never been strangers to hard times. After World War I ended in 1918, depressed prices for agricultural products affected everyone, a condition alleviated somewhat with the opening of the creamery in 1929 and its positive economic impact during the Great Depression of the 1930s. Between 1920 and 1930, Meridian's population increased by four people, from 1,000 to 1,004. By 1940, that number was 1,465 and by 1950, 1,810.

Rural farming activities continued to dominate area life. West of the village, the family of Serafin Lopez de Vinaspre from Castille, Spain, operated Ten Mile Stock Farm. One son, Vincent, became a world champion wrestler in the 1930s and another, Fidel, operated a milk-hauling route for many years. There were common intermarriages between Spaniards, Basques, and other ethnic groups.

Urban evolution had not yet reached the village, where Richard Nourse recalls as a youngster, "all those vacant lots. There were so few people here, I wished people would come and live in Meridian." Carman Loveland from Nampa, who married Meridian High School graduate Lois Law in 1937, said of those days, "I used to know 98 percent of the people. Sam Webb had the grocery store and Frank Nourse at one time owned half of Meridian. You could buy a 25-foot lot for $100, $10 down and $10 a month." Frank's son, Richard, said his father often bought up area properties whose owners were unable to pay the taxes.

But life had its lighter moments. Clysta Gray recalled that in the 1930s, fire broke out in the liquor store adjacent to a grocery store she and her husband, Elden, operated at Idaho Avenue and East Third Street. "The volunteer fire department spent a lot of time in our store, passing liquor through a hole in the wall. No liquor survived, and it took them forever to put out that fire."

Despite the Depression, some new businesses sprang up, including George Davis's grocery store in 1932. Besides orchards and dairy farms, Meridian has had a robust beekeeping industry since 1909, when G. F. Atwater sold bulk comb honey, 12 pounds for $1, and advertised "no less amount will be sold. Bring a pail." In September 1934, ten railcars carried 40,000 pounds in 5-gallon cans to market from 10 local apiaries owned by Earl Biddick, G. A. Koger, and others.

The economy improved after World War II, when Meridian began a growth spurt to a population of over 2, 000 in 1960. Civic leaders, including Herald Cox, Don Roberts, Ernest Lembke, and George Ambrose, worked to transform the community club into the chamber of commerce.

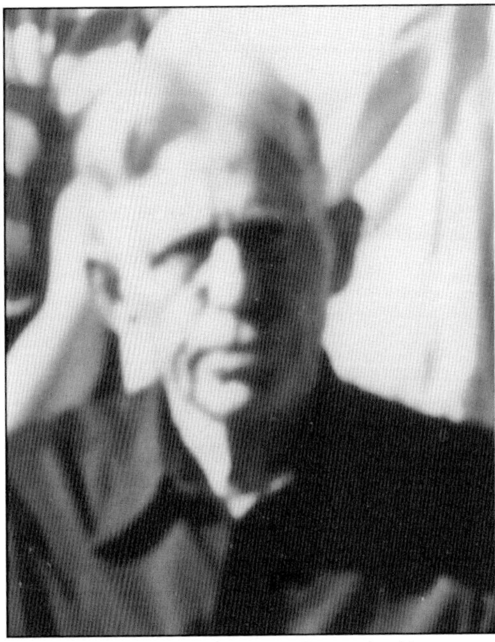

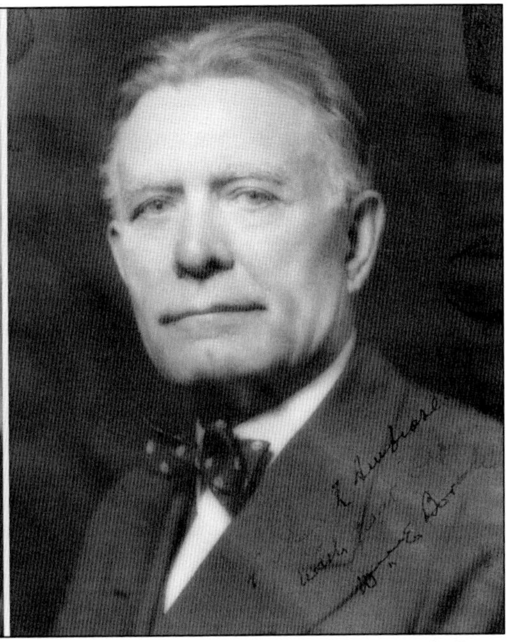

William Edgar Borah, near the end of his six-term career in the U.S. Senate, is pictured above right. The inscription on the photograph was written to George L. Ambrose, above left, a state legislator from Mackay, Idaho, and later magistrate with an established law practice in downtown Meridian. The "Lion of Idaho" had close political and personal ties to Meridian, where his good friend, Dr. S. M. C. Reynolds, managed the opening of Borah's early campaigns that were always held in Meridian. While GOP politicians generally dominated the local scene, the other party also remained active. A Democratic rally and barbecue in Meridian on November 4, 1916, is pictured below. (Above, PAP; below, MHC.)

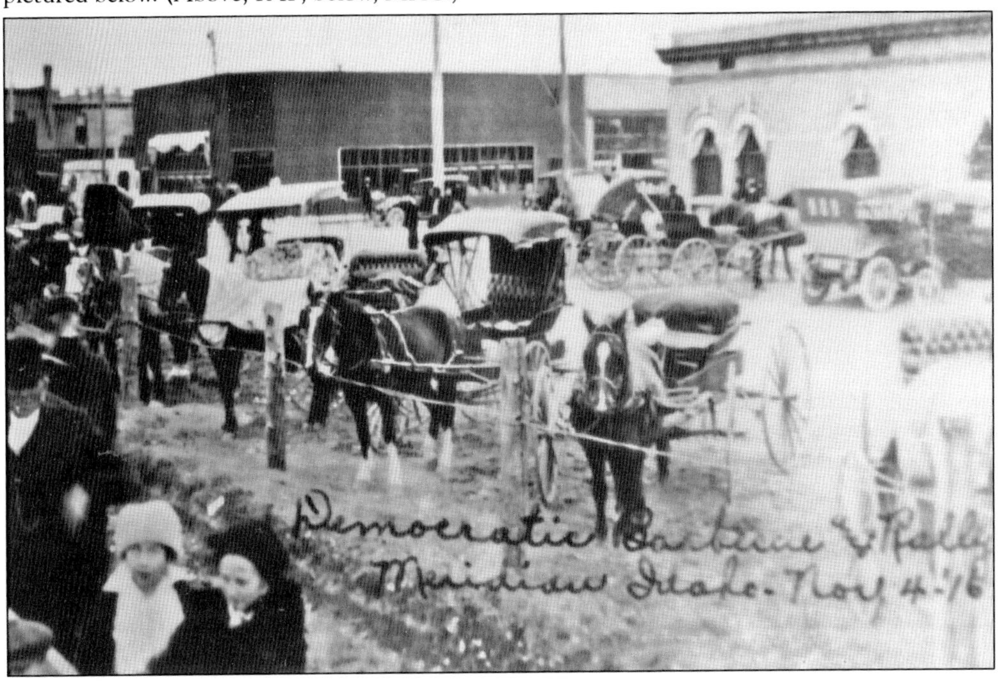

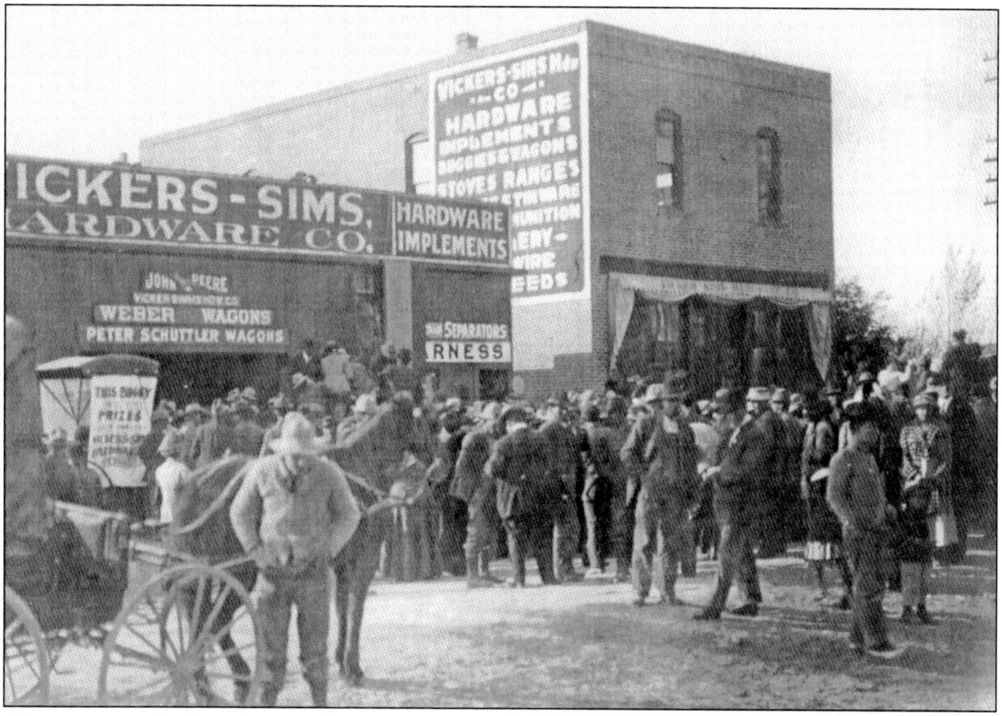

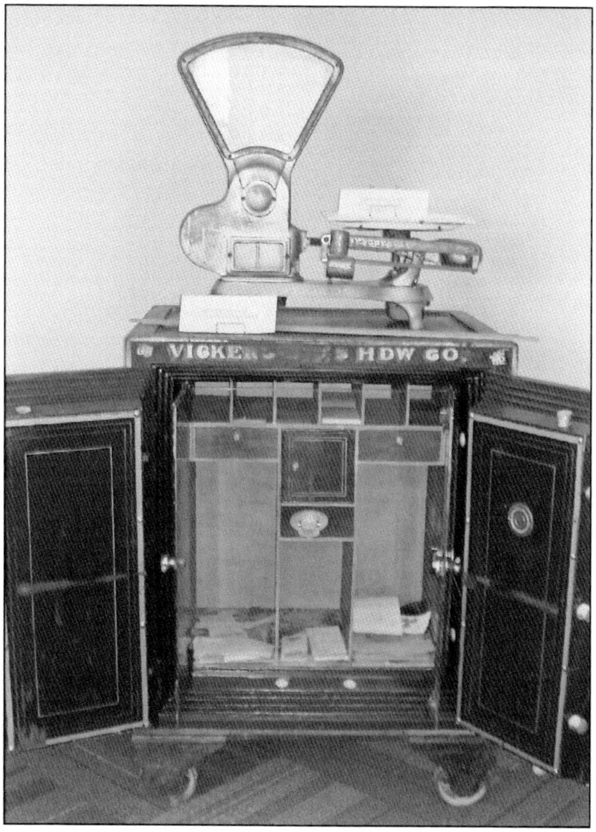

Above, a crowd of cowboys and others fill East First (now Main) Street north of its intersection with Idaho Avenue in 1917. Eight years earlier, in the May 7, 1909, weekly *Meridian Times*, editor/publisher John Baird described a walking tour of Meridian businesses, including several dozen firms on the main streets. Foremost was Vicker-Sims Hardware, located on the lower floor of the Modern Woodman Building, and operated by E. E. Sims, J. W. Harrell, and M. M. Louderbough. The store sold hardware and implements, Weber and Peter Schuettler wagons, cream separators, harnesses, stoves/ranges, and guns and ammunition. Not pictured are young Meridian and Ada County men drafted into the army starting with half a dozen on August 10, 1917. The Vickers-Sims Hardware Company safe, pictured right, was later with Louderbough Hardware and is now in the Meridian History Center. (Above, MHC; right, PAP.)

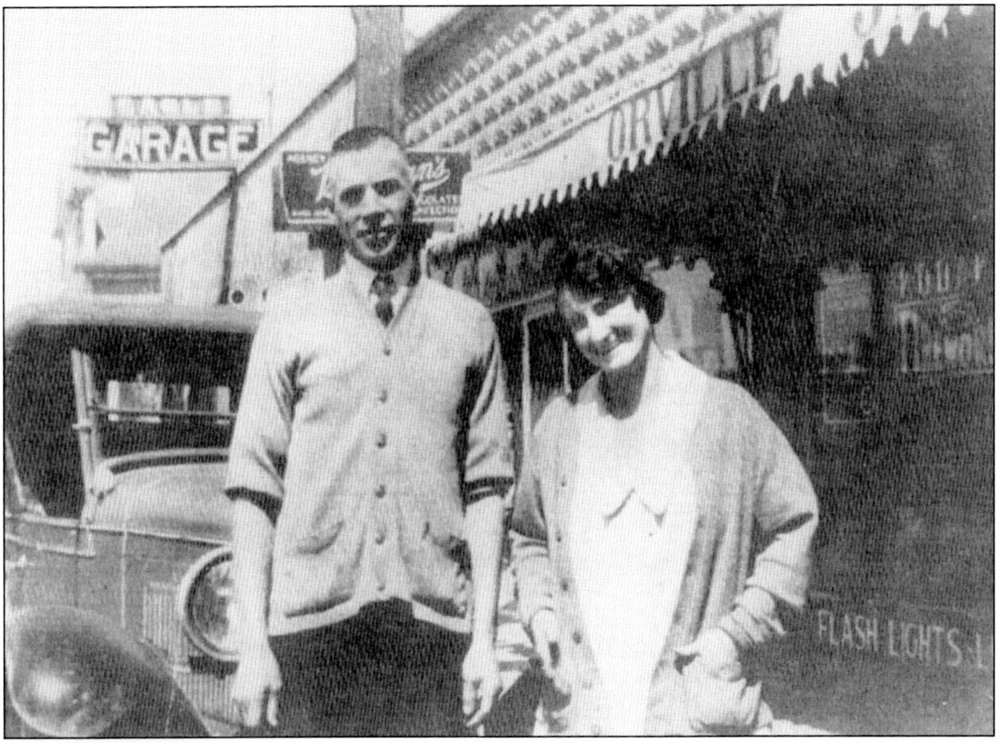

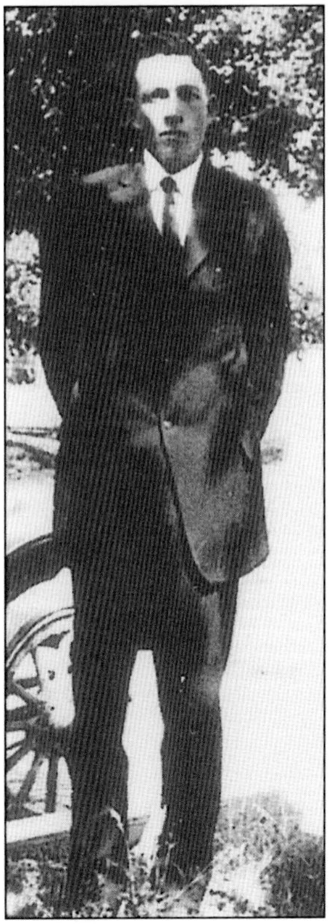

Orville Jackson, pictured above, of Eagle served in the U.S. Army Medical Corps and in 1917 was stationed at Camp Fort Douglas near Salt Lake City, Utah. He wrote in a letter home on July 30, "Eat at the hospital at a table; have good eats, and a fine place to sleep." Jackson worked in Meridian before purchasing his famous drugstore in Eagle and maintained close business and social ties to Meridian. George A. Nourse, pictured at left, wed Frances Kerr in 1917. Kerr was the daughter of T. N. Kerr, proprietor of the Dewey Palace Hotel in Nampa. They divorced after having two children. George and his father, Frank Alonzo Nourse, were stockholders of the Idaho Building and Loan Association, and in 1927, George inherited his extensive farm properties in Meridian. (Above, EHS; left, RN.)

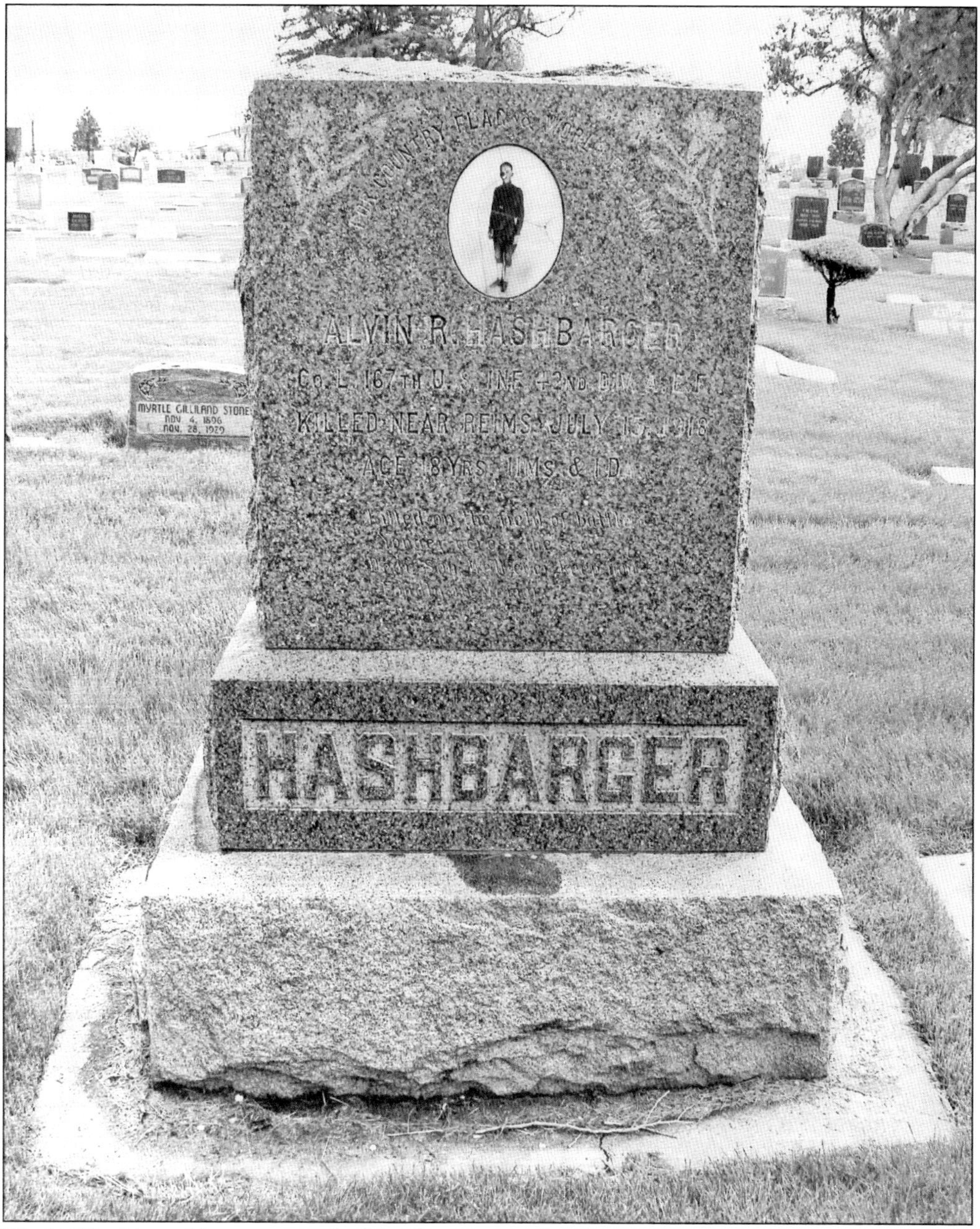

World War I lasted four years and affected many area families in a most direct and painful way, as many young men's lives were lost in battle. Alvin R. Hashbarger, one of over 100 Meridian-area men in the service, was a month shy of his 19th birthday when he was killed near Reims, France, on July 15, 1918. His tombstone in the Meridian Cemetery has a photograph of him in uniform, and the epitaph reads, "For country, flag, and world freedom." He served in Company L, 167th U.S. Infantry, 42nd Division, Allied Expeditionary Forces. There is also a poem inscribed, "Killed on the field of battle, yonder across the sea; Dear Son, we'll ever keep you fondly in memory." Another Meridian soldier, Walter Anderson, grandson of James Matthew Anderson, spent the war stateside and survived the flu epidemic of 1918 but in 1923 contracted the virus and died in Mountain Home, Idaho. (PAP.)

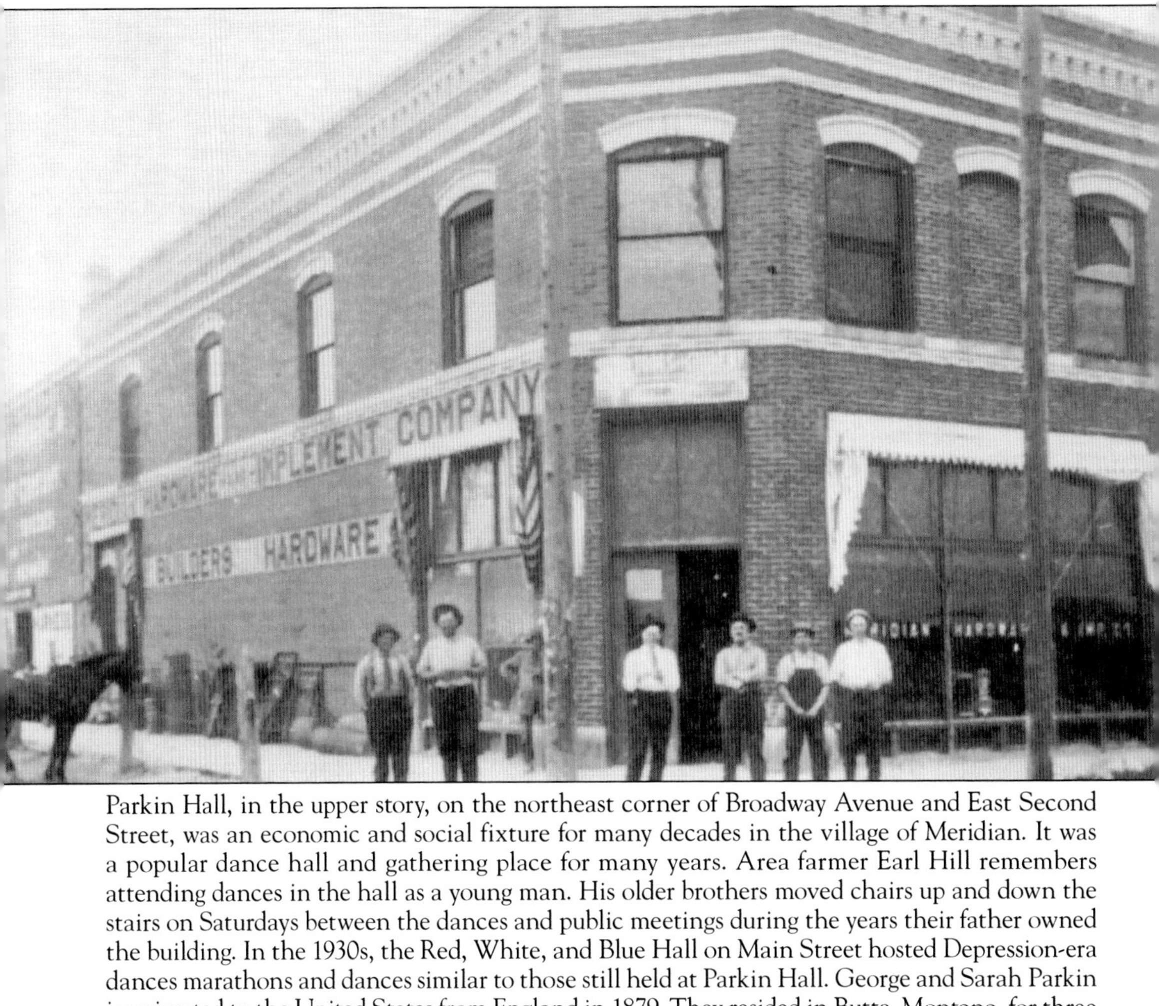

Parkin Hall, in the upper story, on the northeast corner of Broadway Avenue and East Second Street, was an economic and social fixture for many decades in the village of Meridian. It was a popular dance hall and gathering place for many years. Area farmer Earl Hill remembers attending dances in the hall as a young man. His older brothers moved chairs up and down the stairs on Saturdays between the dances and public meetings during the years their father owned the building. In the 1930s, the Red, White, and Blue Hall on Main Street hosted Depression-era dances marathons and dances similar to those still held at Parkin Hall. George and Sarah Parkin immigrated to the United States from England in 1879. They resided in Butte, Montana, for three years prior to relocating in 1883 to Meridian, where they homesteaded on the southeast corner of McMillan and Locust Grove Roads. The building was torn down in 2009 to make way for a new complex called The Hub.

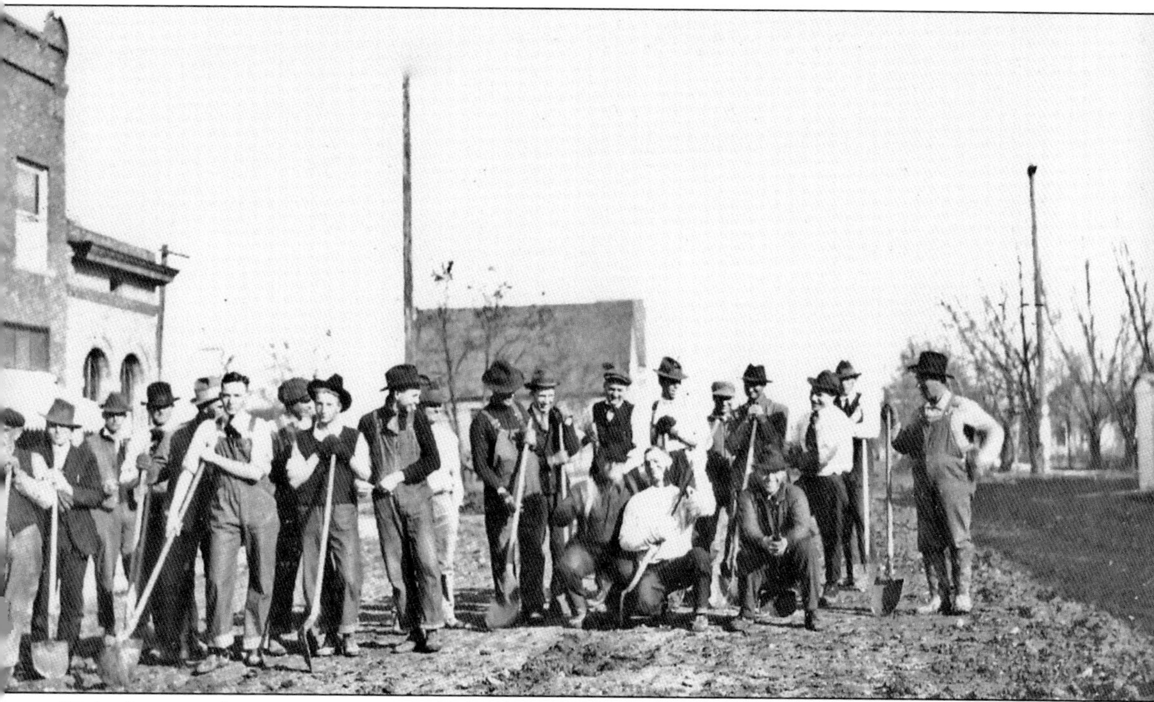

This photograph captures a group of Meridian businessmen with shovels doing voluntary street work in the 1920s on Idaho Avenue. Volunteerism was the very essence of village social and economic life during a time when public safety and passable roadways depended upon those who lived and worked in the area. The late Pastor Evert Roberts recalled life in Meridian in the 1920s: "It was a totally different society and era of thinking. We played a lot of checkers if we were penned up in winter, and we worked in the summers. There were always berries to pick, onions to chop, and lettuce to hoe. On weekends, we went to church; my father was a minister, also. Were we bored? Heavens, no. It never entered my mind that we were being cheated or missed anything or had nothing to do."

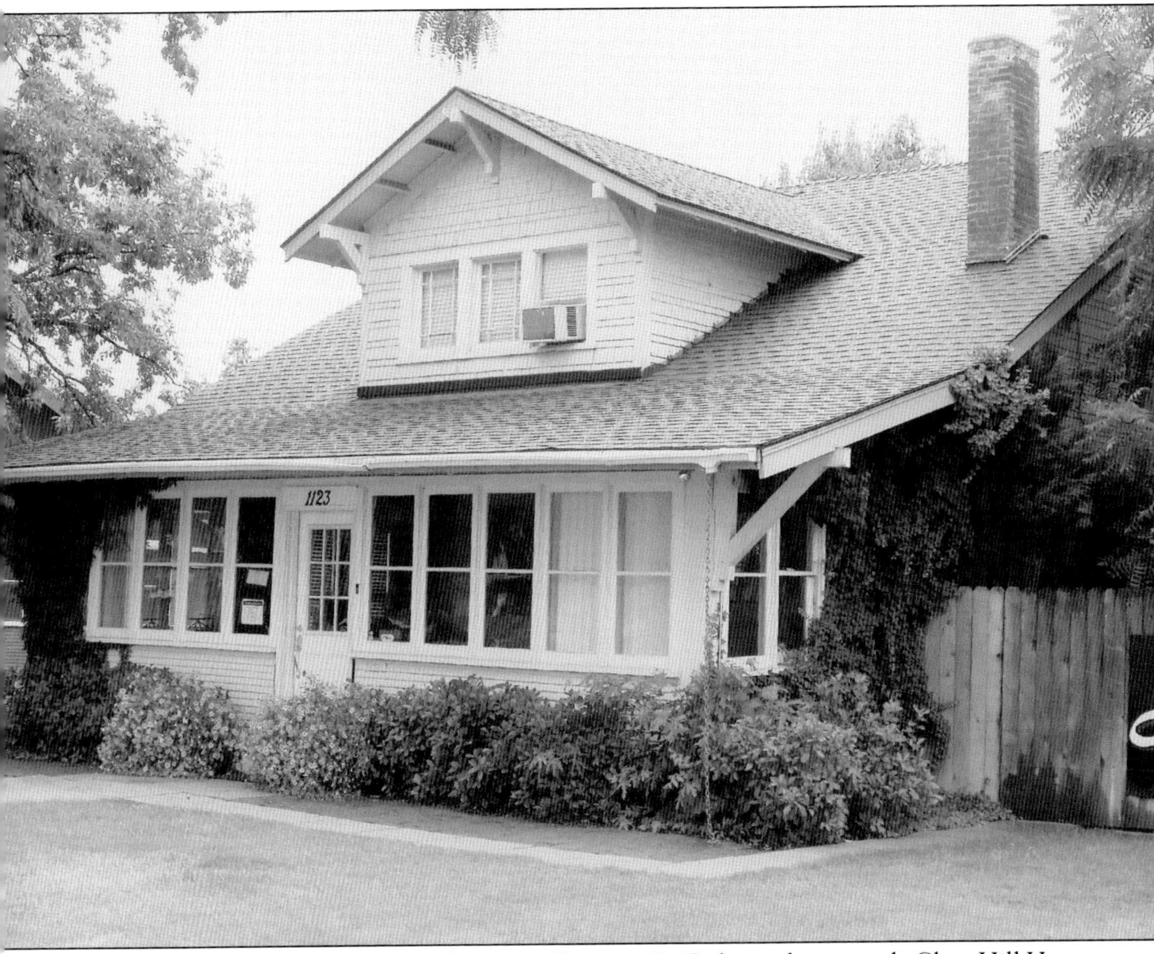

Listed on the National Register of Historic Places in 2005, the craftsman-style Clara Hill House, at 1123 North Main, was built by Charles Arzt in 1920 and occupied by Mae Estes until Clara Hill purchased the home in 1938. An example of the American Movement's craftsman style, the building attains a natural look through use of wood, earth tone colors, simple features, and geometric forms. The house models the transformation of Hunter as an outpost into the growing and prospering village of Meridian. Built on the original through-town state highway, the Hill House still stands out as a domestic dwelling of moderately large size and modern style of the times. The craftsman style of domestic architecture was most popular in the United States between 1905 and 1930. It spread from California and was one of the building types featured in a regular architectural column in the *Meridian Times*. (PAP.)

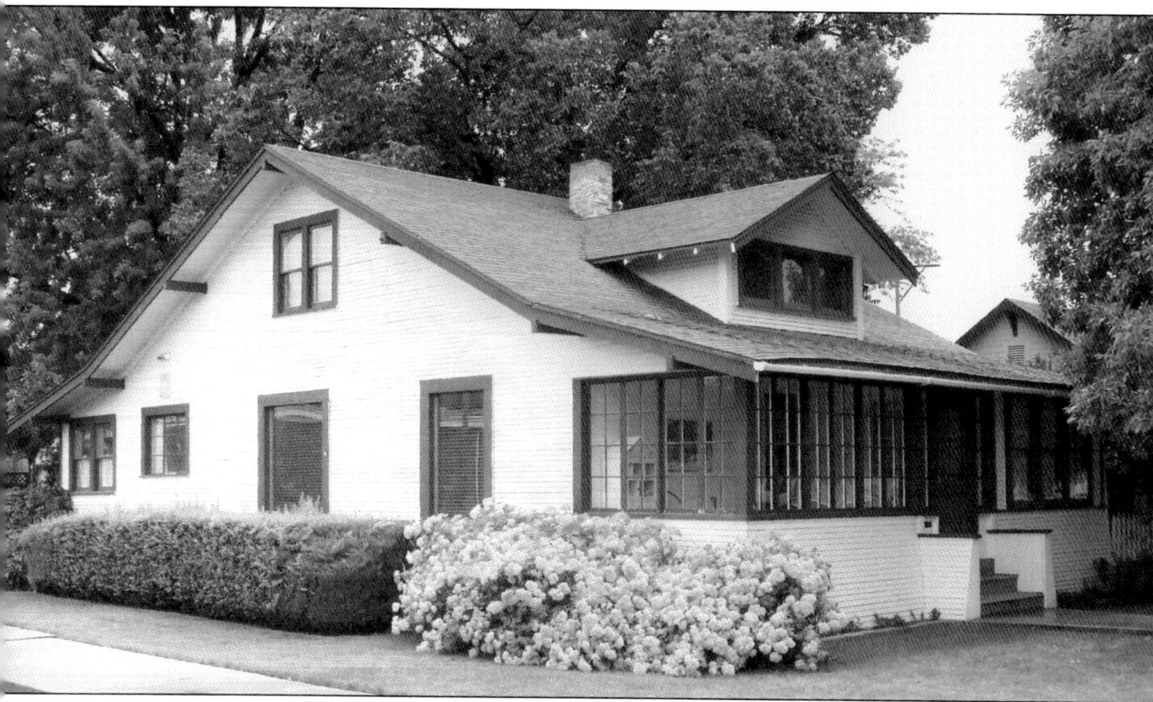

The R. H. Bell House, a craftsman-style residence at 1376 East Pine Avenue, was constructed in 1922. It stands out modestly but proudly as a modern, domestic dwelling located on a prime downtown corner lot on the original town-site plat. The *Meridian Times* reported in its issue on May 6, 1921, that S. H. Griffith, a local coal merchant who once served as mayor of Meridian, has a contract to build a "strictly modern (house) including a furnace" on land he owned at the corner of Second and Pine. These homes were featured in publications, including the *Ladies' Home Journal*, the *Craftsman Homes* guide by Gustav Stickley, and the Sears, Roebuck and Company's *Modern Homes* catalog. Ralph H. and Jessie Bell purchased the residence in 1925 and maintained ownership for 52 years. It was listed on the National Register of Historic Places in 2005. (PAP.)

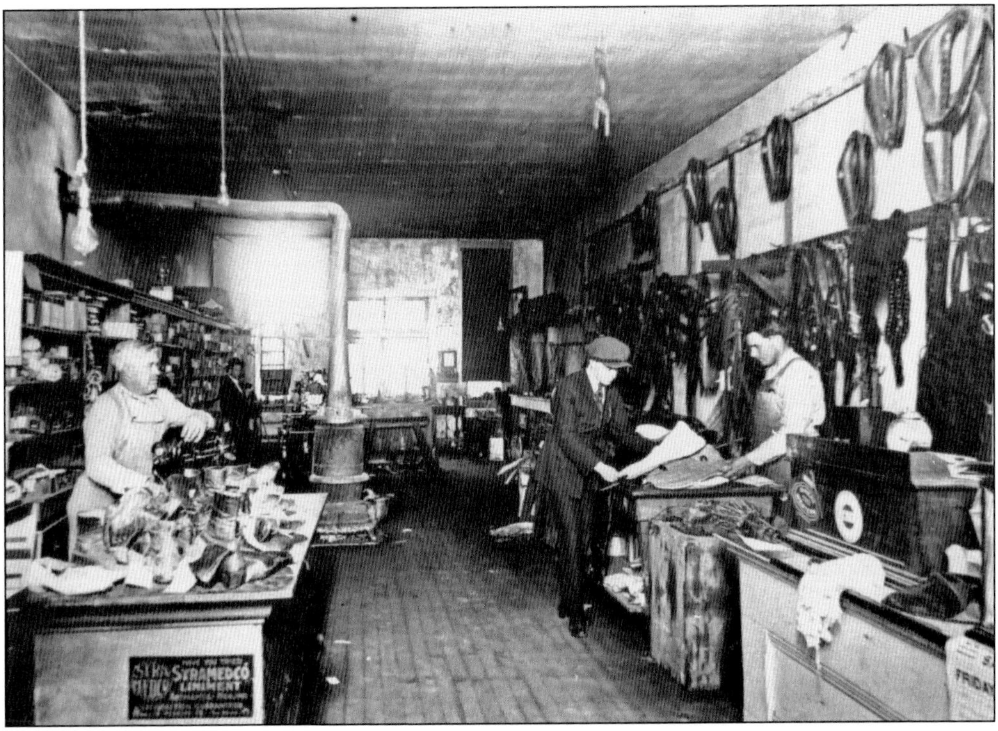

Pictured above in the 1920s is an interior scene from a harness shop at 126 East Broadway Avenue. There are harnesses hanging at the top of the far right wall along with a large heating stove with a long elbow pipe as well as naked light bulbs on the left side. They illuminated the area where the cobbler worked on leather footwear across from the pair examining the tooled leather samples. Note the advertisement for liniment and the slatted wooden floor. Pictured below, a woman at a barbershop is getting a haircut in a chair next to the stovepipe used for heating. On the left is Sim Cunningham. The shop was on the north side of Idaho Avenue, possibly at 120 East Idaho.

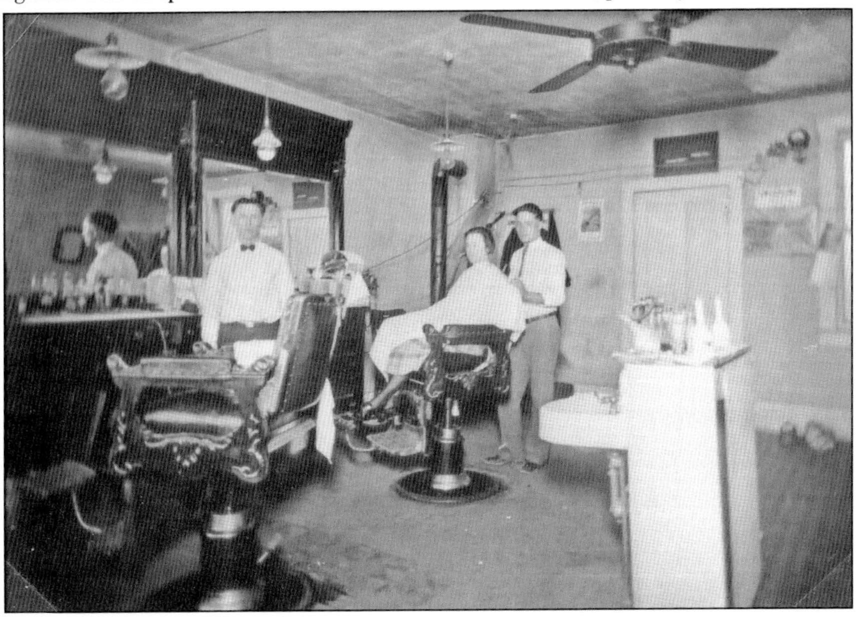

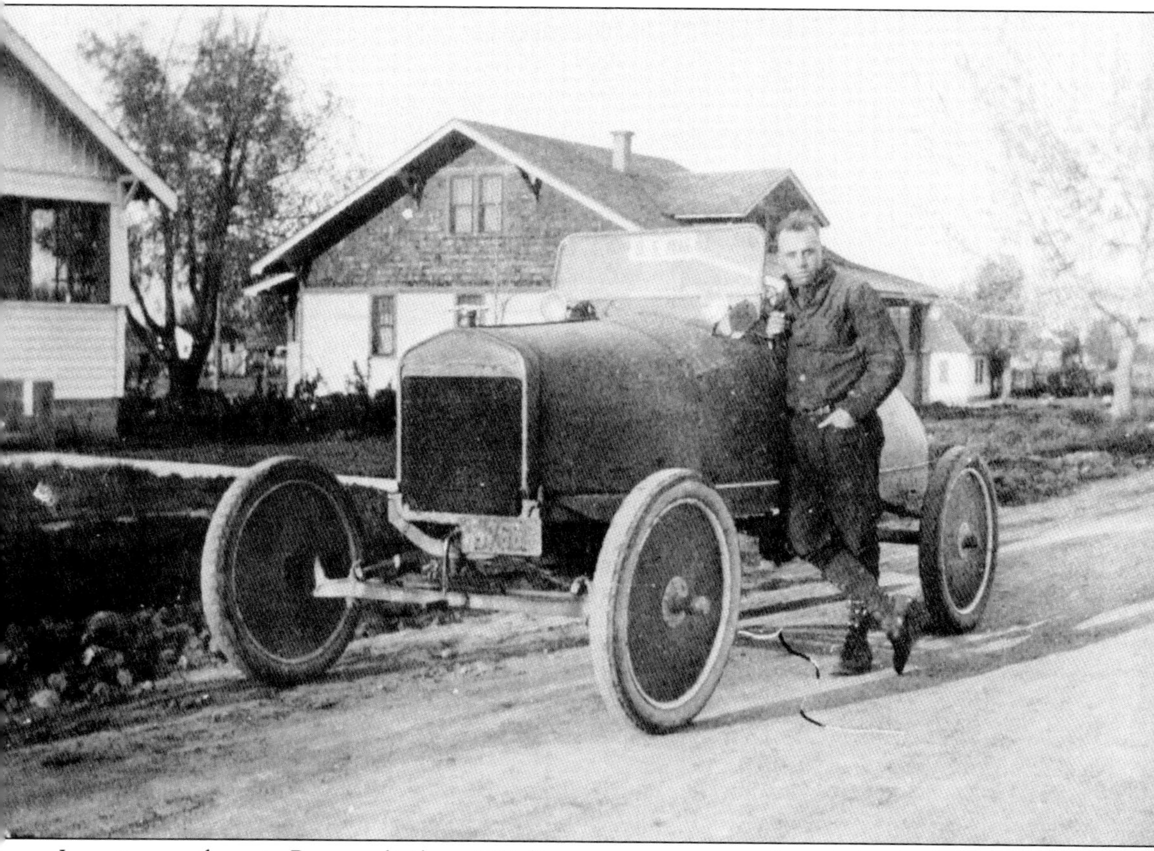

Longtime mail carrier Raymond "Shorty" Wolfe poses next to his roadster for his 1925 Christmas card. Meridian's post office was located inside various business buildings in the downtown area after starting out in a residence. In 1894, "Postmaster N. W. Bower (or possibly his daughter), was there to get the mail," wrote Mary French of stepping off the train. In fact, Julia Bower had the appointment and was postmistress. Later the post office moved downtown and around from business to business, before the post office building was constructed on the southeast corner of Idaho Avenue and East Second Street in the 1950s. On July 11, 1957, the *Meridian Times* profiled postmaster Lorenzo Frank Jolley. Jolley brought in the very first truckload of milk to the 1929 creamery as a contract hauler and also served as the village's one-man police force from 1941 to 1944, when he became acting postmaster. In 1950, he received his postmaster's commission.

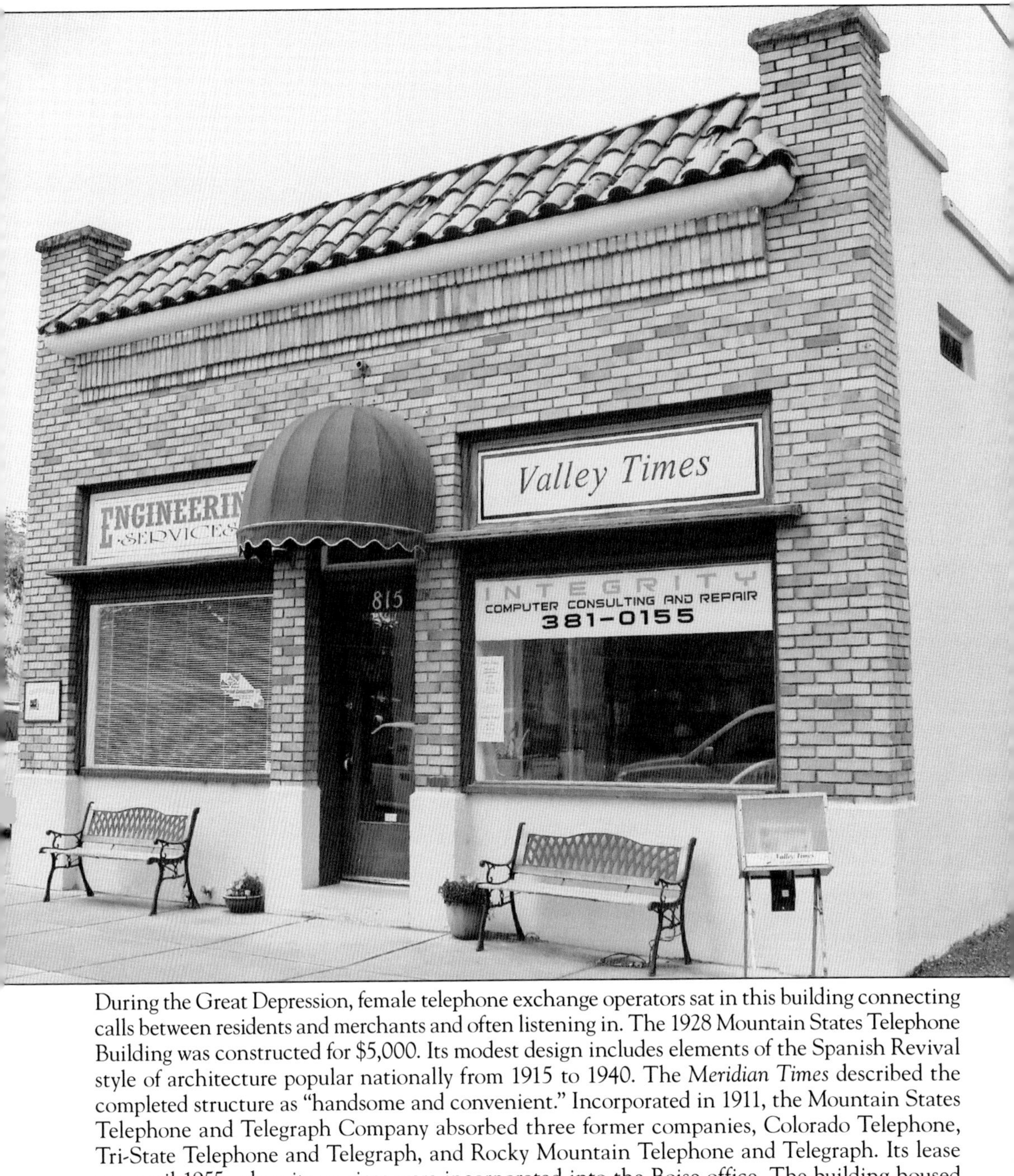

During the Great Depression, female telephone exchange operators sat in this building connecting calls between residents and merchants and often listening in. The 1928 Mountain States Telephone Building was constructed for $5,000. Its modest design includes elements of the Spanish Revival style of architecture popular nationally from 1915 to 1940. The *Meridian Times* described the completed structure as "handsome and convenient." Incorporated in 1911, the Mountain States Telephone and Telegraph Company absorbed three former companies, Colorado Telephone, Tri-State Telephone and Telegraph, and Rocky Mountain Telephone and Telegraph. Its lease ran until 1955, when its services were incorporated into the Boise office. The building housed former Mayor Voris Botkin's real estate business before his family sold the building in 1981. This is one of only a few unaltered historic businesses along Main Street. It was added to the National Register of Historic Places in 2009. (PAP.)

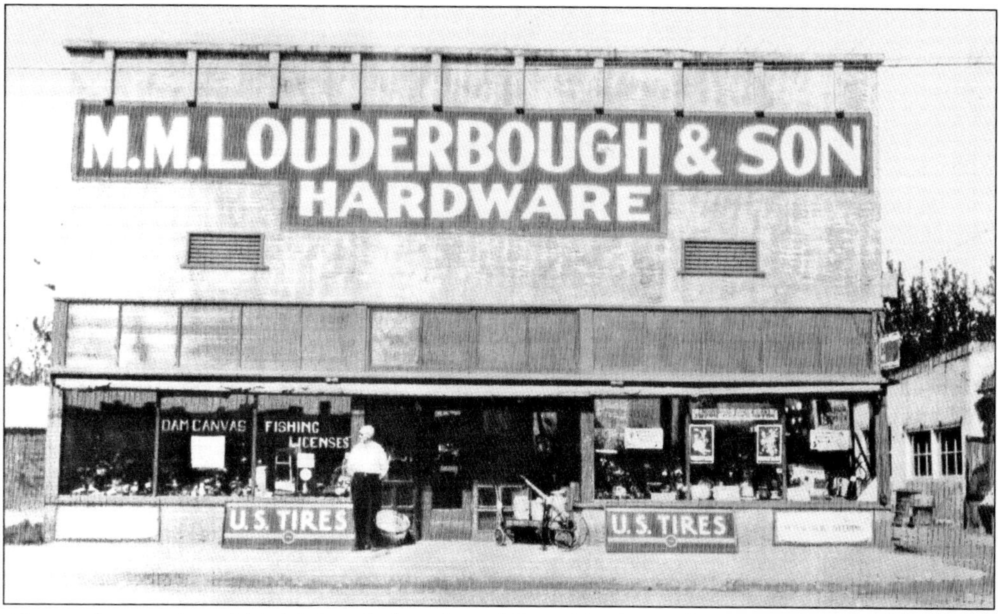

Above, the exterior of M. M. Louderbough and Sons Hardware Store is pictured, with Milton Louderbough standing in front beside a large metal bucket. Between the two U.S. Tires signs there is a wagon with three milk cans and window advertisement for dam canvas—used by local farmers during irrigation. The store also sold fishing licenses, *Popular Science* magazine, and other wares. According to the *Meridian Times* in its July 20, 1934, issue, "Louderbough's announce that they will soon move to their new building. Hammer handles sell for 13¢, boy's ax handles for 25¢ and men's ax handles for 30¢." Below, two men in suits are pictured inside the early hardware store that sold a myriad of nails and other supplies, including horses' harnesses and farming implements such as shovels and pitchforks.

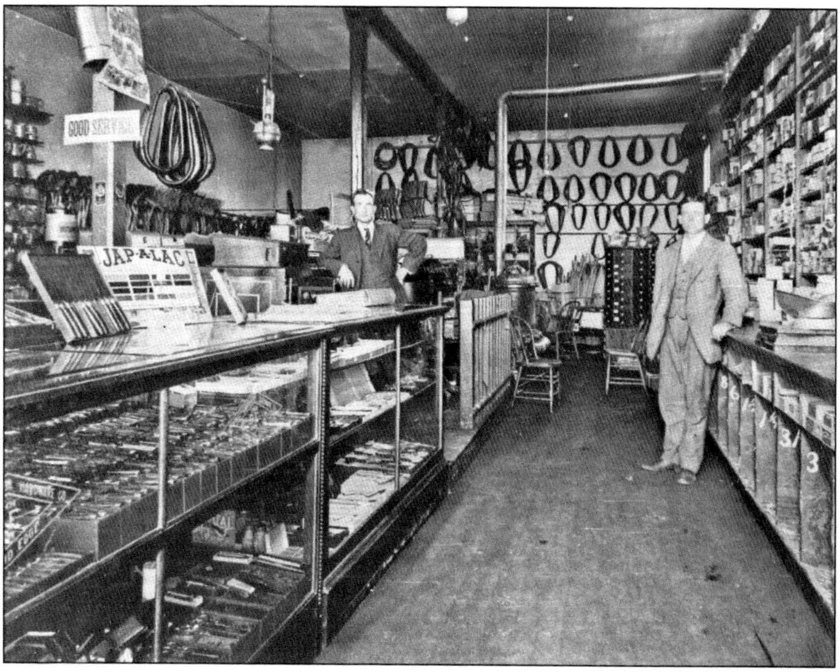

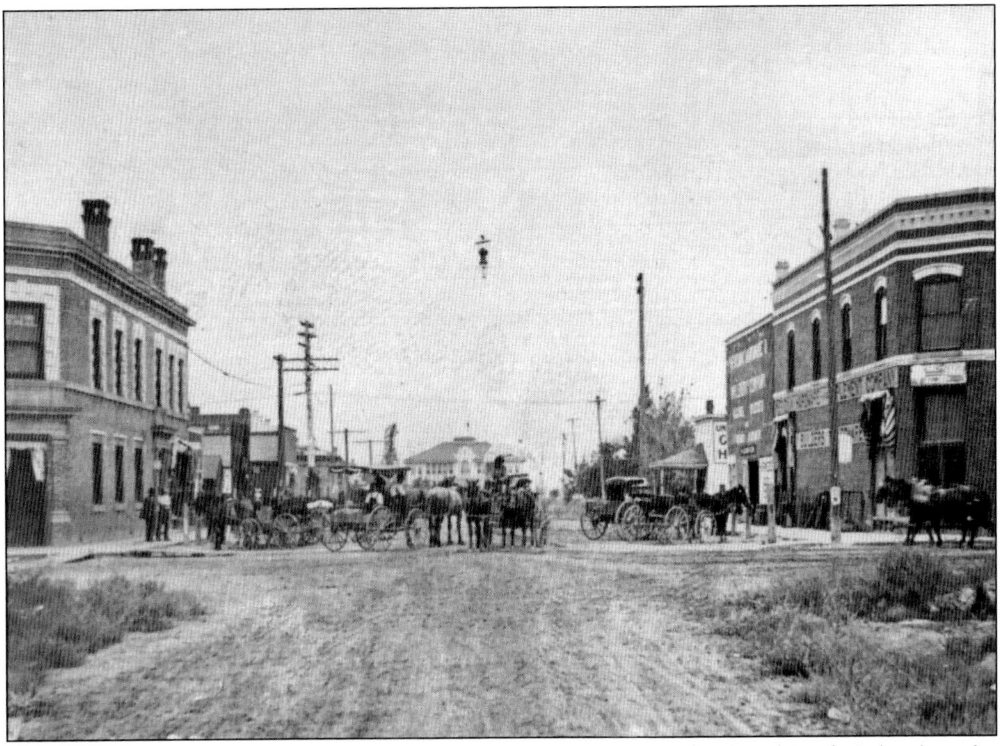

Above, horse-drawn conveyances clog the dirt street leading to the Rural High School in the distance. On the left, Dr. H. F. Neal's sign is visible in the second-floor window, while across the street, Meridian Hardware and Implement Company/Builder's Hardware occupies the ground floor of Parkin Hall. This photograph was taken before the 1920s. Below, a later photograph of the same intersection shows that the same businesses occupy the same spaces, but gas-guzzling autos have replaced the horses of yesteryear, and Boise Valley Realty Company's office is on the west side of East Second Street within the bank complex on the first floor.

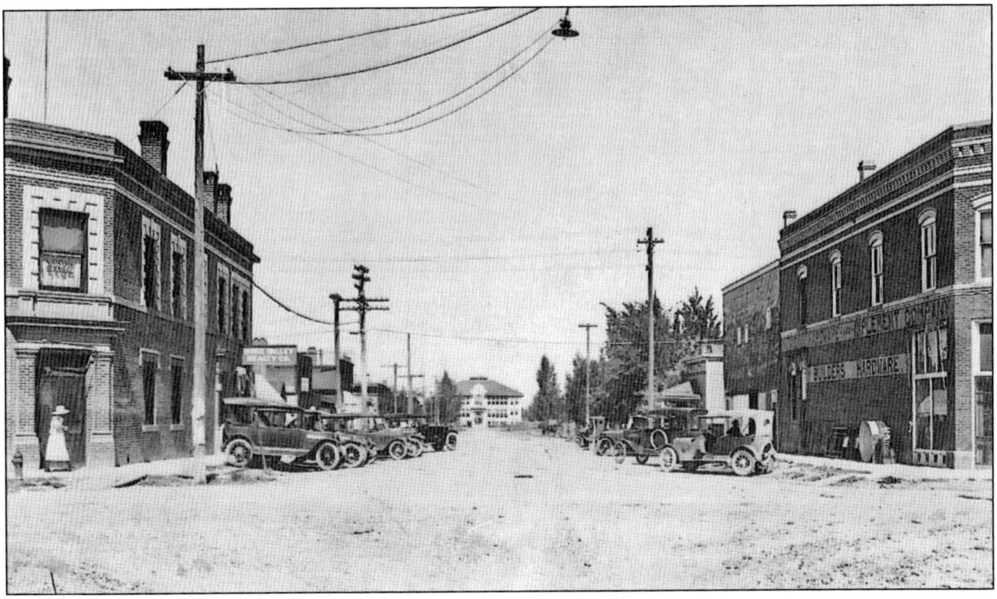

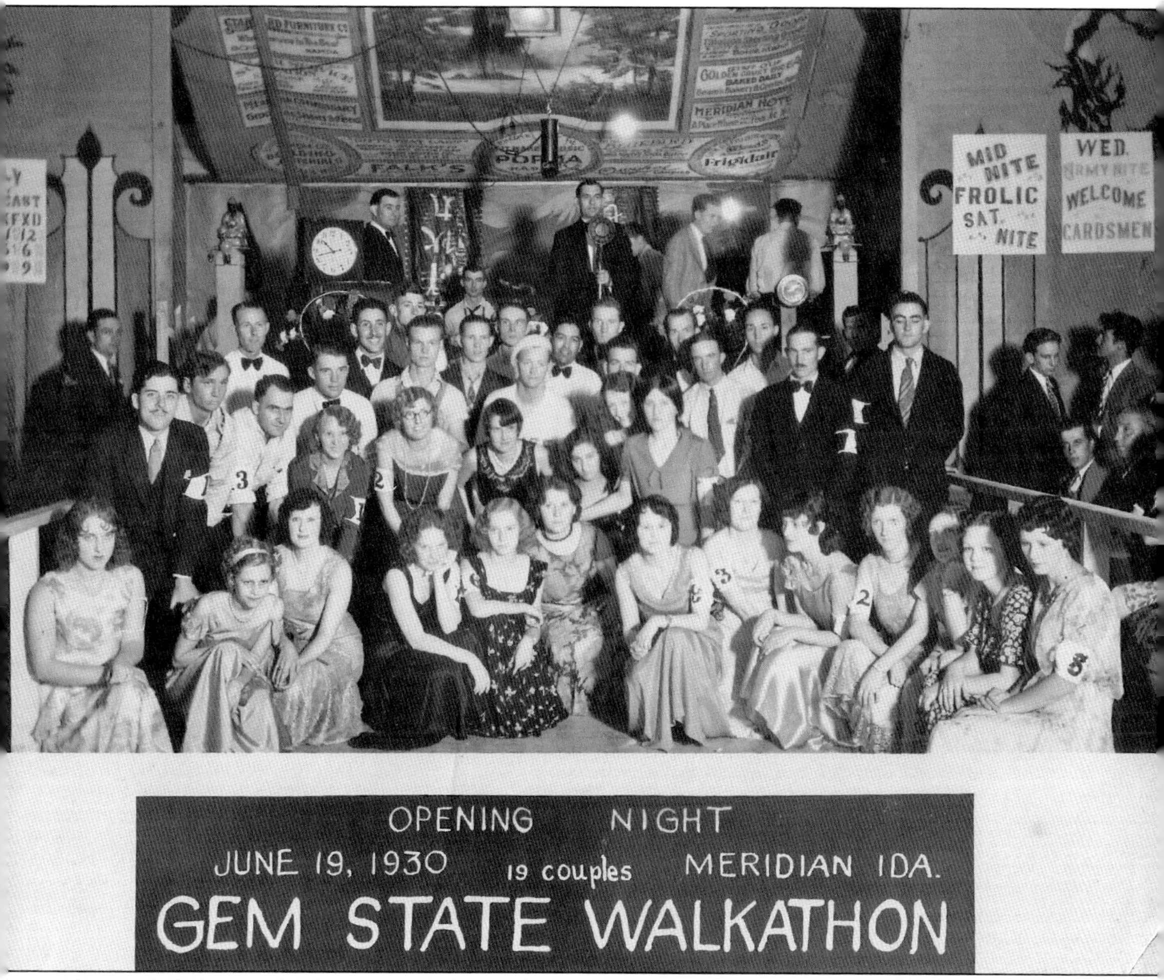

The Red, White and, Blue dance hall was built in 1927 on Main Street and was the scene of many organizational dances. When it was the scene of Walkathon dances, many parents loudly discouraged their youth from attending. A cash prize was awarded to the couple that could stay on their feet for the longest time; short resting periods were observed and a local physician, often Dr. H. F. Neal, was present. On one occasion, a local couple of note won the cash prize. After their original partners quit, they continued dancing and held each other up long enough to be the last dancers. They won the cash prize and decided to get married. They rode to Boise in the back of a truck to obtain their license and were wed at the dance hall. The building was razed in the winter of 1937–1938 and Charles Starr, who announced plans to build another dance hall 3 miles east of Caldwell, secured the lumber. (Lila Hill.)

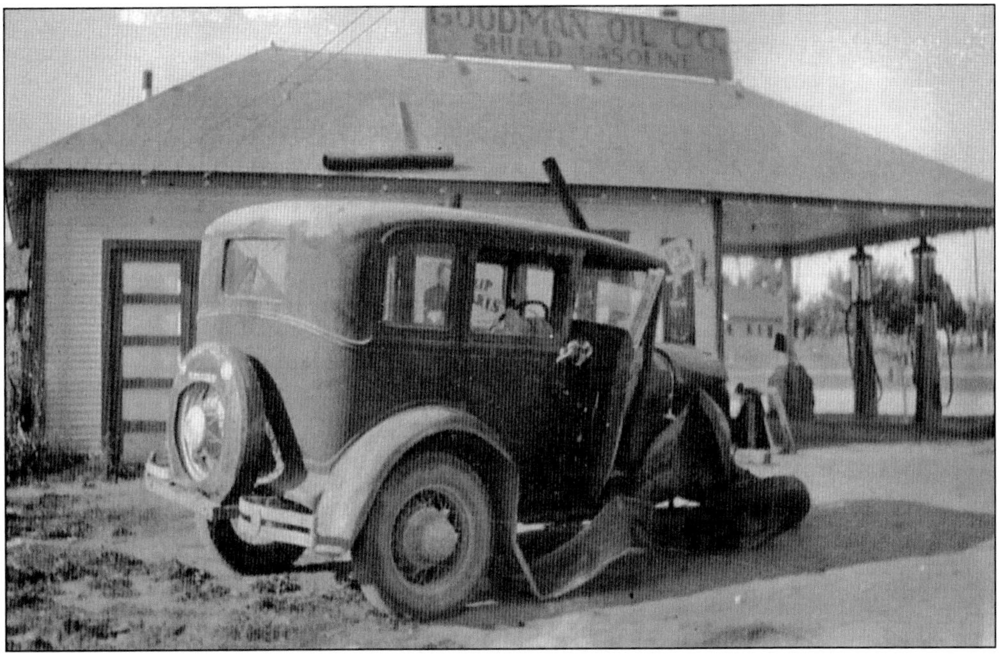

Above, Frank C. Nourse built Nourse's Curve Station in 1931, selling gasoline from Goodman Oil Company in Boise on the north end of the village along the state highway. Note the vintage vehicle with the smashed-in front end waiting its turn to be "parted out." Nourse is pictured below standing at left with his left hand on the hood of the roadster and chatting with two employees in this photograph taken in September 1936. After leasing out the service station, Nourse built a wrecking yard in 1933–1934 behind an auto parts store, on the east side of Main Street approximately 250 feet south of Fairview Avenue on the North Curve. The business offered trade-ins and advertised "garage parts for most cars." (Both RN.)

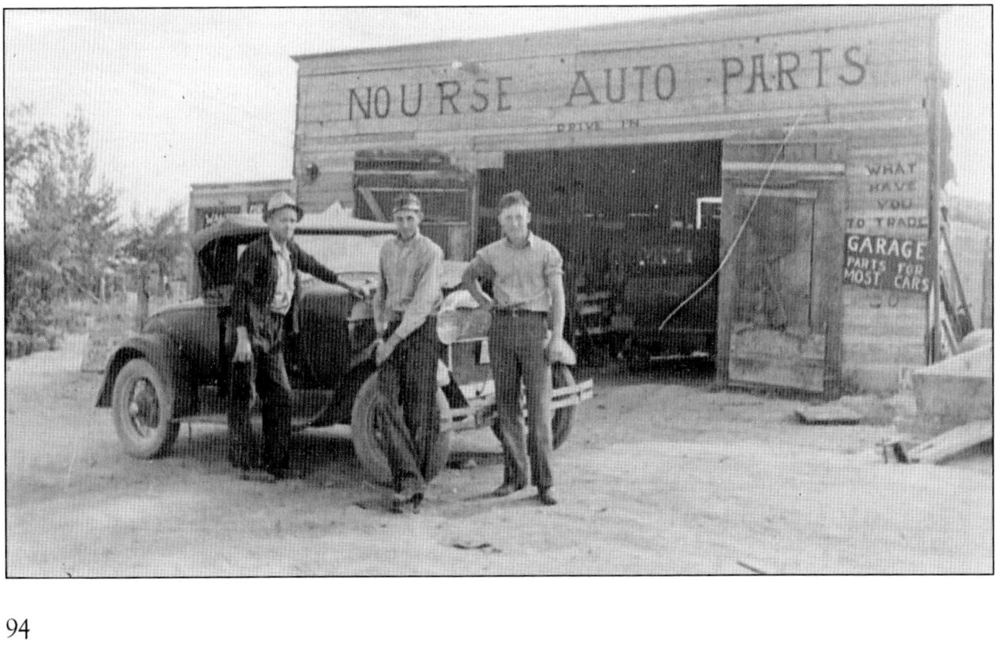

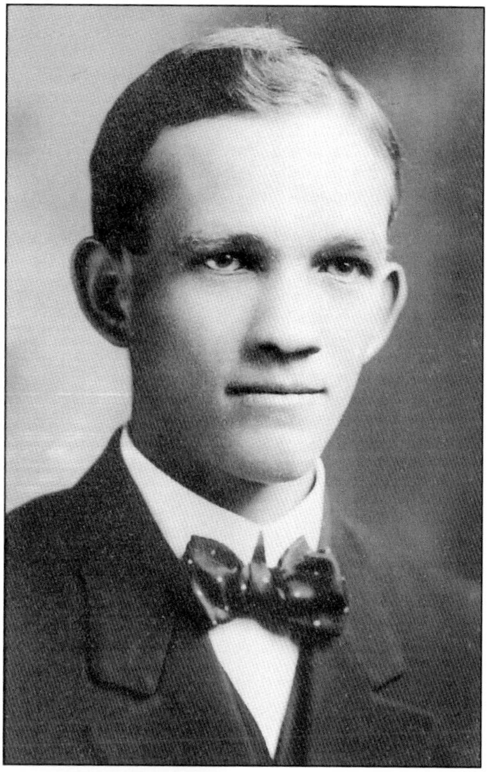

Frank C. Nourse is pictured at right as a young man. He was born in Boise in 1887 and in 1911 married Rosalie Unternahrer; they had six children. He was active in the chamber of commerce and the Elks and was a nominal Republican and Protestant. He was listed in the Who's Who for Idaho and the Western States (1950–1951). Frank C. Nourse is pictured below in front of his first real estate office, 1943–1946, with his son, Walter, who was home on furlough in 1943. Frank C.'s gimmicks included handing out personalized matchbooks and quality cigars. When he died in 1948, he left a bill for $30 for cigars and nearly 30 pairs of shoes. Since Frank C. Nourse walked with a limp from a previous auto accident, he required special built-up shoes, and his many years of walking on concrete in the auto parts garage was hard on footwear. (Both RN)

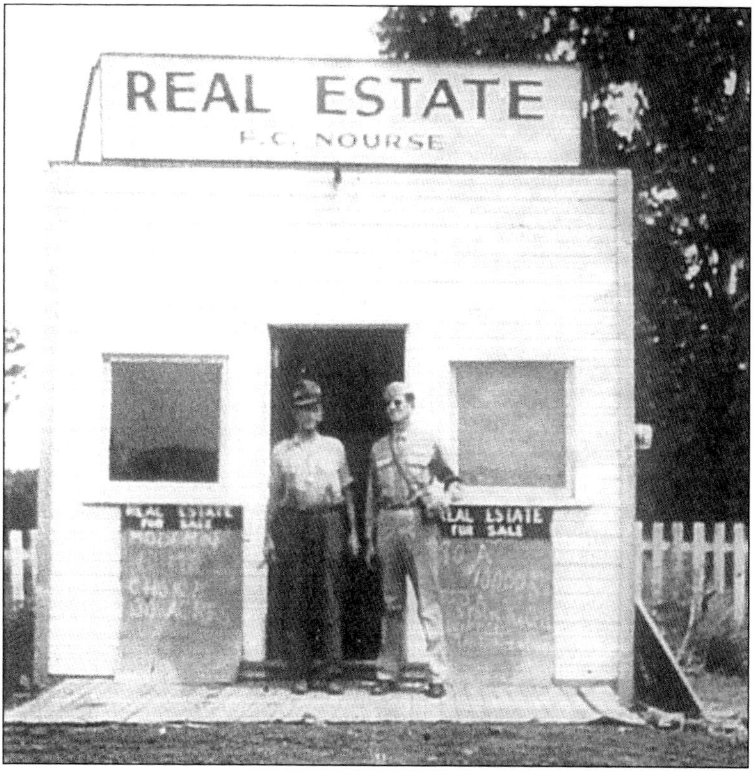

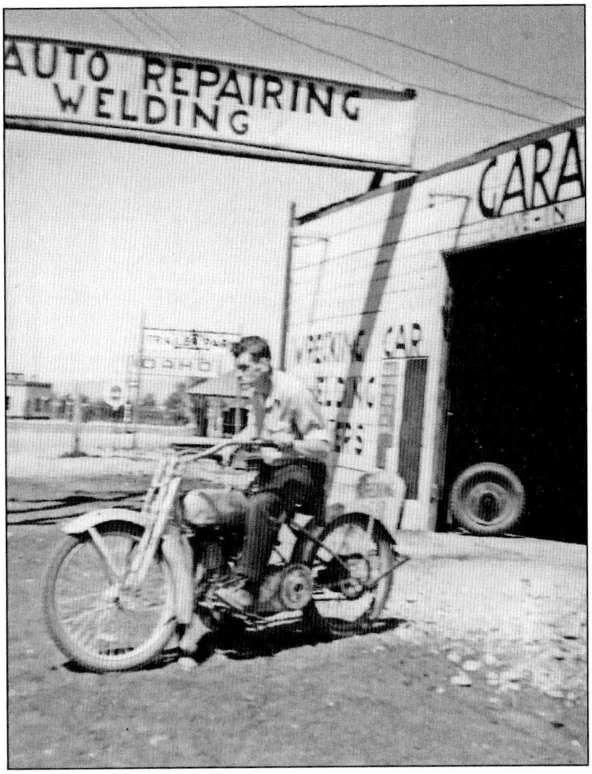

Pictured at left, Frank Alfred Nourse (1917–1996), son of Frank C. Nourse and grandson of Frank Alonzo Nourse, suffered a severe head injury in a fall from the bed of a moving truck when he was young. In 1936, he was at Pierce, a small logging town, in northern Idaho, where he helped fight blister rust while stationed at Camp No. 149 of the Civilian Conservation Corps, pictured below. His brother, Richard, still has two letters from that experience. Frank Alfred Nourse returned to Meridian, graduating from Meridian Rural High School in 1940 at age 22. After army service, he was employed for many years unloading freight in the Ketchum and Nampa yard before retiring from the Union Pacific Railroad. (Both RN.)

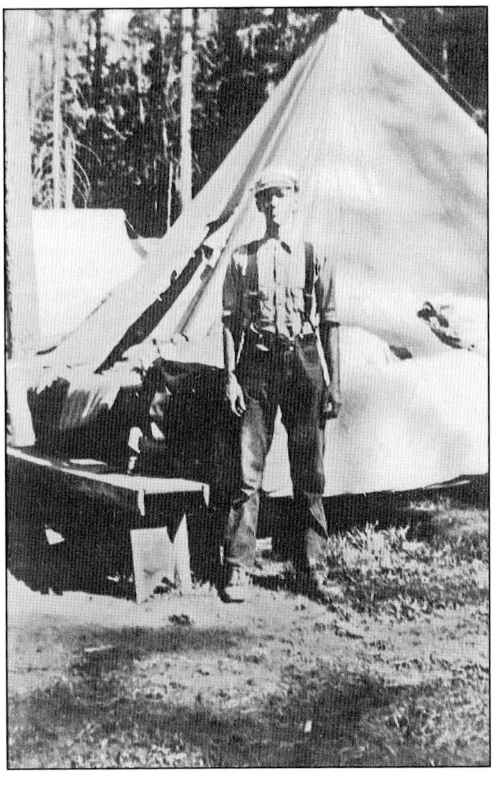

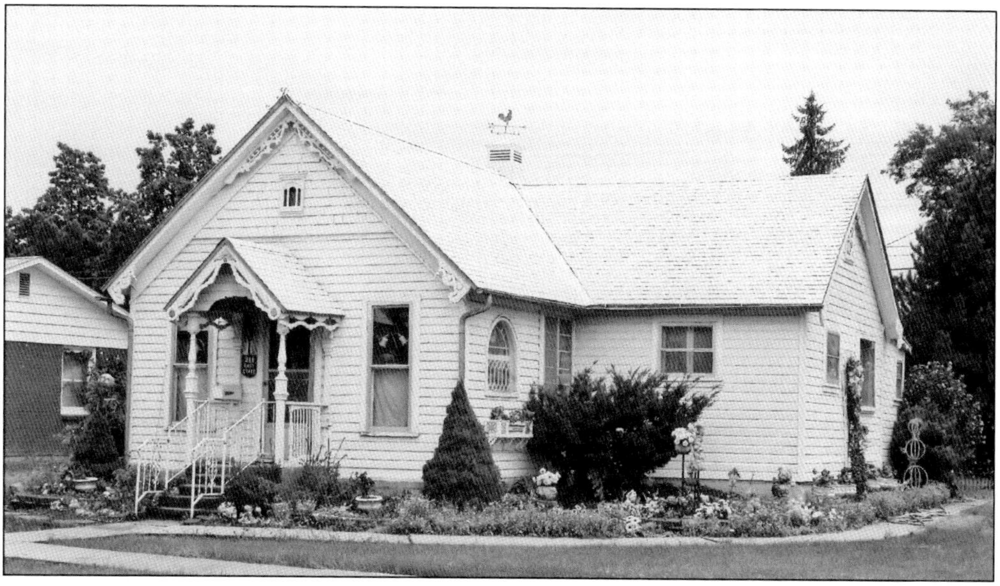

At the age of 11, Frank C. Nourse helped his father build one of the first homes in Meridian, a cottage-style house of eclectic architectural design that still stands at 211 East State Avenue (pictured above). His auto garage on "Nourse's Curve," where the state highway curved at what is now Fairview and Main, was destroyed along with the Fountain Cup drive-in in a huge fire in 1945. Frank C. Nourse died in 1948. Some Meridian elk hunters are pictured below after flying in an airplane into the wilderness on September 30, 1947, and camping at North Star Lake. Frank C. Nourse is kneeling in front, and at the far right are Jack Thorne and Earl Coleman. (Above, PAP; below, RN.)

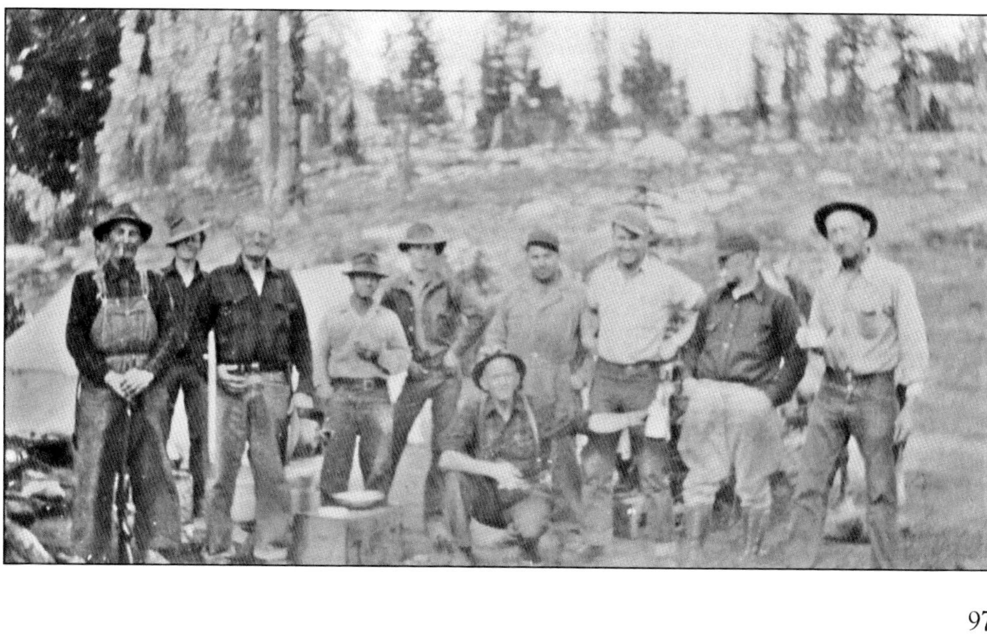

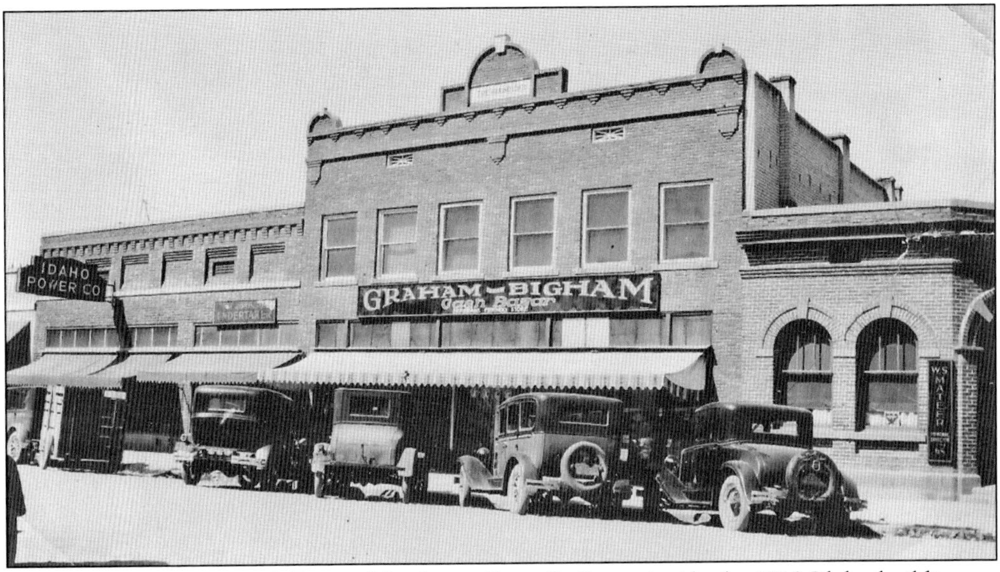

The Graham-Bigham Cash Bazaar Merchants Friendly Store, inside the 1913 Idaho building on Idaho Avenue between East First and East Second Streets, is pictured above. To the left is Robinson's undertaker shop, and to the right is the office of funeral director, W. S. Mateer. The store would later become the Cash Bazaar, a popular family clothing business, especially when the school term resumed. Below, pickups and autos are parked next to Herb's Ice Cream and Biddle's Grocery on the right. On the left are Veltex gas station, Vicker-Sim's Hardware Company, and other buildings, including the 1902 Modern Woodmen structure. In 1939, Meridian did not yet have paved streets, but the boy on his bicycle munching on an ice cream cone does not seem to mind. Since 1928, the interurban had been gone, and Meridian's population had climbed from a few hundred to over a 1,000, but there was still something idyllic in pre–World War II village life. Pastor Roberts recalled, "We went swimming in the ditches and had picnics in the summertime."

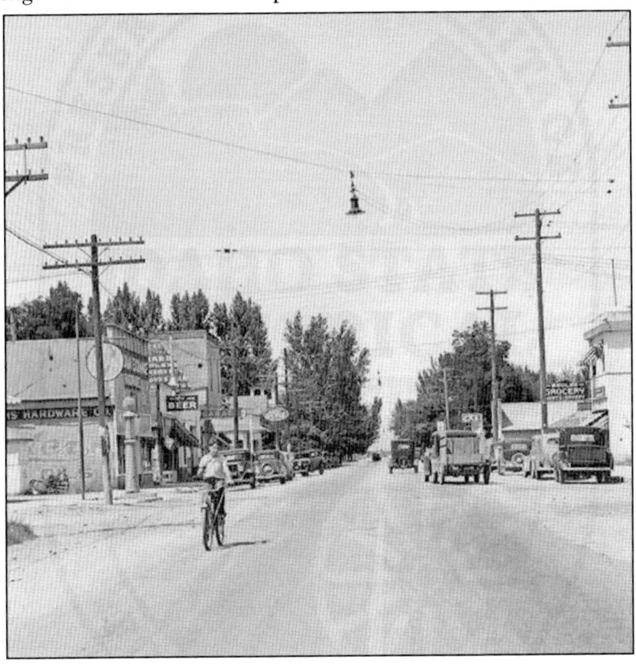

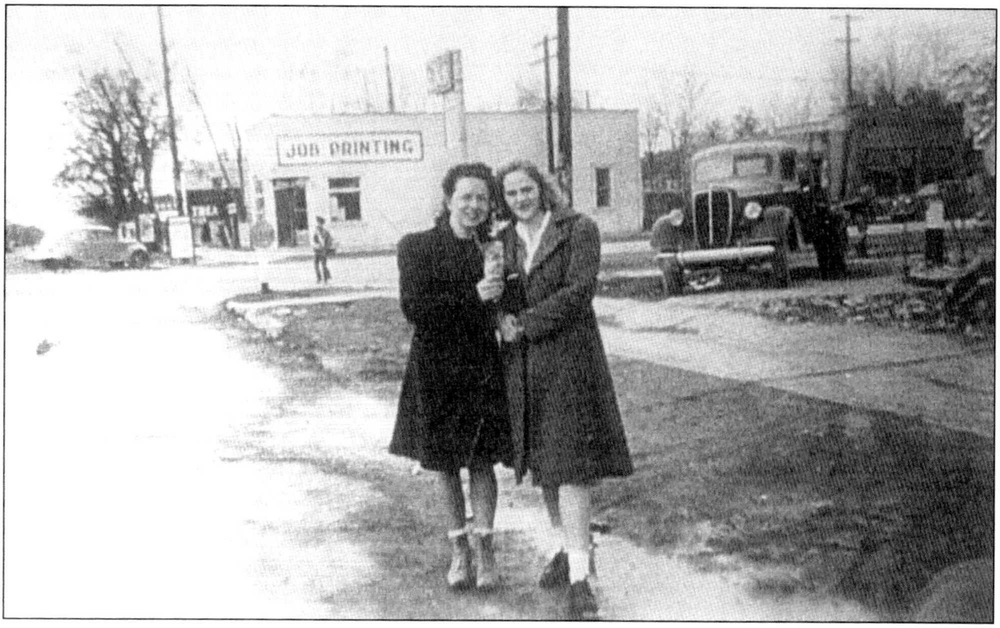

Meridian High School freshmen Naomi Fitzgerald and Ellaise Hailey are pictured above, in 1941, in front of the words "Job Printing" on the east side of the *Meridian Times* office building. The *Times* building was located on the northwest corner of Main Street and Idaho Avenue in the current site of the Sunrise Café. The bobby-soxers are standing next to what is today Generations Plaza on the northeast corner. Clysta Mayes Gray (September 24, 1911–January 12, 2000) and Loren Elden Gray (August 17, 1910 –January 2, 1991), pictured below, were married for 60 years. Clysta, the daughter of cemetery sexton Ward Mayes, grew up in Meridian during the Roaring Twenties and later was a distinguished journalist and columnist for the *Meridian Times*. Elden was a businessman who operated G and B Redi-Mix. In 1972, their son, Lawrence, became Elden's partner. Laurence, or "Larry" as he was known, died in 2009. (Above, RN; below, MHC.)

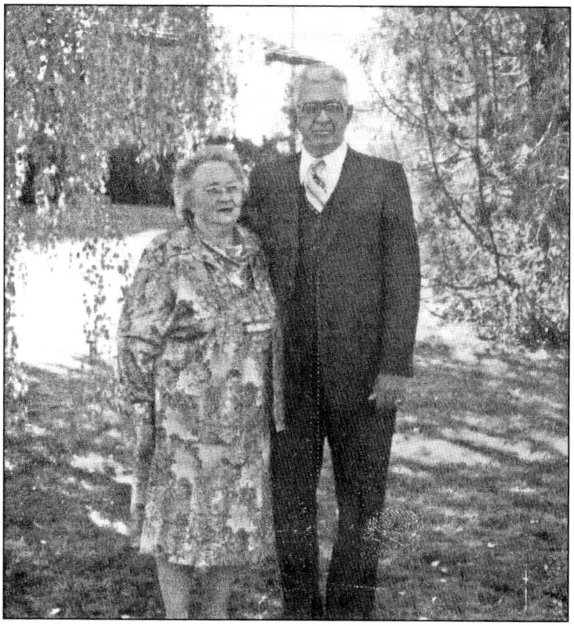

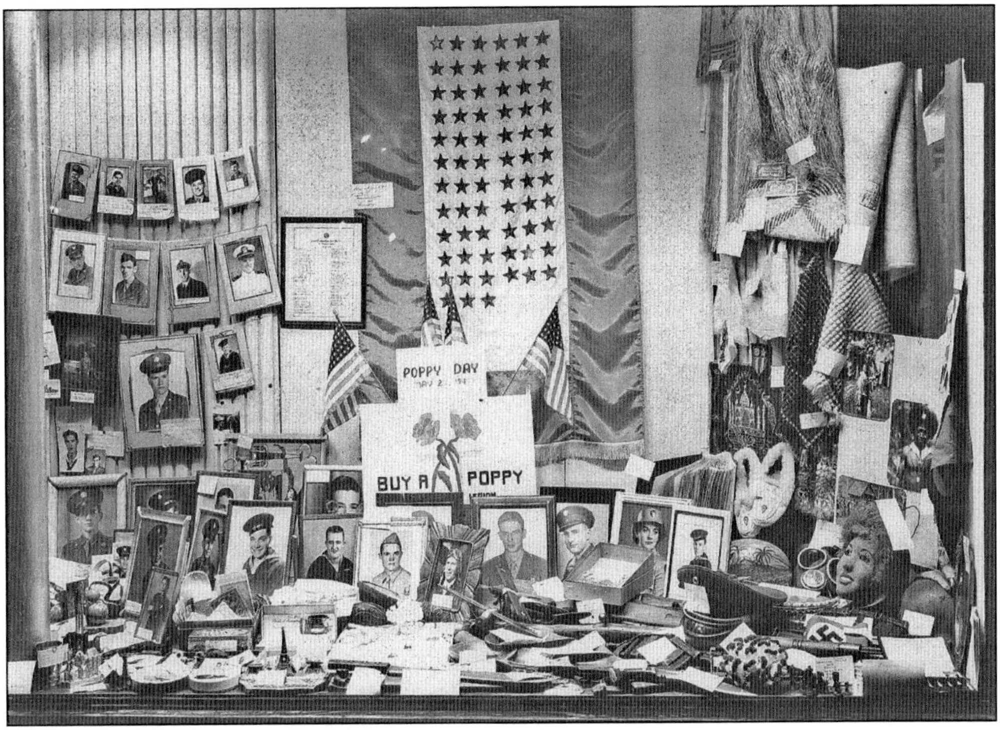

Pictured above, the Victory Window at the Idaho Power Company on Idaho Avenue during World War II displays memorabilia, including pictures of servicemen and servicewomen. Walter J. Nourse is pictured at the bottom on the far left end. Below, members of Meridian Patrol in 1941 helped enforce traffic and student safety. The students were supervised by teachers O. M. Manion (back row, far left) and Damon Flack (back row, far right) and the image shows Richard Nourse (next to Manion). Mayor W. L. Lawson and the four council members had charge of the four wards into which Meridian was divided for blackouts. The blackouts were sometimes unannounced and were held so Japanese bombers could not see their targets. The American Legion sold poppies and auxiliary ladies held card parties to buy stamps and war bonds. Rosalie Nourse was a board member and 1943 award-winning auxiliary historian who helped lead those efforts. (Both RN.)

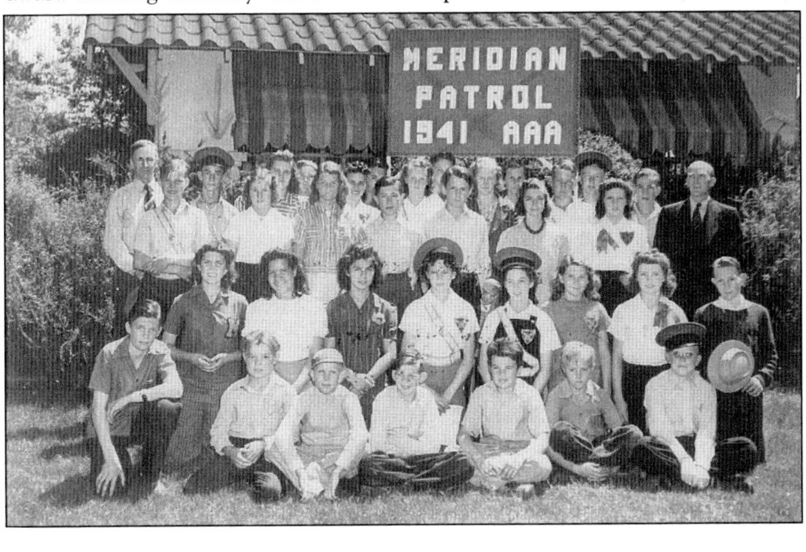

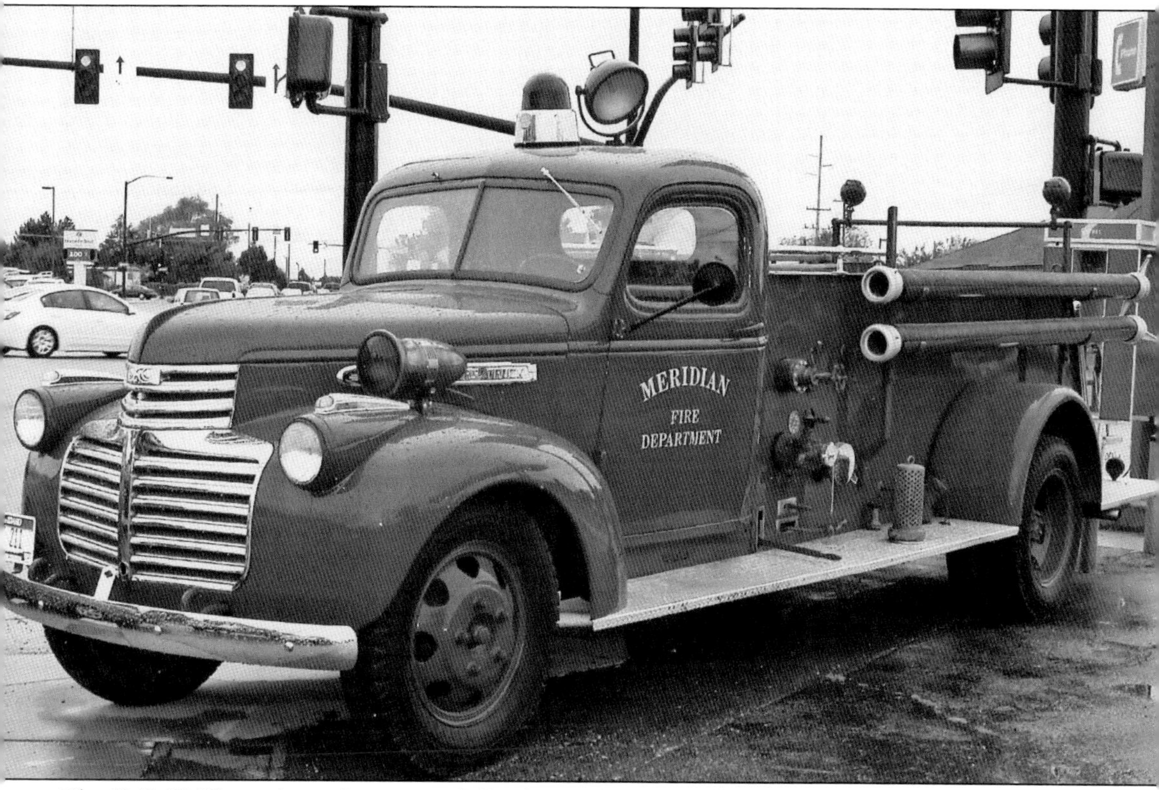

The 1943 GMC parade truck is pictured. On August 31, 1903, Village Ordinance No. 4 established fire district limits and provided fire protection. On September 22, 1904, ordinance no. 17 issued bonds to pay for required equipment and construction of a combined jail/fire engine house. In the spring of 1908, the village ordered a Champion double-cylinder chemical fire extinguisher from Portland, and its first test inspired the organization of a volunteer fire company with LeRoy Adams as chief and 20 charter members. Since 1999, when there was still only one old three-bay building, the city has built five fire stations and employs 54 full-time firefighters. In September 2007, the Meridian Fire Department completed construction of a new five-story training tower with several unique features, including a live fire prop, a live fire and sprinkler demonstration, and a ventilation prop for practice of roof ventilation on three different styles of roofs. The department also added a 2008 Pierce Arrow XT 100-foot aerial ladder truck to their line of apparatus. (PAP.)

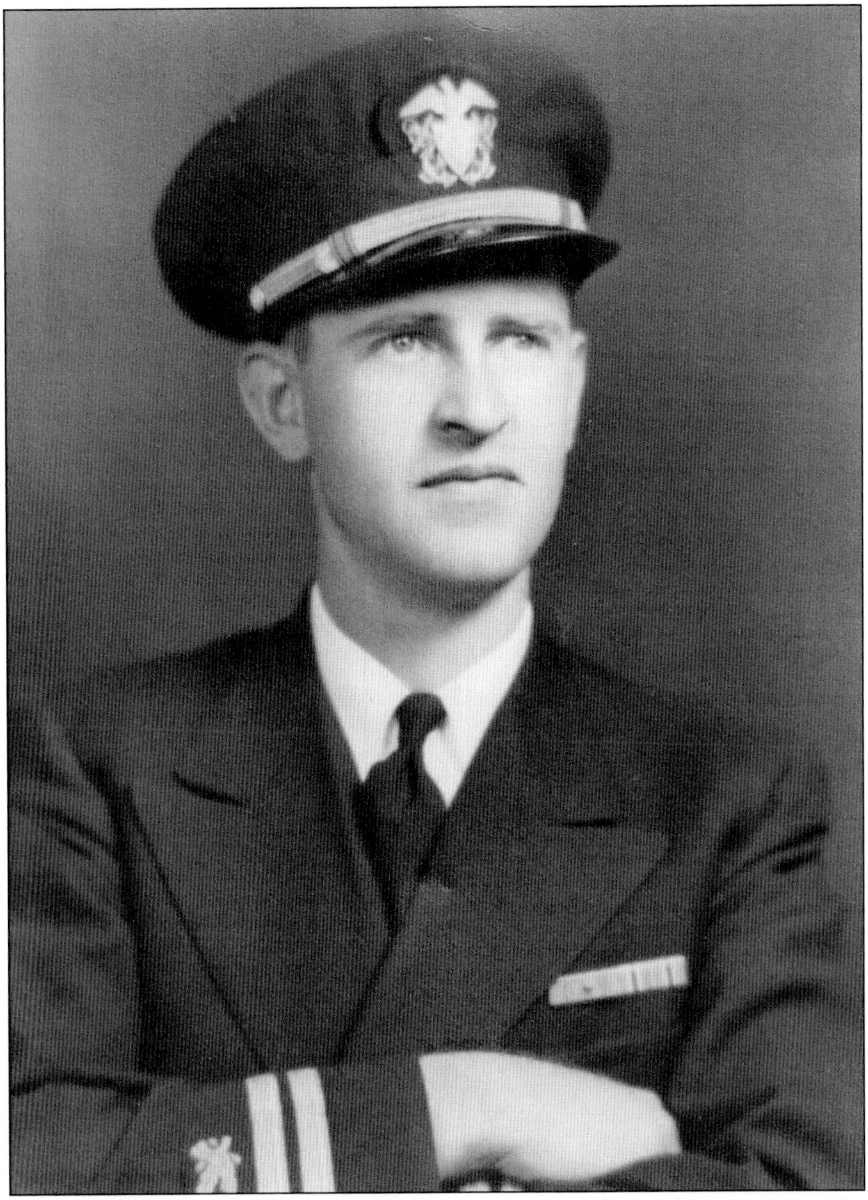

Grant Lewis Ambrose was born in Mackay, Idaho, in 1915 and died in Boise in 1969. The son of George and Amy Ambrose, he moved with the family to Bozeman, Montana, after completing the eighth grade, to help brother Denny gain appointment to the U.S. Naval Academy. The family returned to Mackay, where Grant graduated from high school. He herded sheep for $30 a month on Willow Creek Summit and saved enough to enroll in Idaho State College in Pocatello. He earned a bachelor's and law degree at the University of Idaho. He enlisted in the navy in March 1941 as an ensign and was assigned to Bermuda, Harvard University (where he instructed navy personnel), and to China. In April 1946, he left the service as a lieutenant commander and brought his family to Boise, where he was a deputy county prosecuting attorney; and then to Meridian, where he was city attorney and continued in private practice. He was the chamber of commerce president, Man of the Year, and helped spearhead a successful $805,000 school bond, all in the 1950s. (PAP.)

Six

From Creamery to City Hall

By the 1960s, the Ada County Dairymen's Association Creamery was in the last decade of its operation before moving to Caldwell in 1970. The lives of area farmers and city residents revolved around its operations. *Meridian Times* articles show there were 1,500 dairymen who were association members, and the creamery was a $7-million business that impacted everyone.

Farmers' or so-called patrons' checks were mailed twice a month, and many small farmers on 40 acres instead of the larger 80-acre dairy and row-crop farms, even where the families still consumed their own raw cow's milk and churned their own butter, depended on that income for daily staples of life purchased at George Davis's grocery (Idaho Youth Ranch today) and elsewhere in town. The association paid dividends in the form of checks each December and mailed equity checks from the revolving fund in June.

The end of the creamery's operation in Meridian also signaled a shift in social patterns in the area. For generations, "town kids" and "farm kids" were very different in their outlooks and activities. Those raised on farms, especially during the Great Depression, evinced a work ethic that did not appear to characterize later generations. Part of that process was having to rise early before school to milk the cows and perform other chores and return after school to repeat the process.

The late Elmer Potter, who taught sixth grade at Mary McPherson Elementary for many years, said those differences were fading even in the last years of the dairy association. "It's harder to tell town and farm kids apart," he said.

The process of social amalgamation that began prior to the end of the creamery's heyday in the Meridian area intensified in the years after its demise. Youngsters raised in subdivisions had much more in common with "town kids" than those who had been raised on farms surrounding the growing city.

Sociologists may see this transformation in a positive light, as diminishing or erasing the socioeconomic distinctions between classes. Those who were raised on the vanished farmsteads might see it differently, as the passing of a lifestyle on which the entire area's economy depended and which will not come again.

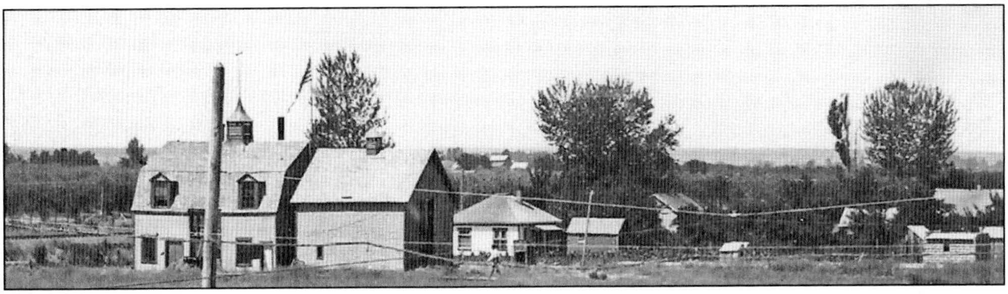

Christian Zenger, a Mormon who brought his family from Utah in 1886, built the second house in Meridian next to and south of the 1897 creamery just north of the railroad tracks on today's Main Street, pictured above. The house also served as a store and post office. The land, claimed in the name of his wife, Eliza, became the area where the business portion of the village evolved. Below is the creamery following the fire, during construction in 1929. The association paid dairy farmers 80¢ per hundredweight for their whole milk, from which they separated the cream and churned butter. On the first payday at the facility, operators paid $1,000 to local farmers for the milk. The interurban and area teams and wagons hauled milk and fruit after the former opened in Meridian in 1908. The sight of a dairy farmer hauling containers of raw milk to the local creamery presaged the later transporting process from larger farms to the new creamery beginning in 1929.

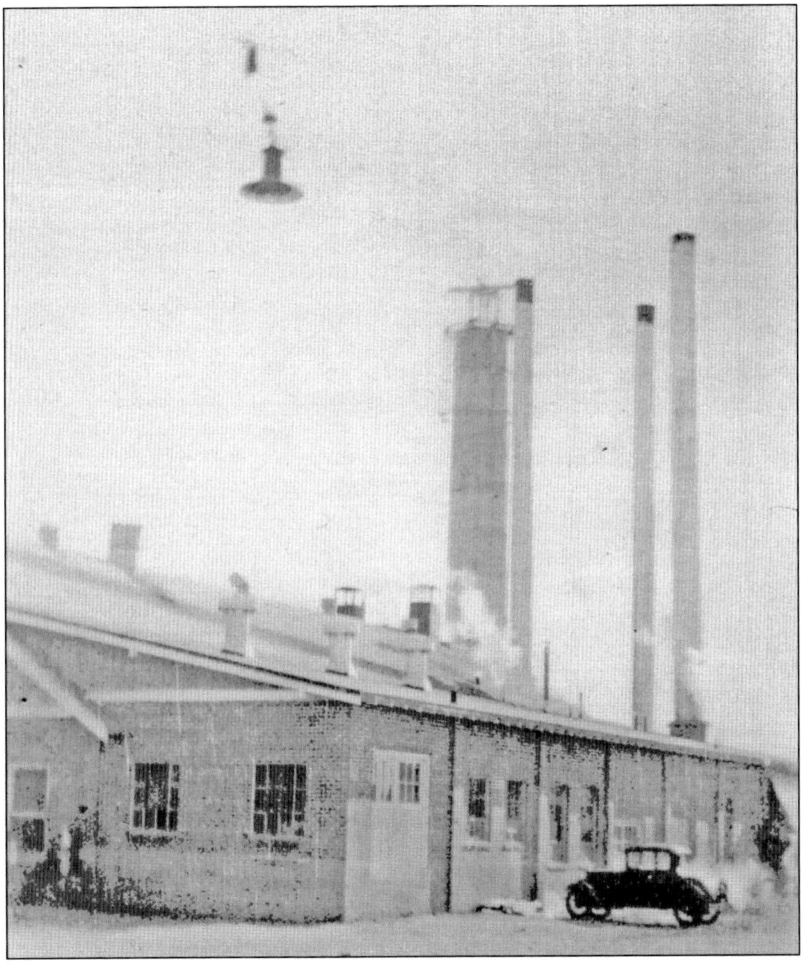

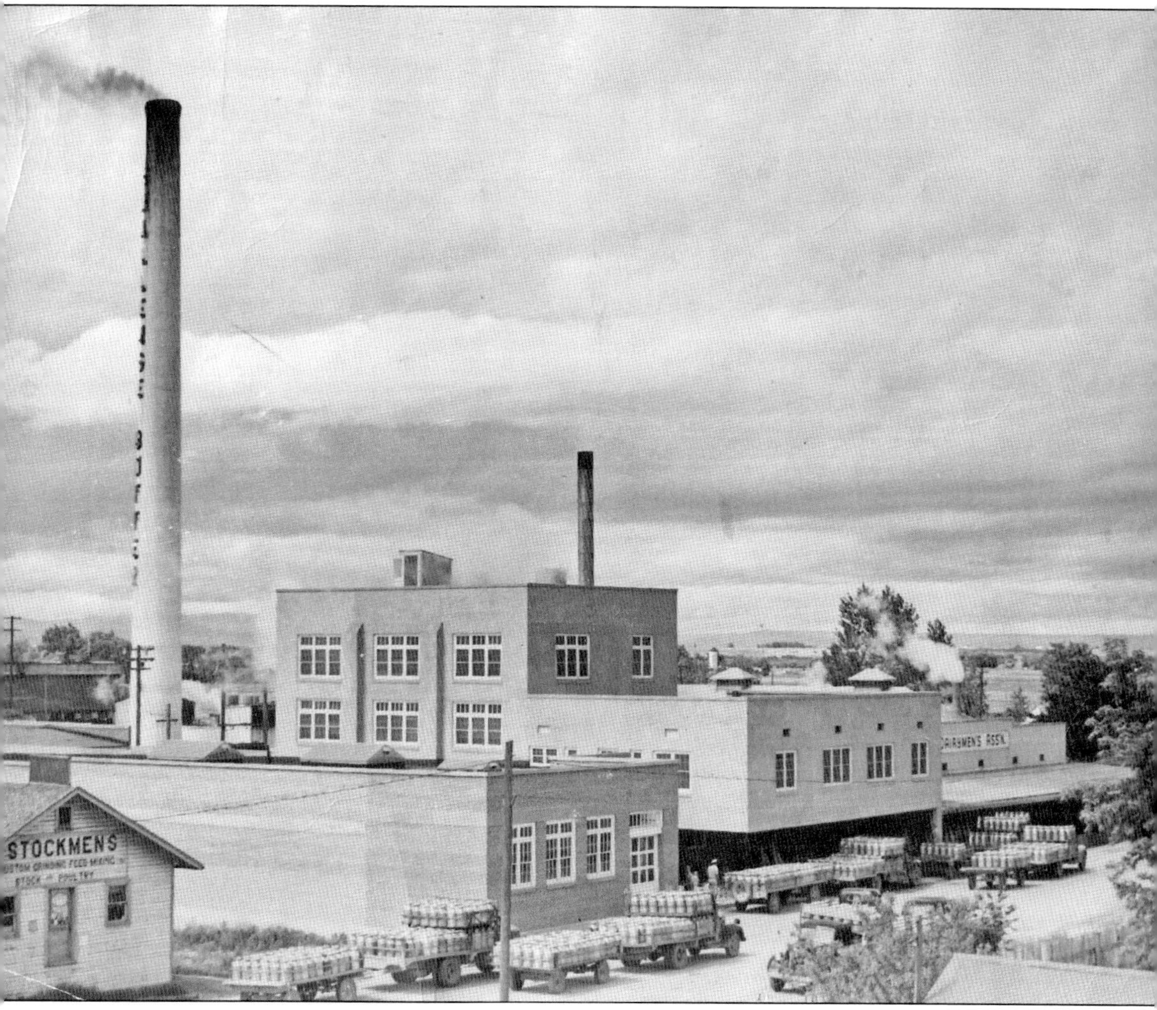

Meridian's first creamery was built in the 1890s for $7,500, but the area entered its dairy phase in earnest in 1929, when a larger facility was constructed and quickly rebuilt thanks to insurance after a fire. On opening day, June 20, haulers delivered 29,000 pounds of milk, a figure that would soon increase to a half-million pounds a day, a business level of $5 million to $6 million annually. The Ada County Dairymen's Association, known locally as the creamery, ushered in the first local wave of prosperity since the plummeting of farm prices after World War I. It employed many local workers and was a reliable revenue source for farmers on the many acreages around Meridian where cows were milked and crops were grown. The creamery whistle blasted at 7:00 a.m., at noon, and again at 5:00 p.m., signaling the start, midday break, and end of each workday.

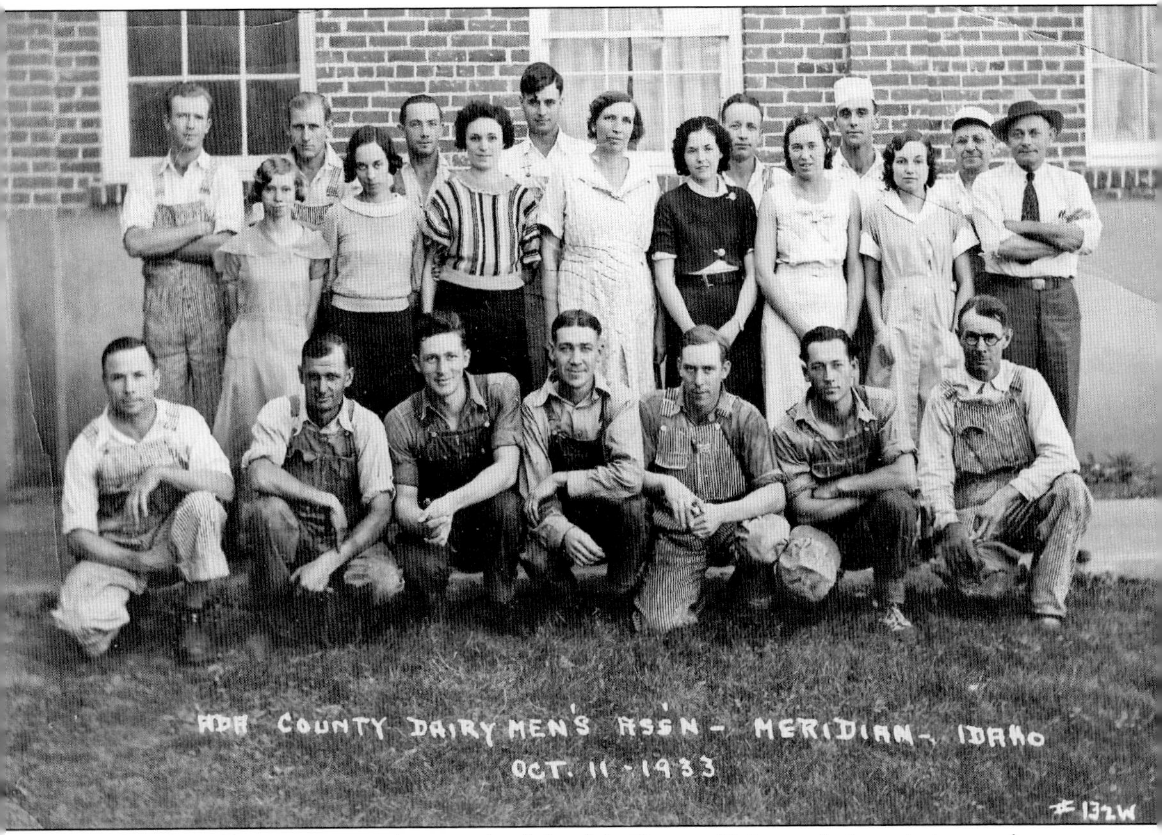

The above Depression-era photograph of the Ada County Dairymen's Association workers was taken on October 11, 1933. In a real economic sense, the creamery was a local counterbalance to the Great Depression, whose advent and course coincided with the emergence of the dairymen's association. Its life-giving tentacles reached from the core of the downtown area to hundreds of area farms of varying sizes and types, all of which had a few milk cows. From left to right are (first row) Frank Matcham, Row Wisner, Whipol Law, Ralph Ausman, Bill Hansen, Ernest Lembke, and Alfred Matcham; (second row) Irene Bowers Sykora, Thelma Bushby, Helen Cairns Bryce, Mabel Gregory Davidson, Hazel McClure Taylor, Ethel Langley, Madeline Wallace-Pape, and H. P. Hansen; (third row) Fay White, Ed Frymyer, Warren "Bud" McGill, Henry McFaddan, Ray Matcham, Gerald Records, and Tom Hall.

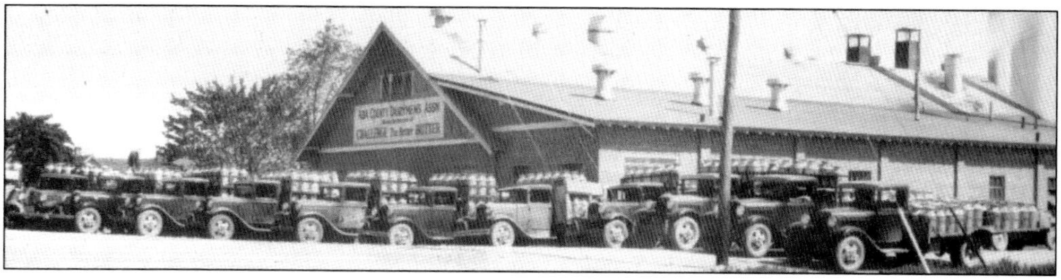

Trucks laden with milk cans, pictured above, line up in front of the creamery. The Ada County Dairymen's Association also maintained its own vehicles. The *Meridian Times* reported on June 29, 1934, "Dearduff and Hoseley are building the body for another big Ada County cream truck this week, and it will hold many cans. The plan is for a capacity of 84 and 28, which means that 112 cans of milk will be hauled if it is loaded to capacity. The way that whole milk is coming into the creamery now, it will be needed in the service immediately." Milk hauler Fidel Lopez is pictured below in a truck pulling a wagon, both loaded with milk cans; his dog sits to the right.

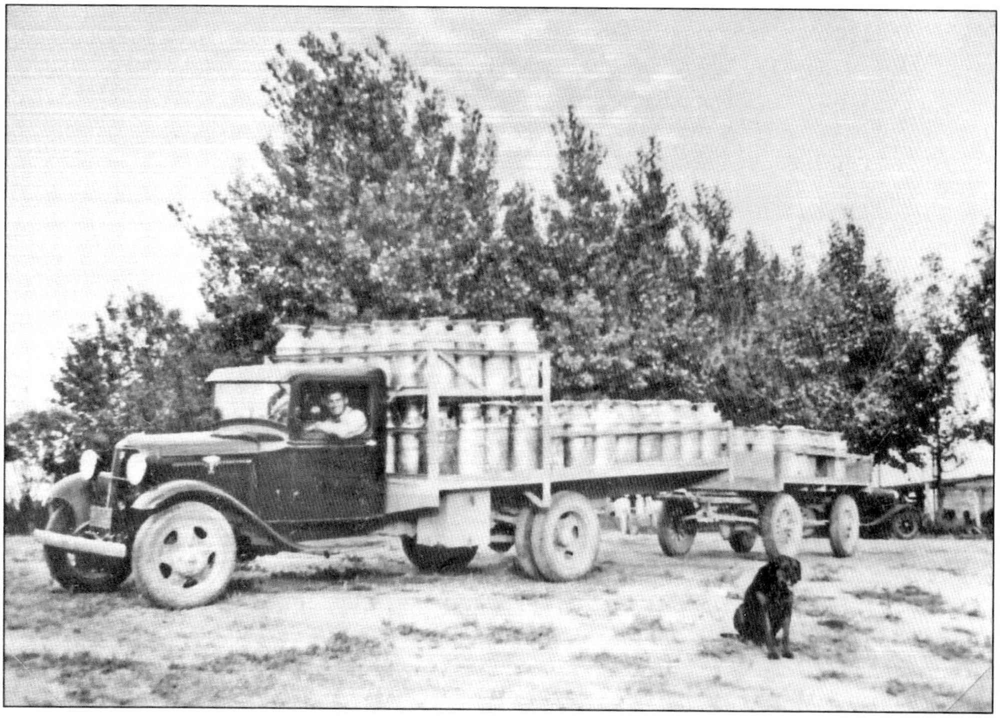

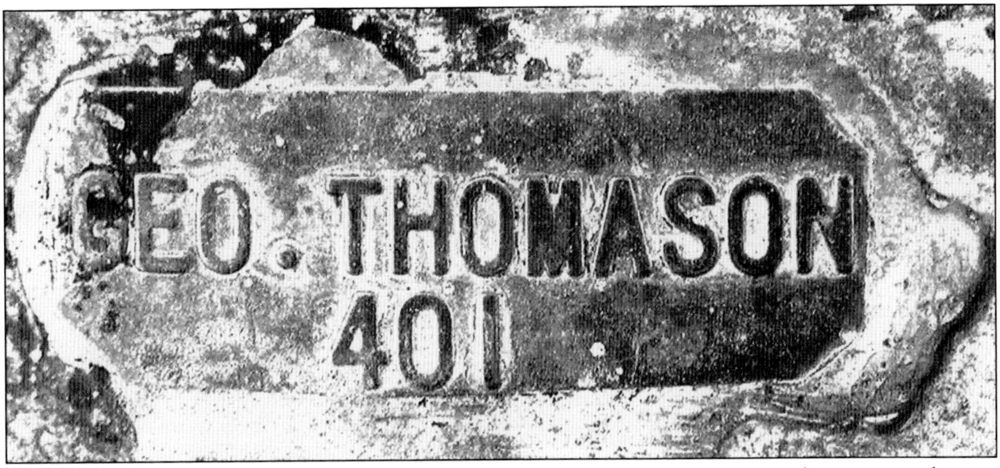

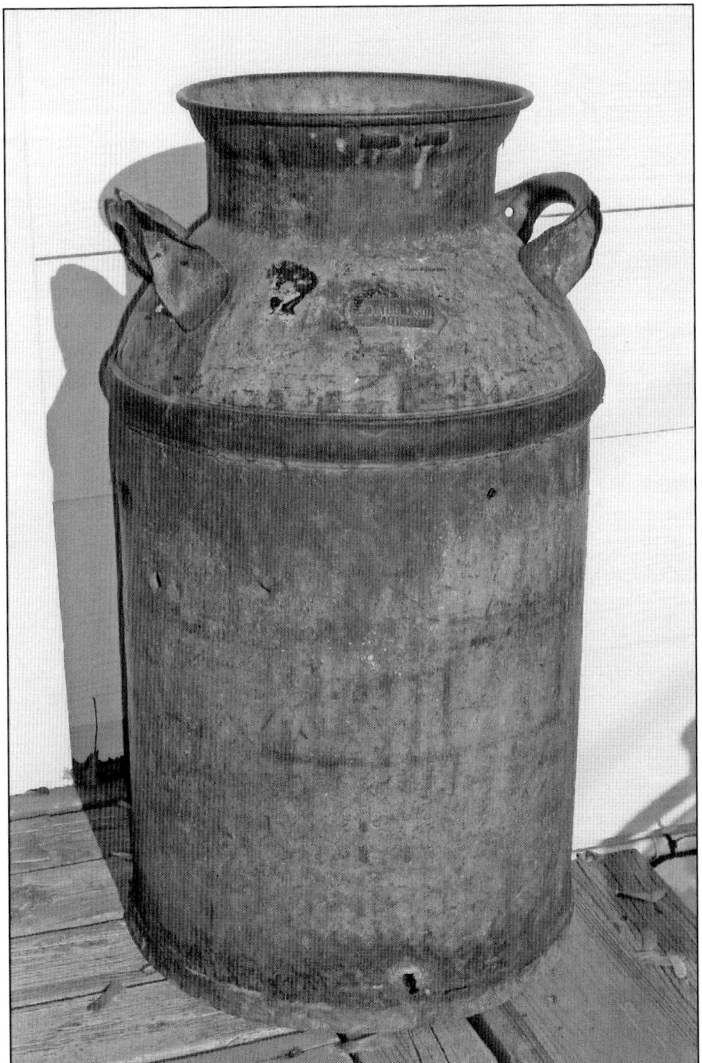

A rare brass nameplate, pictured above, reads "Geo. Thomason 401," a reference to George L. Thomason, creamery account number 401. He relocated from Oklahoma to Meridian in the 1940s and helped operate a small family herd of dairy cows within the village limits until his death in January 1947 at the age of 62. Later milk cans feature only a three-digit number applied in black paint to the upper part of the can for identification. Thomason's surviving family members, including grandson Frank Thomason, relocated in November 1948 to a 40-acre homestead south of town, where they continued milking cows and expanded their row-cropping activities. (Both PAP.)

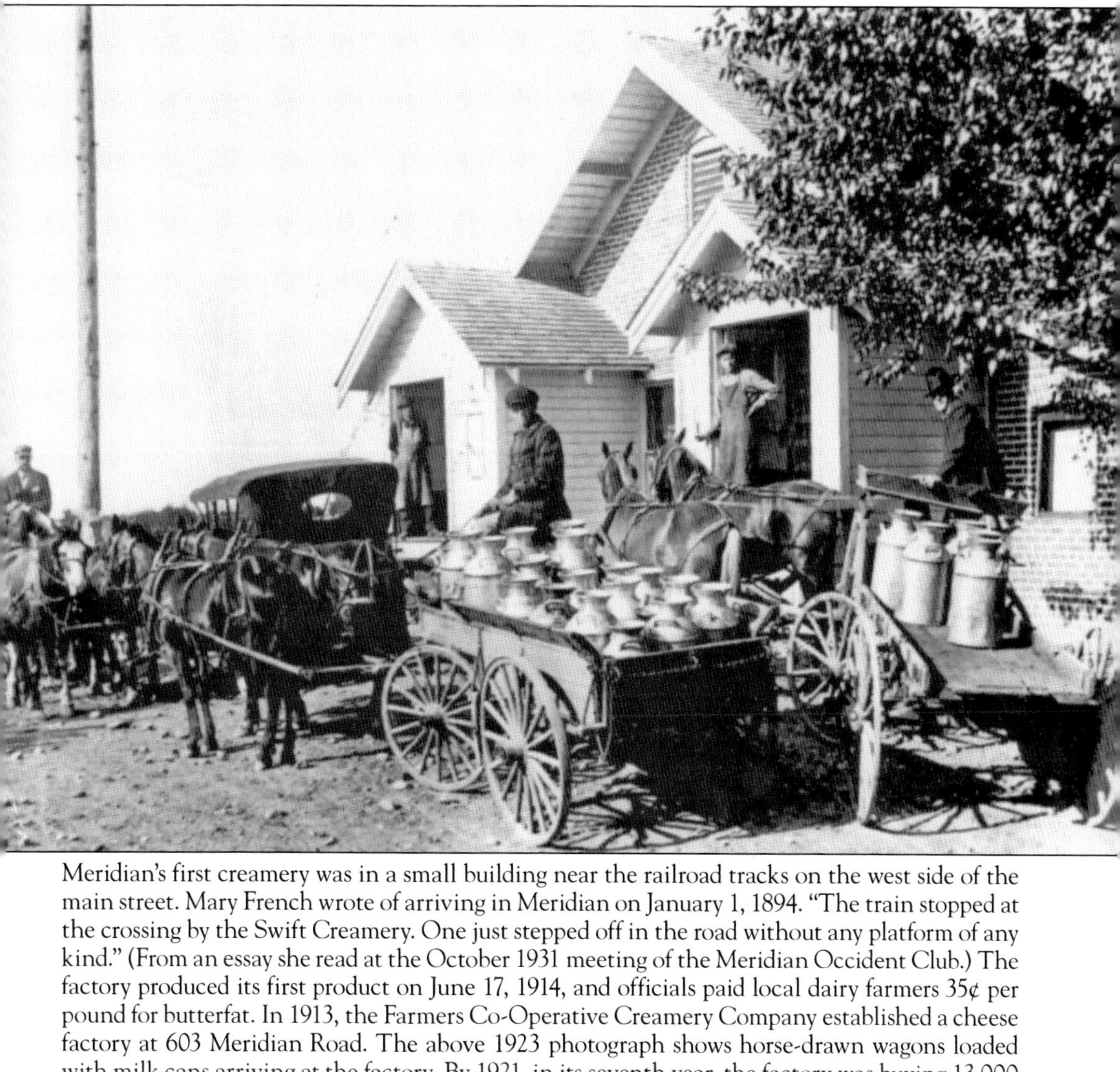

Meridian's first creamery was in a small building near the railroad tracks on the west side of the main street. Mary French wrote of arriving in Meridian on January 1, 1894. "The train stopped at the crossing by the Swift Creamery. One just stepped off in the road without any platform of any kind." (From an essay she read at the October 1931 meeting of the Meridian Occident Club.) The factory produced its first product on June 17, 1914, and officials paid local dairy farmers 35¢ per pound for butterfat. In 1913, the Farmers Co-Operative Creamery Company established a cheese factory at 603 Meridian Road. The above 1923 photograph shows horse-drawn wagons loaded with milk cans arriving at the factory. By 1921, in its seventh year, the factory was buying 13,000 pounds of milk every day. Although the cheese factory went out of business the year before the new creamery was built, it bridged the gap between the first small creamery and its later larger counterpart by providing a local market for milk brought in by dairy farmers.

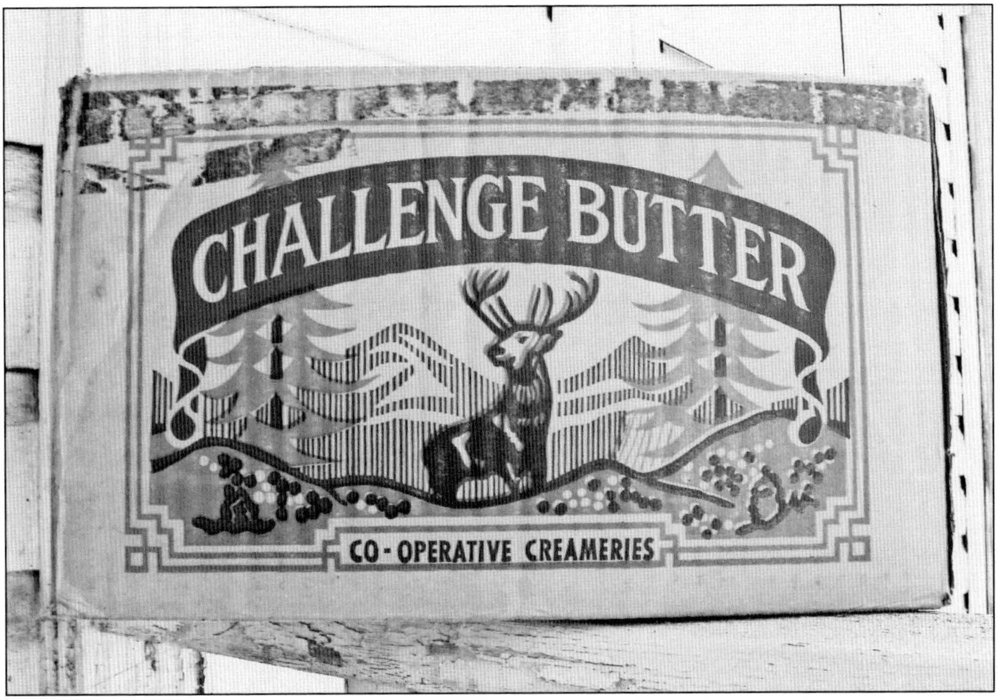

Above, following the construction of the new creamery in 1929, the Ada County Dairymen's Cooperative bought extensive amounts of whole milk from local dairy farmers. It processed and produced dried milk in powder form and also sold its butter to Challenge Food Company. Established in 1925, Challenge marketed butter regionally in Idaho, Colorado, and other states. Below, this photograph of an early dairyman's Ford pickup shows the close connection between the Meridian-based Ada County Dairymen's Association and Challenge Butter. The photograph was probably taken during an early Dairy Days parade. (Above, RN; below, MHC.)

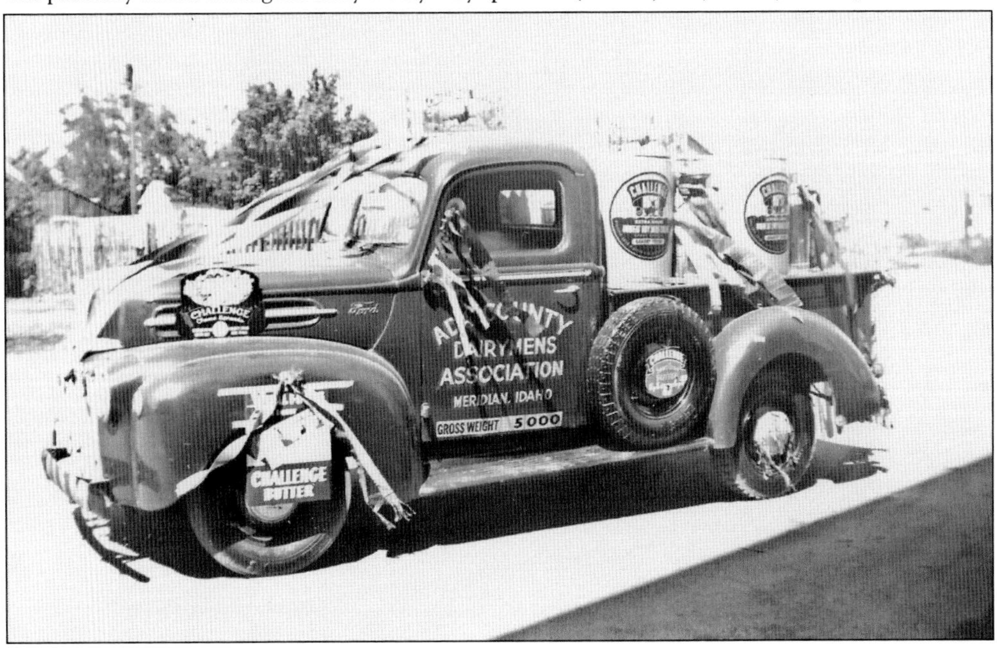

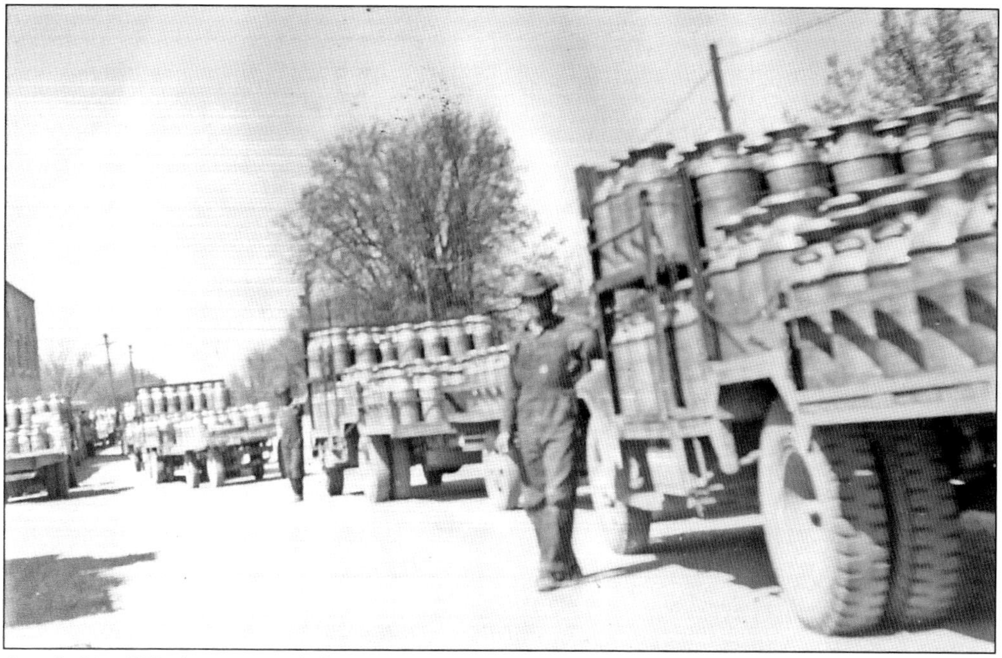

Asoph "Ace" Kusler, pictured above, poses during milk route 13, which he operated from 1945 to 1946. Milk haulers enjoyed camaraderie, staying until the last hauler finished and helping during breakdowns. Ace relocated to Meridian in September 1945 from North Dakota, where he worked in a power plant. He bought a milk route in Meridian and his wife, Betty, drove herself here in October. She taught for seven years in North Dakota and resumed her career in Idaho in 1946 after obtaining a state teaching certificate. Ace died on January 22, 1982. A classic barn that sat near the southeast corner of Ten Mile and Franklin Roads is pictured below. (Above, MHC; below, Ada County Historic Sites Inventory.)

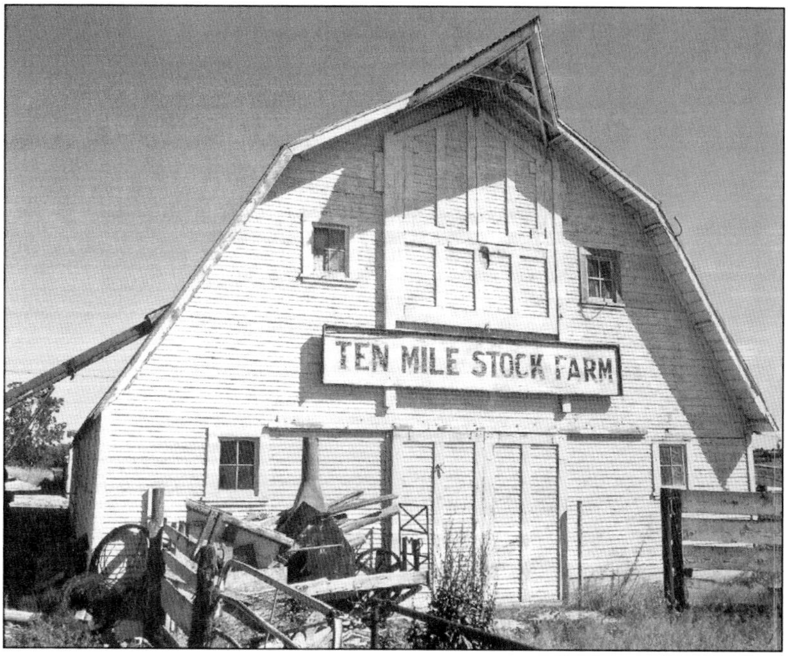

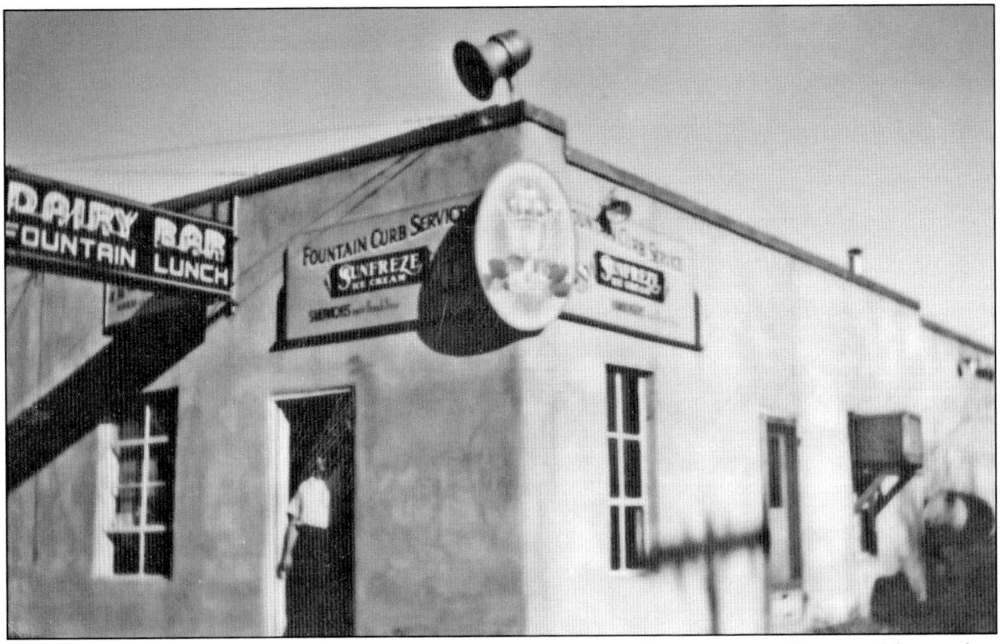

The Dairy Bar, pictured above, was a popular local hangout for young residents and located at the corner of East First (Main) Street and Fairview Avenue, the so-called North Curve. Before the freeway, the state highway snaked down Franklin Road, turned left onto the main drag and then right along the North Curve toward Boise. A new A and W Drive-in opened on this site in the summer of 1959. Below, this 1947 street scene depicts a large banner across East First Street promoting the "Community Dairy Show" and advertising Meridian as a dairyland and America's dairy center. Taken in the middle of the dairy era, the photograph shows hardware stores on both sides of the street as well as many automobiles and several pedestrians.

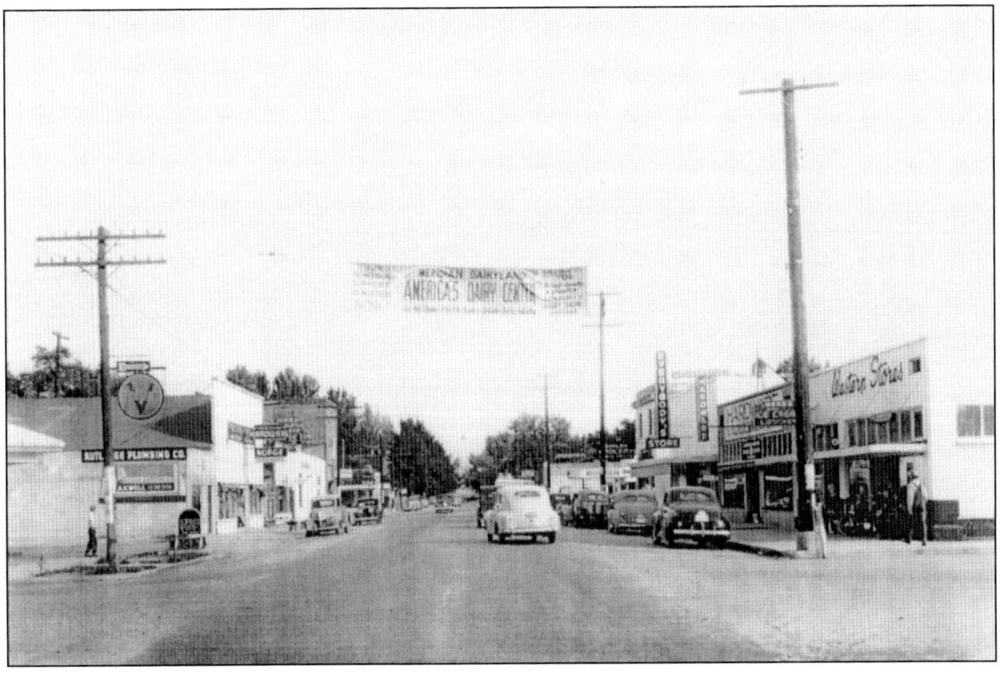

This photograph shows an unidentified girl with a cow at the dairy picnic in 1938. The first Meridian Dairy Show was held on June 18, 1929, two days before the opening of the creamery. The second dairy show was held on August 7, 1930, and the third on October 3, 1931. Below, Julius M. Kleiner, who emigrated from Russia in 1916, purchased 260 acres from the Morrison-Knudsen Company in 1944 at Eagle Road and Fairview Avenue. He turned the land into a dairy and crop farm and oversaw operations until his death in 1972. He earlier owned creameries in Caldwell and Nampa, raised turkeys, and formed a cooperative to address milk prices. Through his son Eugene, the Julius M. Kleiner Memorial Park Trust donated $25 million to construct a 60-acre park by spring of 2011. (Right, ISHS; below, Julius M. Kleiner Memorial Park Trust.)

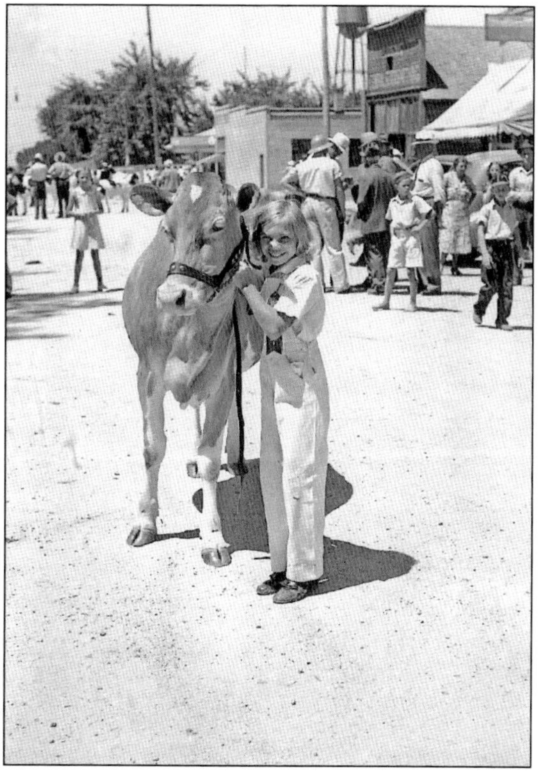

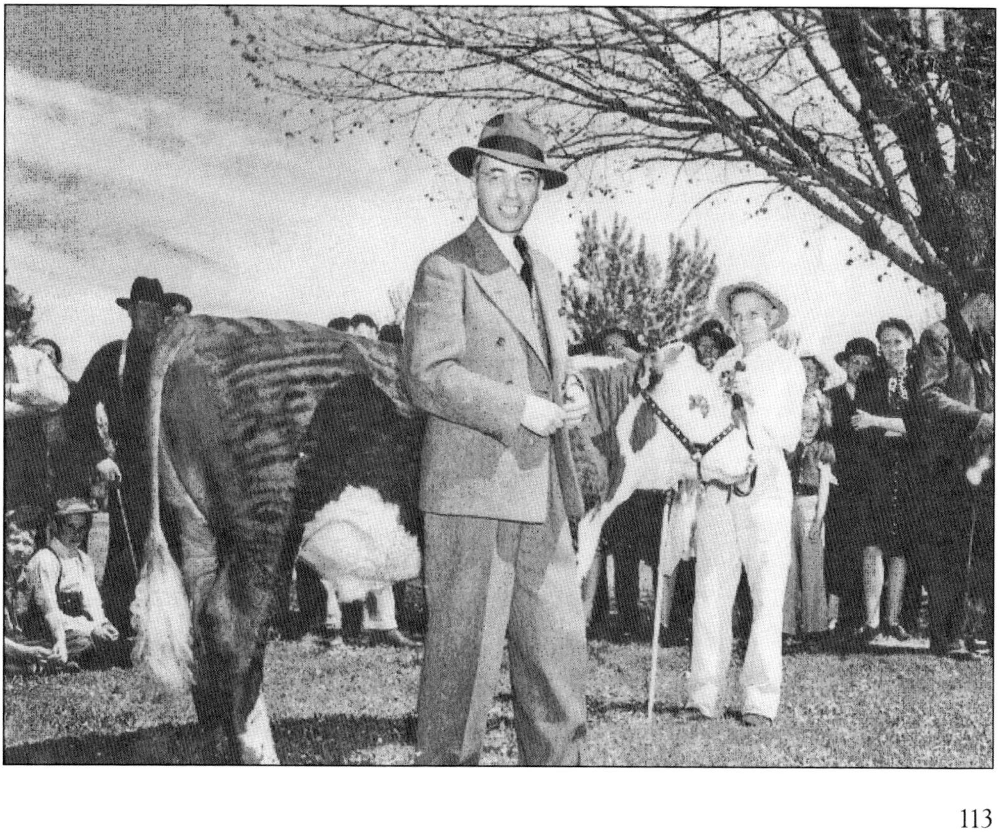

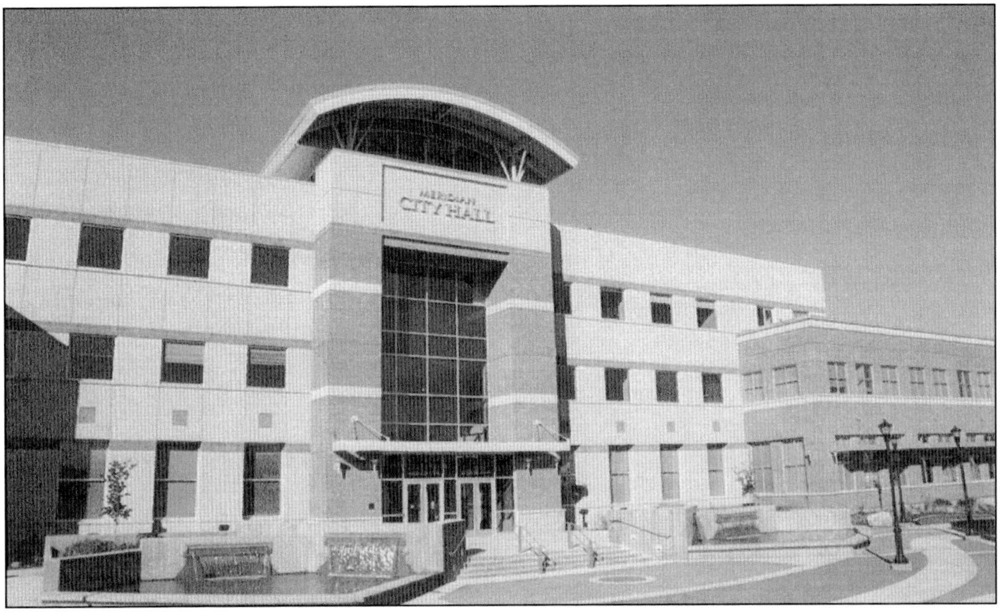

The photograph above by Shelly Houston is of the $22 million city hall building. The building was paid for by savings instead of a bond and erected in 2008 on the site of the old 1929 creamery. Its design and landscape elements capture and symbolize the irrigation, farming, orchard, and dairy eras of the village's past as well as the high-tech, medical/health sciences, and mixed-use features of the city's future. Below is the view looking east along Broadway Avenue from the third floor of city hall. The Odd Fellows building and other structures have been replaced and Parkin Hall has vanished from the northeast corner of Broadway Avenue and East Second Street, but the remnant of the old Hayden Pharmacy/McFadden Market and the old bank building still occupy the northwest corner. (Below, FT.)

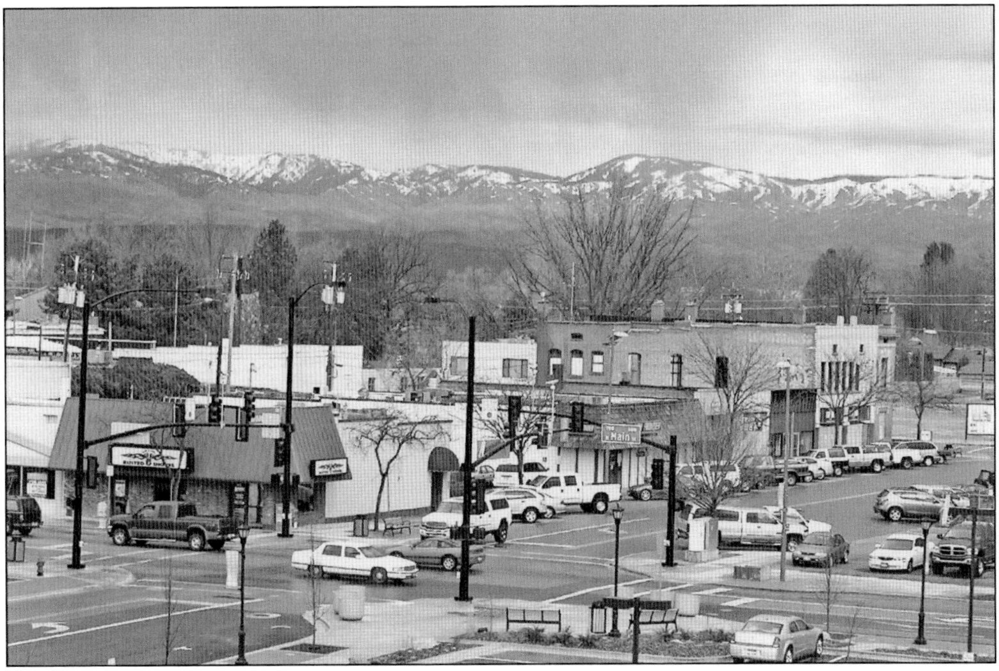

Seven

Church and Community

Rugged individualism had its place in the first years of Meridian's settlement. Isolated settlers built primitive dwellings, waged war on jackrabbits, and hauled water to eke out a bare existence in harsh conditions. Later the power of institutions, including churches, led to a village and then a city. Lila Hill and Glen Davidson have chronicled the influence of Methodists.

The first family to file land claims in the area were Roman Catholics whose daughters intermarried with Methodists. By the early 1880s, Methodists, Baptists, and other denominations were holding services in churches and schools along the Boise River. The Methodists helped other congregations to organize, including the Christian church in 1904 and later the Nazarenes, who in 1916 purchased the building from the Methodist Episcopal Church, South, as distinct from the Methodist Episcopal Church.

The first family to file ownership documents on land that became the village were Utah Mormons. While white families and groups settled and developed Meridian, they were not homogenous in social or political views.

The issue of alcohol and its consumption were central in Meridian's religious history. The village voted to "go dry" by a 3-1 margin as early as 1907 and was the first municipality in Idaho to ratify Prohibition, and ordinances enforcing the legal parameters of consumption and sales were strictly enforced. At least one early establishment was shut down for selling alcohol to minors.

Area churches have combined resources and community outreach through the Meridian Ministerial Association, which sponsors the annual Mayor's Prayer Breakfast. Individual ministers and members of congregations have been stalwarts in local church history and are examples of local youngsters "making good." Young Vernon Law, who helped preside at the 1941 sacrament ceremony as a member of the Latter-day Saints priesthood quorum, graduated from Meridian High School and won the Cy Young pitching award for helping the Pittsburgh Pirates defeat the New York Yankees in the 1960 World Series.

This chapter includes seven denominations, but there were and are other area churches of importance. The history of Meridian's churches is a rich and diverse tapestry. Cassie Palmer, daughter of pioneer W. A. Palmer—who was married to a 1920s gospel soloist named Carmen Mell—once said, "Life has taught me that my Christian faith is the only anchor that will hold me fast."

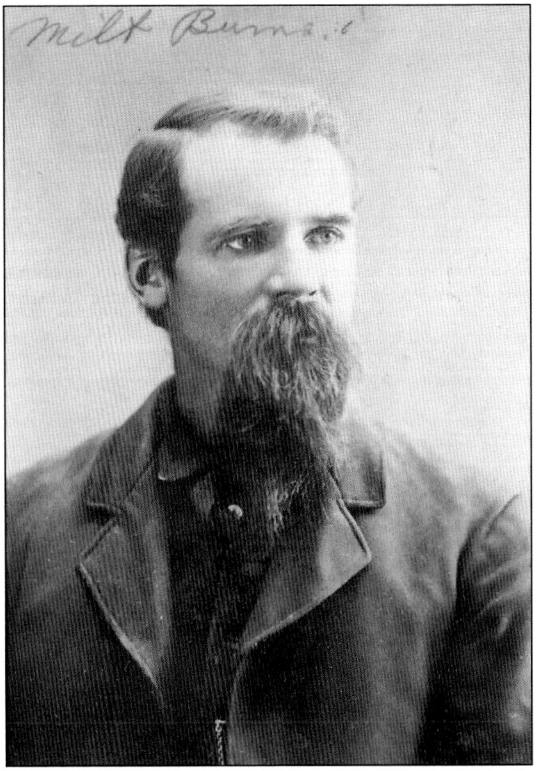

Milton Burns, pictured at left, was a Methodist preacher in the 1880s who was active in the congregation that met at the Five Mile School in that decade's later years. He presented a brief talk at the church's Christmas celebration on December 29, 1888. In early September 1891, his children came perilously close to being consumed by fire while sleeping beside a haystack to which an escaped prisoner had set fire. Pastor Burns was an important figure in the community and the Methodist Episcopal Church, South. A mortgage document from 1896 lists him as one of three trustees. The other trustees were Frank Davison and Samuel Martin Burns, who had signed the deed for the property. Ara Ann Burns is buried in the Five Mile Cemetery, where several early settlers repose in the five acres deeded in 1890 by David and Mollie Regan. The Methodist Episcopal Church, South, pictured below, was built in 1895 and sold in 1916 to the Pentecostal Church of the Nazarene.

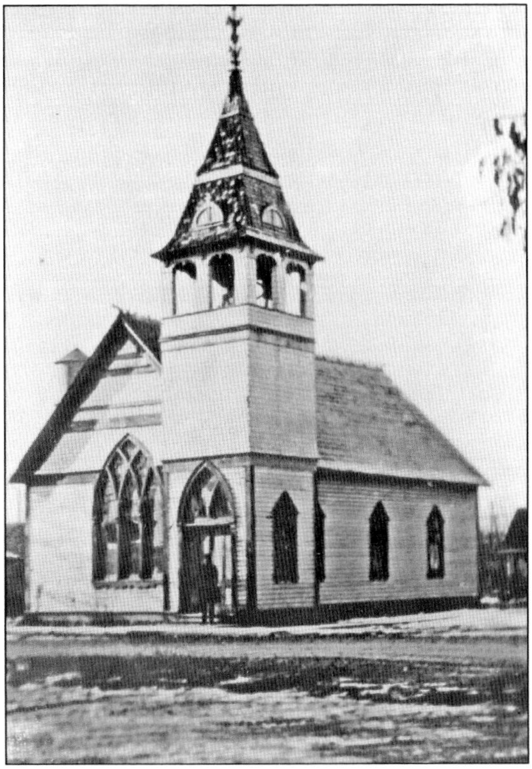

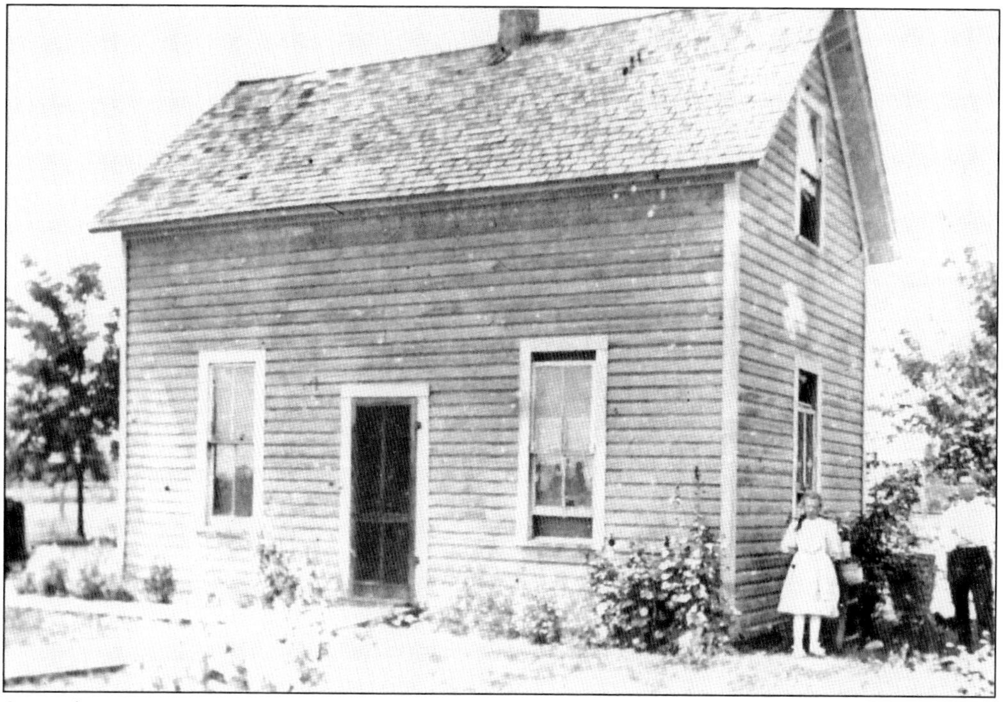

Several ministers and their families used this parsonage (above) built in 1896–1897 until the late 1920s, when a new one was built and the old one sold to Tom Gray for $90. The old structure was relocated to his ranch, south of the village. Below, on November 14, 1908, the Meridian School District sold two lots to the Methodist Episcopal Church for $50. Church volunteers hauled lumber for the new church from Fields Mill on Cottonwood Creek. Work began on the building and continued through the winter, weather and funding permitting. All labor was donated for the facility, located on the northeast corner of East Third Street and Pine Avenue. Officials and the congregation dedicated the new church in late May 1909. The Tourtellotte Company of Boise designed the building.

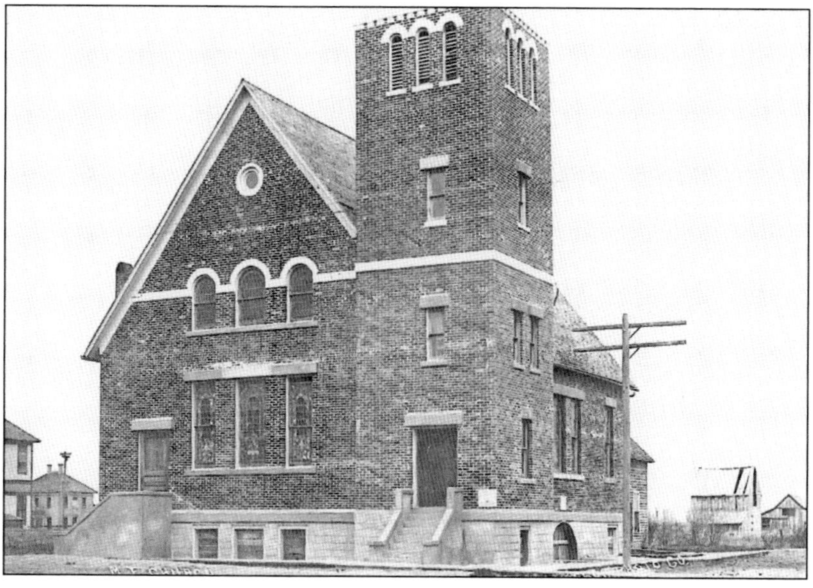

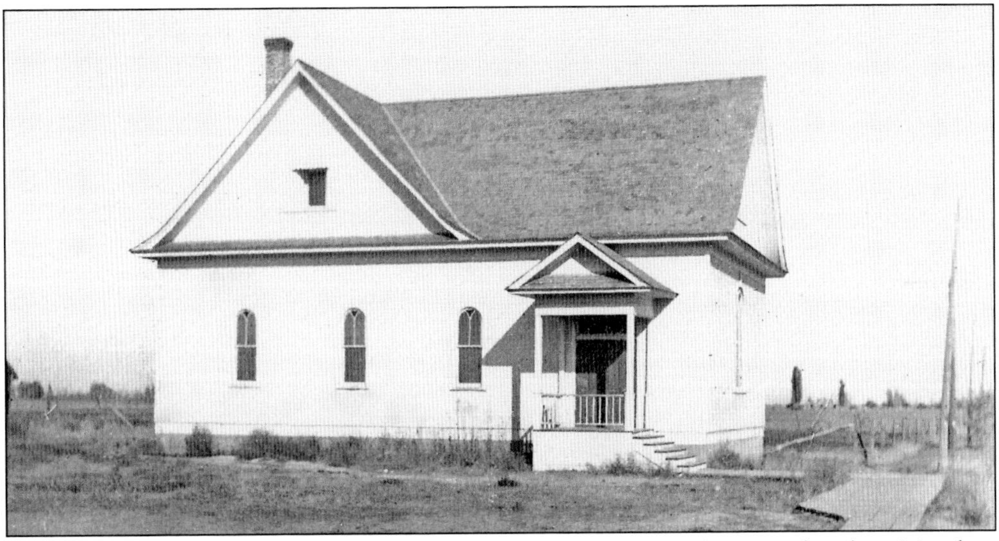

Above, settlers from Nebraska and elsewhere organized the first Christian church in Meridian on June 6, 1906, with 77 charter members at 1001 Meridian Road. Growth in the 1970s under Pastor Ray Beans, followed by Steve and Beth Moore, brought many members. In 1980, the church purchased 4 acres on Cherry Lane and relocated in October 1983 to a new facility that increased the church capacity. During the time that the church was called Cherry Lane Christian Church, attendance soared to over 1,000 each week with multiple worship services. In November 2003, the congregation bought 39.5 acres at Ten Mile and Franklin Roads, and on Easter 2009 moved into a greatly expanded new facility with 2,700 attending the first service at Ten Mile Christian Church. The new church campus and complex, pictured below, are a far cry from the early days, when members bought the old Christian Church on Ustick Road and used the material to add on a classroom wing. (Above, MHC; below, TMCC.)

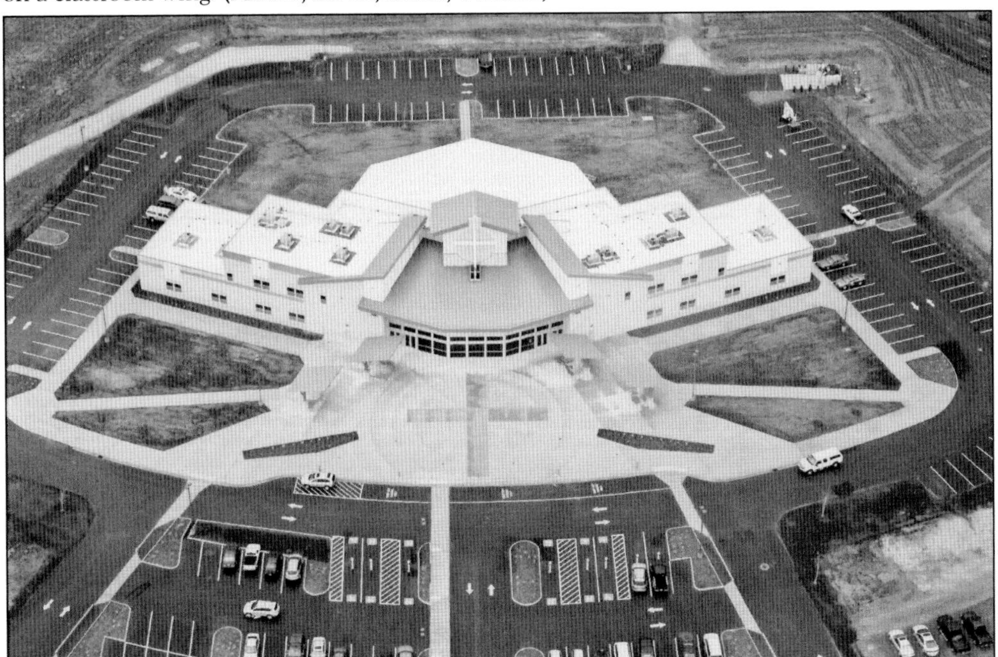

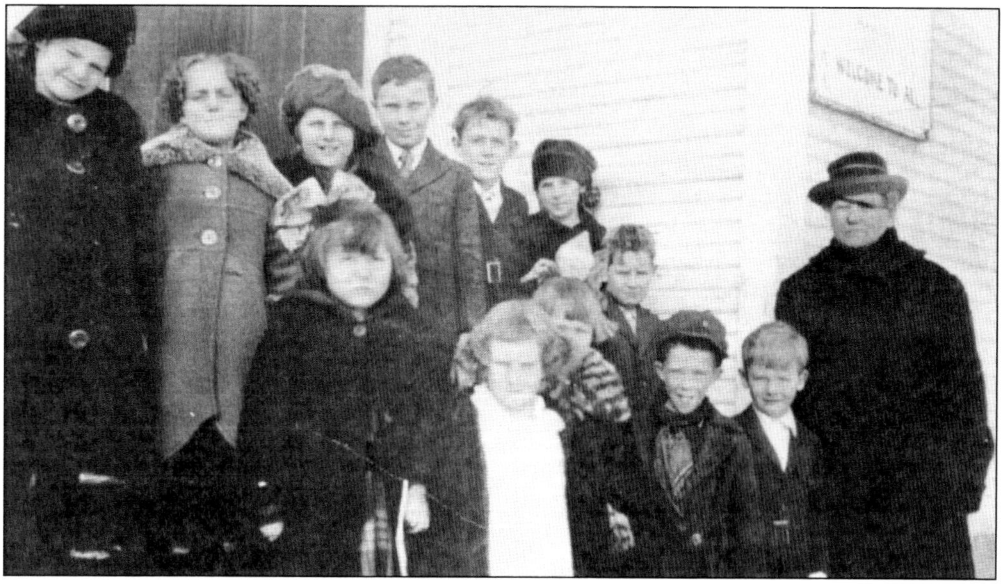

Above, members of the Christian church Sunday school class of 1919, not necessarily in order and with only some identified, are Jonathan Shannan, Genevieve Alger, David McCoy, Roy Alger, Gertrude Webb, Jack Chipman, Ellen Prestinich, Leland Matlock, and Incesi Adams. The first church was organized two years before the interurban arrived in Meridian, with its main line tracks running down Meridian Road, near where the church was located. Members of the congregation are pictured below in 1919. In the early 1930s, a basement was dug under the church for a kitchen and Sunday school classrooms. The congregation grew and relocated to Cherry Lane and then into the current new facility on the northwest corner of Ten Mile and Franklin Roads. It continued and increased its outreach programs into the community for children, youth, adult bible studies, seniors, small home groups, and recovery classes for those with addictions.

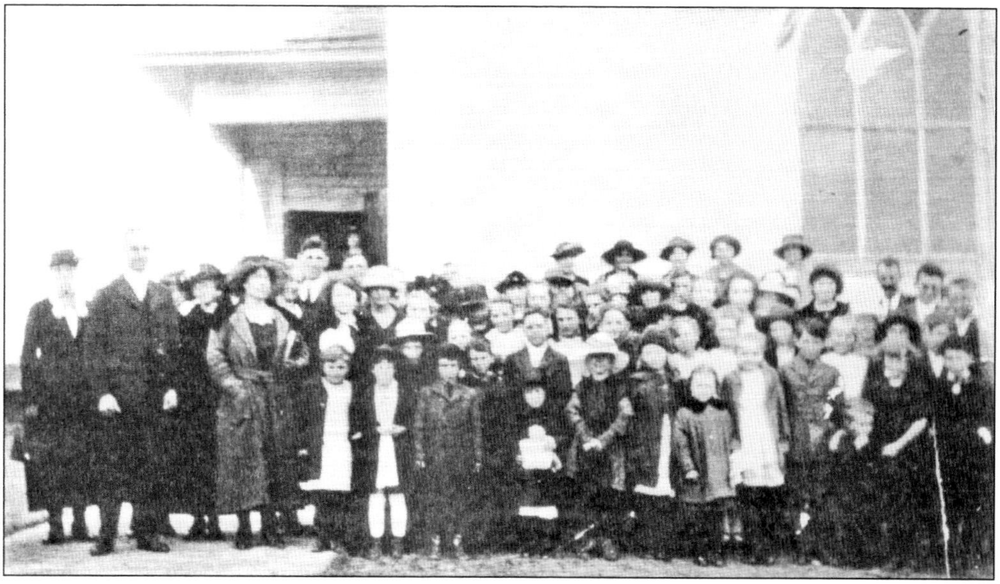

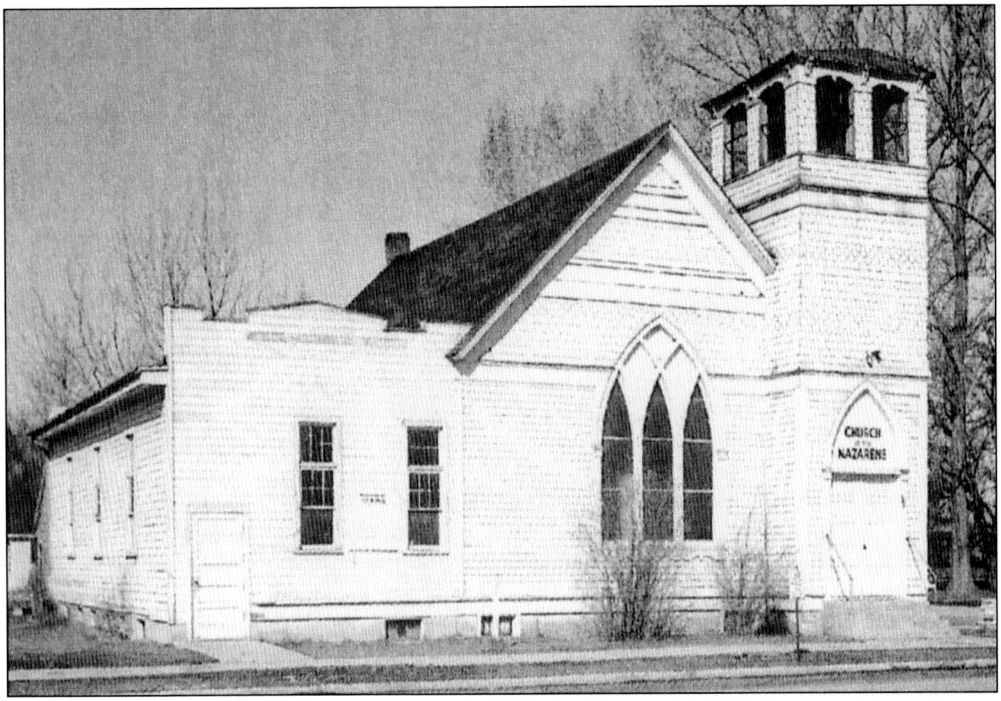

Above, Rev. George S. Culver, pastor from 1933 to 1938, led a membership drive that increased the congregation by several families. The families came from other states, and Culver assisted in relocating them to the Meridian area. By this time, the word Pentecostal had been dropped and the official name was the Meridian Church of the Nazarene. The 1940s brought a building remodel and south-side addition, among other improvements, including a new parsonage in 1947–1949 on the west side. The church rented the old one to the family of Willard and Elizabeth Rowley until 1951. In 1954, the old parsonage was demolished. During the 1954 ministry of Rev. Lester Braddock, pastor from 1953 to 1957, the old white church was torn down to make room for the new brick church building. The photograph below shows Reverend Braddock turning dirt in 1954. (Both VSCN.)

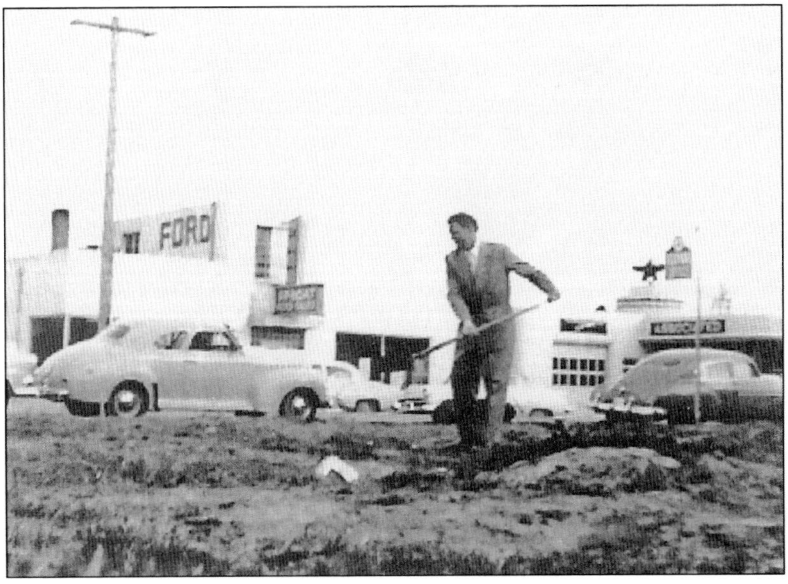

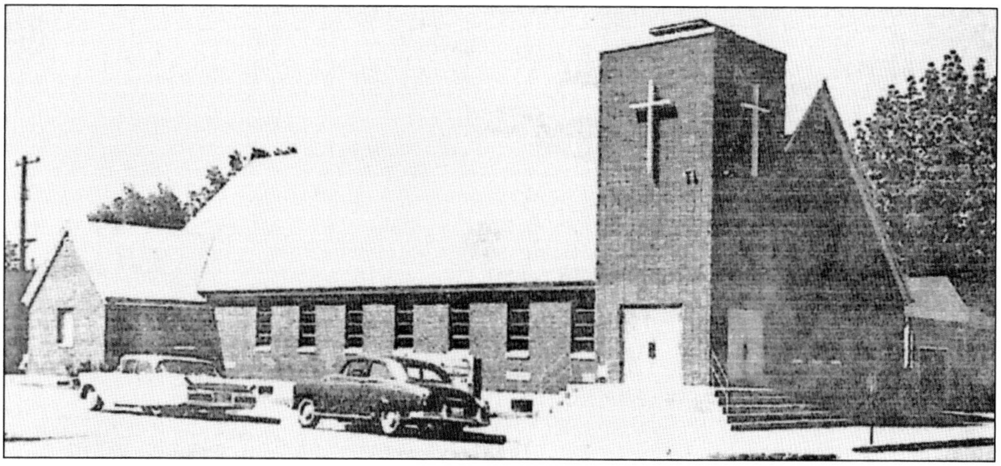

Above is the church in 1957 with its new sanctuary and classrooms and a parsonage on the right side of the building that dates from the late 1940s. The new structure cost $40,000. While it was under construction, the congregation held services in the American Legion Hall at 22 West Broadway Avenue. On May 15, 1955, Dr. Samuel Young, general superintendent, held a dedication service for the new facility. The new Valley Church of the Nazarene complex, pictured below, is located at 150 West Maestra Street south of the city on the west side of State Highway 69, north of Victory Road. The new church held its first services in November 2007. Pastor Tim Pusey said there are approximately 500 congregation members. (Both VSCN)

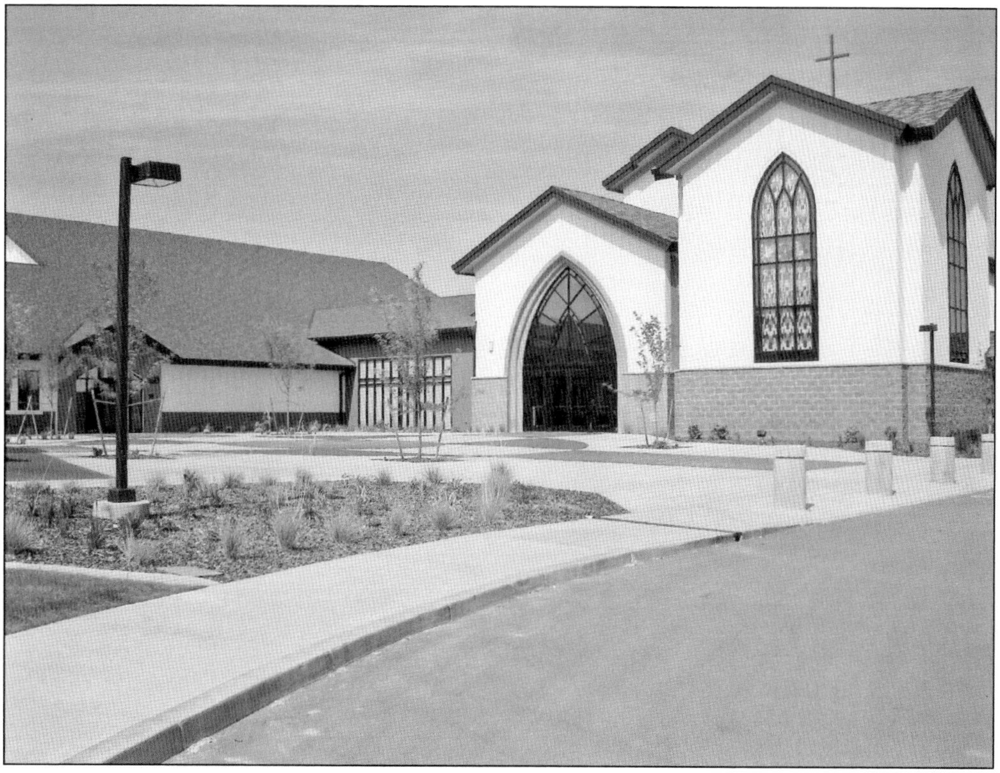

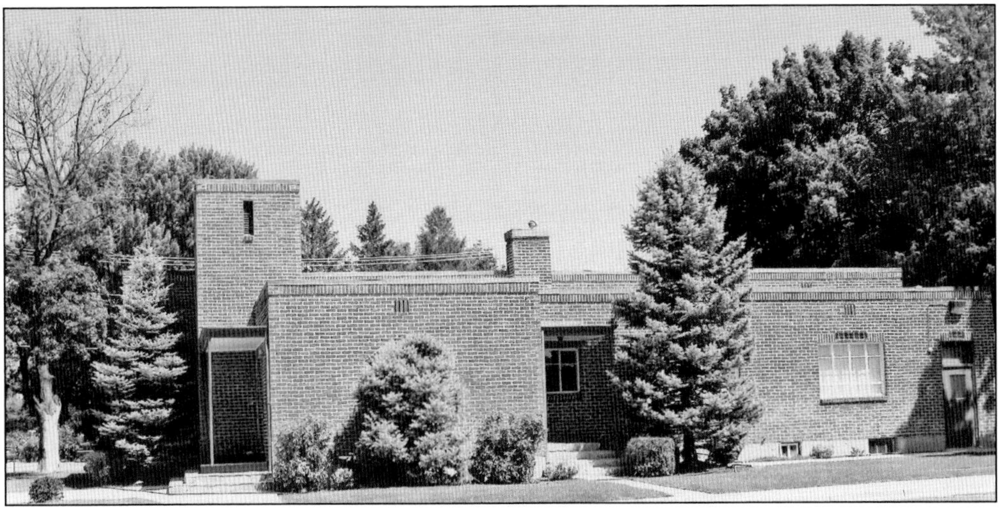

Above, ground was broken on the first Latter-day Saints (LDS) chapel on October 13, 1939. The dedication occurred in June 1941. In later years, the church was used as the Meridian Seminary Building, accommodating Meridian seminary students from the high school across the street. Most LDS families in the area came from eastern Idaho, particularly Montpelier, Soda Springs, Toponce, and Chesterfield. Many were descendants of colonizers sent north by Brigham Young to the Bear Lake country "to expand and firmly establish the boundaries of Deseret," wrote Charles Sturgell. The new arrivals discovered there were no church services or good roads as they traveled to establish wards in Nampa or Boise. A small local Sunday school of the Boise Second Ward was eventually established in Meridian on April 29, 1932. Below, the church at 3020 West Cherry Lane is one of many Mormon wards in the area. (Above, PAP; below, LDSC.)

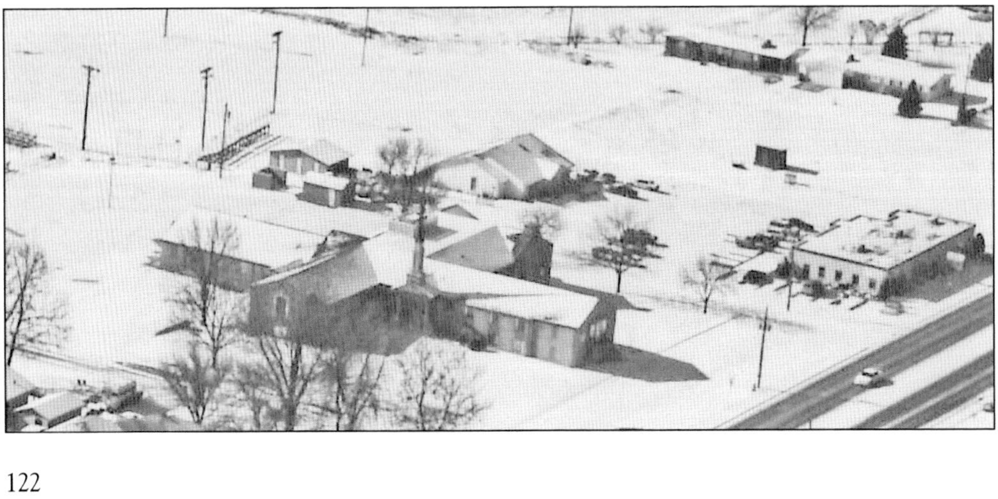

Pictured at right, Pastor Evert Roberts, a native of Arkansas, founded Meridian Gospel Tabernacle in the fall of 1940. Pastor Roberts served for 62 years with two brief hiatuses and considered the entire community to be his congregation. He passed away on August 11, 2006, at the age of 93. The first building on East Carlton Avenue between Meridian Road and Main Street burned down in the spring of 1946. Church elders purchased land at what is now the church's present location at 1507 North Meridian Road, which at that time was outside the city limits. During construction of this second building, pictured below, services were held in the American Legion building on the northwest corner of Meridian Road and West Broadway Avenue. The new building was finished in 1947 and seated about 140 people. (Both MGT.)

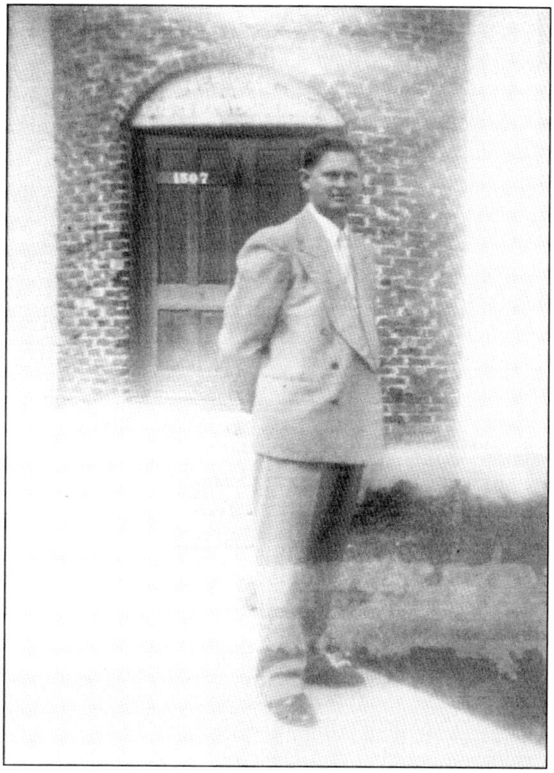

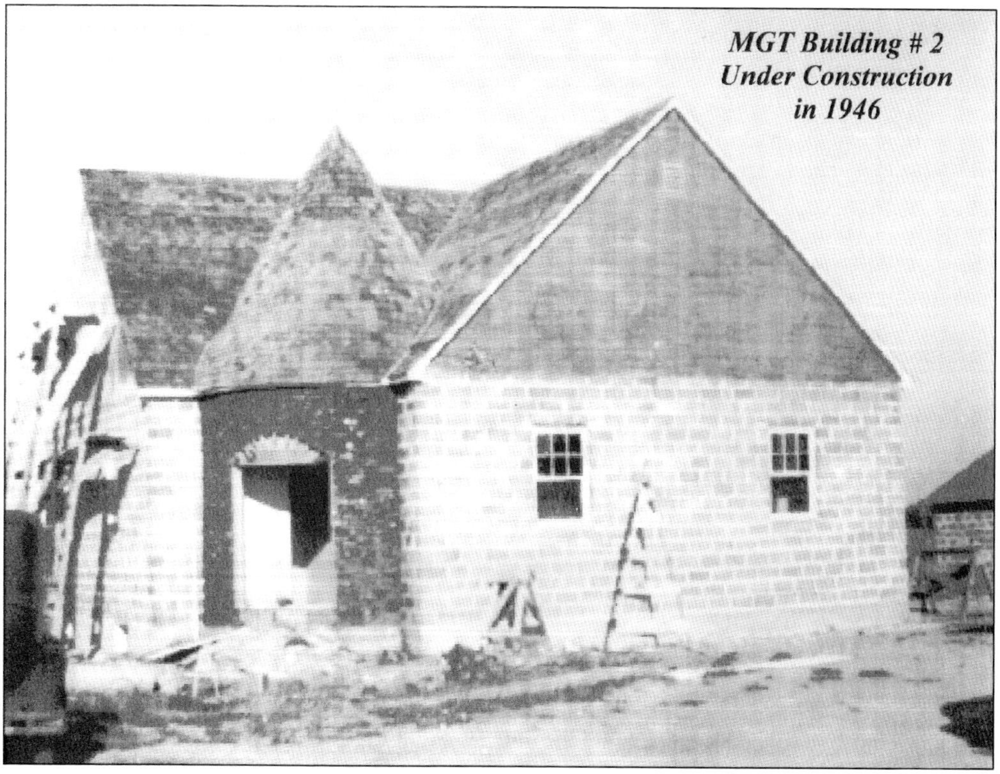

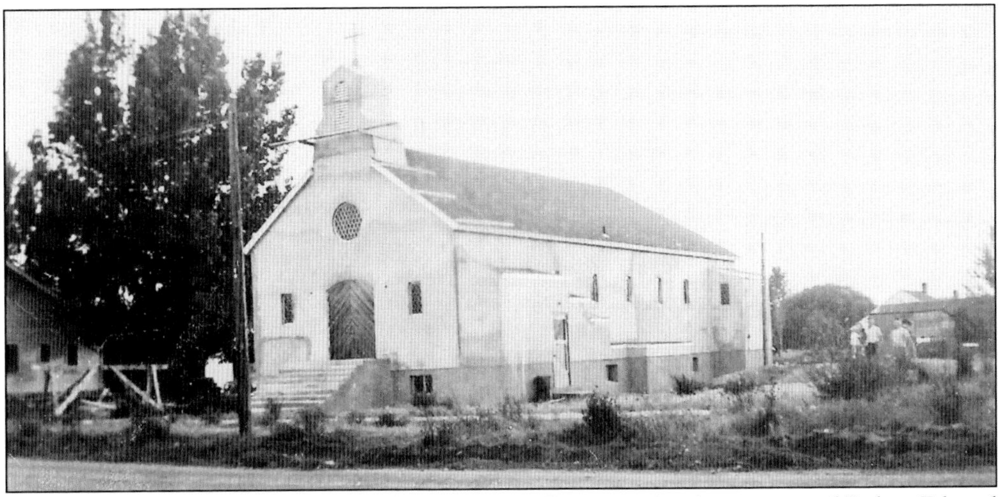

The Catholic community of Meridian began in 1941. Forty-two families petitioned Bishop Edward Joseph Kelly for a parish, and on December 27, 1944, he transferred the Meridian Mission Church (MMC) under St. John's Cathedral in Boise. On January 14, 1945, the MMC celebrated mass at the American Legion Hall, and on July 7, 1946, Fr. Urban Schmidt said mass at St. Frances X Cabrini Catholic Church, pictured above. Bishop Kelly and Fr. Nicolas Hughes dedicated the church on December 8, 1946. In July 1963, the church purchased 20 acres on Cherry Lane. Rectory construction occurred May 1966–September 1966. On November 13, the Parish of Meridian was formally established. In 1974, the new church on Cherry Lane became Holy Spirit Catholic Church. Below, in July 1998, Meridian joined Eagle's St. Matthews Catholic Church to become Holy Apostles Catholic Church (North and South), located at 6300 North Meridian Road. (Above, RN; below, HACC.)

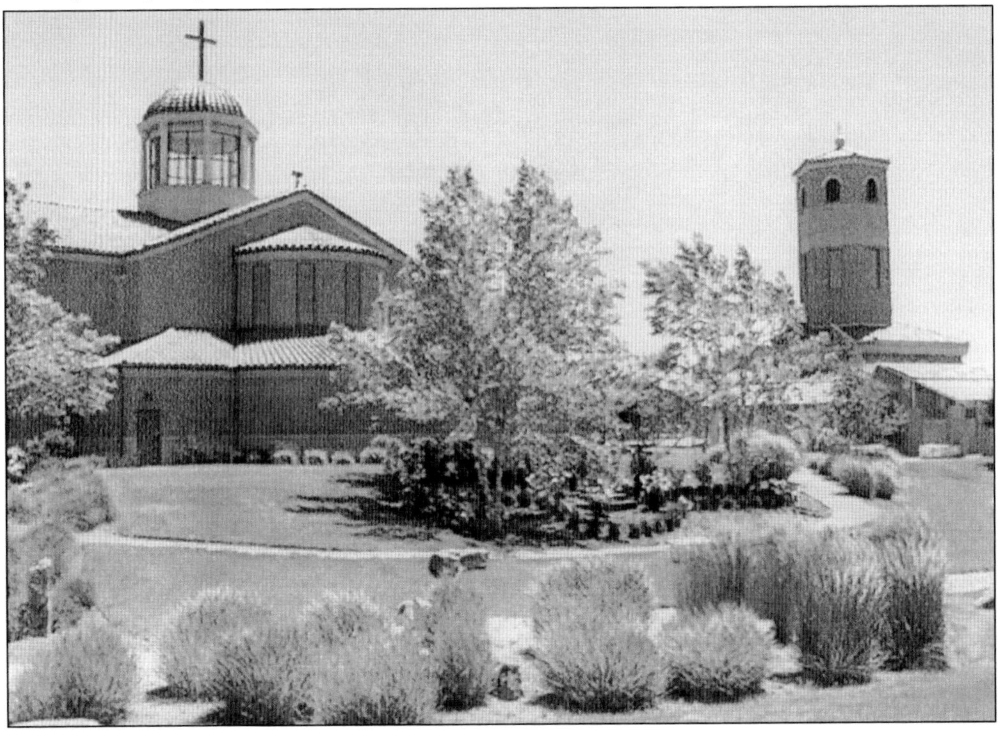

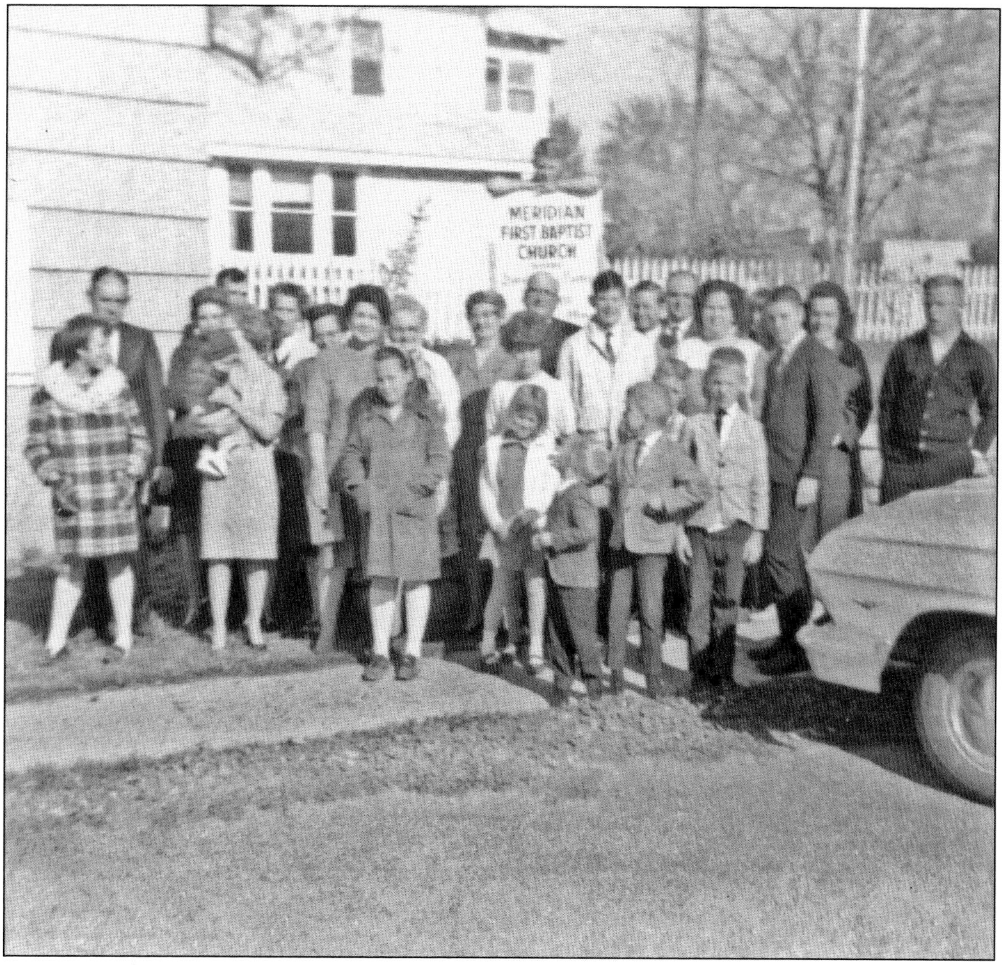

Pastor David Piper, pictured above, started the First Baptist Church in Meridian in 1967. The first service on February 18, 1968, included 33 people. Core members for the next 42 months included the Piper, Farrow, Maslonka, Mayer, Quenzer, and Smith families plus Julie Cook, Myrtle Cook, Lula Frost, Alta Hansen, and Marlene Sweatland and her children. While they were meeting at the American Legion Hall, Martha Smith found a fifth of whiskey in the oven, thankfully before she turned it on. Below, the original group held dinners with Pastor Dave asking each family to bring a "passing dish," Michigan lingo for potluck. The congregation purchased 1.5 acres on Pine Avenue for $7,000. The $35,000 building loan came from the Northwest Baptist Revolving Fund (half) and many individuals. The first service was held on September 19, 1971, with 75 attending. Additions followed in 1972, 1975, 1981, and 2007. (Both MFBC.)

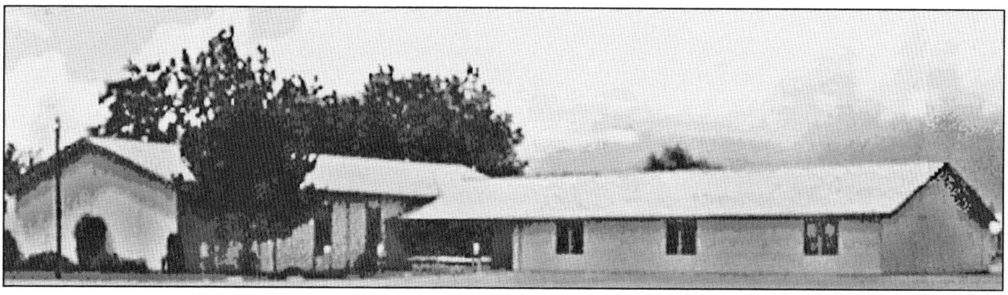

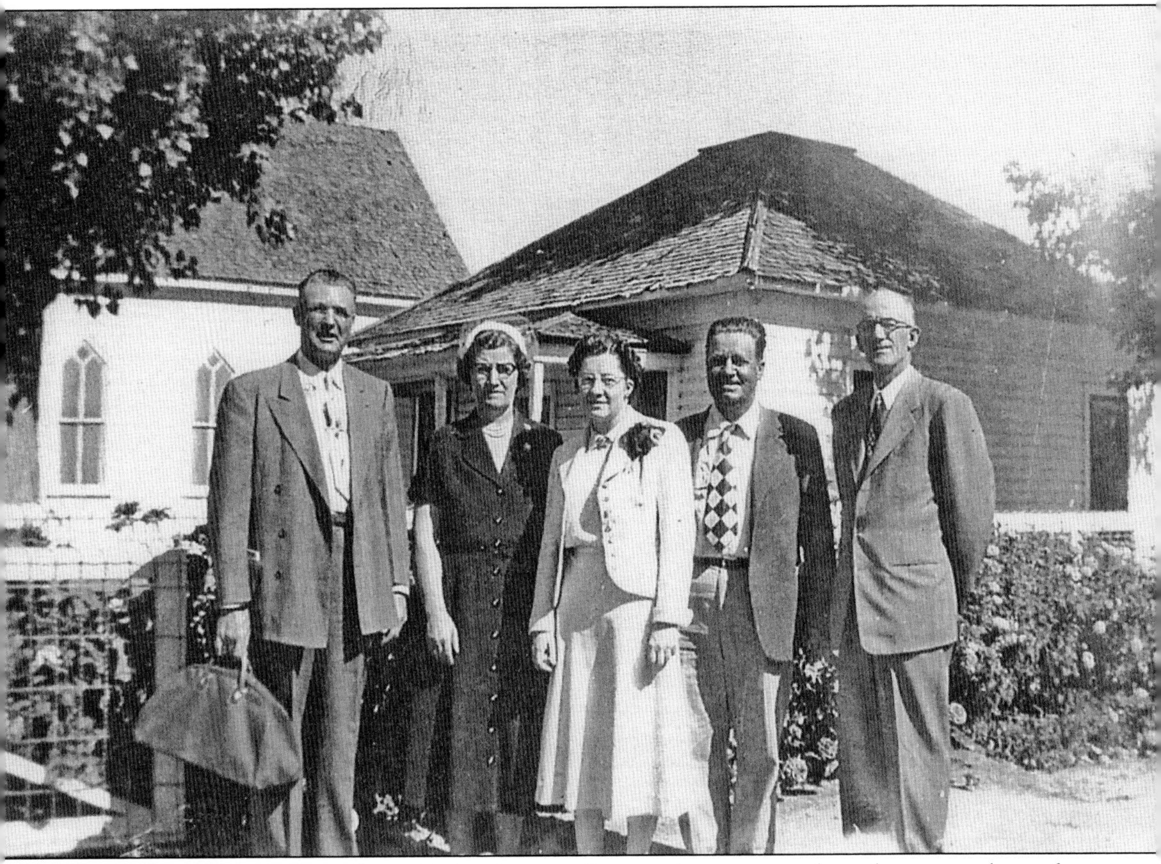

From 1944 to 1979, the Boise Valley Singing Convention sponsored southern gospel songfests every quarter by invitation at churches in Meridian, Kuna, Star, Boise, Nampa, Caldwell, Wilder, Nyssa in Oregon, and other communities. In the early 1960s, it held all-night singings on New Year's Eve in Meridian's Nazarene Church and Gospel Tabernacle. H. H. Ryan of Meridian was among the convention's first presidents, and Meridian High School graduate Jean Fisher, the first woman leader, served from 1952 until 1979. She said that black gospel singers from Boise occasionally attended and performed, including Wilma Shines, who died in 1992, and the choir from St. Paul's Church. "It didn't matter who you were or what religion you were," Fisher said. "The conventions were never a competition; they were about gospel music, and enjoyment of it." The photograph above shows Fisher with Idaho Four Quartet members John Lyda, Lucille Pankratz, Albert Thomason, and Reuben Pankratz, in 1957 in Star in front of the oldest Christian church in Idaho. (JF.)

Bibliography

Ellis, F. W. "The Story of Meridian." The *Idaho Magazine*, March 1904.

French, Mary. Essay read at the October 1931 meeting of the Meridian Occident Club.

Gish, Alice. Reminiscences. (with Don and Lucille Gish)

Hart, Arthur A. *Life in Eagle, Idaho.* Eagle, ID: Eagle Historic Preservation Commission, Caxton Printers, 2008.

Hill, Lila, and Glen W Davidson. *They Came to Build a Community, The History of Meridian, Idaho and the People Called Methodists.* Meridian, ID: Trustees of the First United Methodist Church, 1986.

———*A Look Back in Time*, weekly column in *Valley News* and *Valley Times*, 1991–2009.

Mell, Cassie. Reminiscences, 1984. Cassette tape on Deposit with the Meridian Historical Society.

Meridian Times, 1909–1968.

Reminiscences of the late Clysta Gray and Evert Roberts, manuscripts and published writings, 1993.

Sturgell, Charles. *A History of the Mormon Church in Meridian, Idaho.*

Thomason, Frank J. *Meridian from Sagebrush to Suburbs.* Meridian, ID: *Valley News*, 1993.

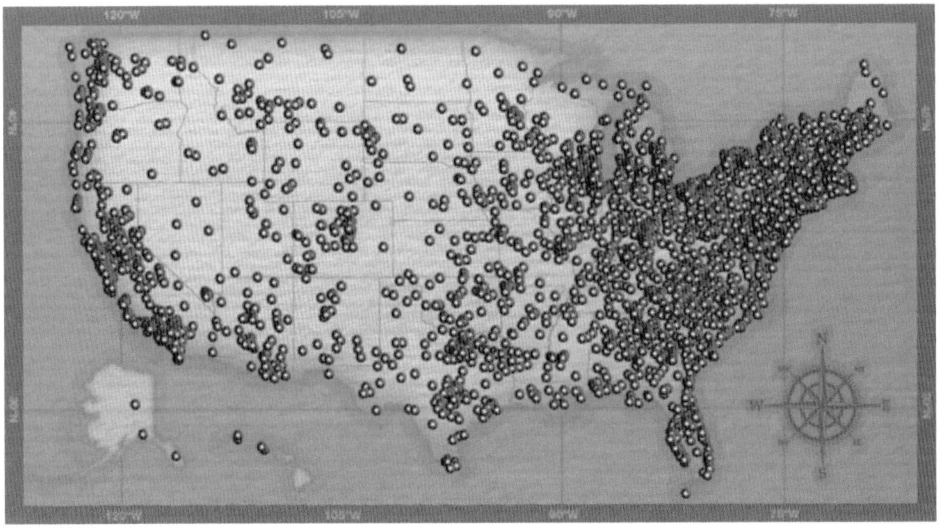